Our Son, a Stranger

Our Son, a Stranger

*Adoption Breakdown
and Its Effects on Parents*

MARIE ADAMS

McGill-Queen's University Press
Montreal & Kingston · London · Ithaca

© McGill-Queen's University Press 2002
ISBN 0-7735-2400-2

Legal deposit second quarter 2002
Bibliothèque nationale du Québec

Printed in Canada on acid-free paper that
is 100% ancient forest free (100% post-consumer
recycled), processed chlorine free, and printed
with vegetable-based, low VOC inks.

McGill-Queen's University Press acknowledges the
financial support of the Government of Canada
through the Book Publishing Industry Development
Program (BPIDP) for its publishing activities. We also
acknowledge the support of the Canada Council
for the Arts for our publishing program.

**National Library of Canada Cataloguing
in Publication Data**

Adams, Marie, 1945–
    Our son, a stranger: adoption breakdown
    and its effect on parents
    Includes bibliographical references and index.
    ISBN 0-7735-2400-2
    1. Interracial adoption – Canada. 2. Adoptive parents
    – Canada I. Title.
    HV875.7.C2A32 2002   362.73'4'0971   C2001-903311-7

Typeset in Palatino 10.5/13
by Caractéra inc., Quebec City

Contents

Illustrations following page 90

Foreword by Dr Harvey Armstrong   vii

Preface   xi

Introduction   xvii

PART ONE FAMILY PROFILES   1

1 The Adams Family   3

2 The Roethler Family   20

3 The Brooks Family   35

4 The Graves Family   48

5 The Verdan Family   61

6 The Pelligrini Family   75

PART TWO CONCLUSIONS   91

7 Why Do Some People Adopt?   93

8 The Effects of Adoption Breakdown on Parents   106

9 The Search for Answers 132

10 Applying What We Learned 169

Epilogue 195

My Personal Advice for Parents 197

Bibliography 201

Index 207

Foreword

DR HARVEY ARMSTRONG

I am moved and indeed honoured that Marie has asked me to write this foreword. I first met Marie and Rod nineteen years ago, when they were hurt and defeated by Tim and the system. I was a psychiatrist at the Clarke Institute Family Court Clinic. For two years Rod and Marie attended my parents-support group. This intelligent, courageous, and insightful couple came back years later when Tim was brought to Youthdale Crisis Center, of which I was director, and a decade after that Marie called as she worked on her thesis. A valued friend and colleague, she led two Parents for Youth groups in Newmarket, which help parents with out-of-control youth, for five years. She and others like her have extended my ability to help parents, a much-needed service.

Experience and expertise in working with aboriginal people qualifies me to comment on Rod and Marie's struggle with Tim's aboriginal origin. For twenty years I directed a University of Toronto program that provided mental-health services to about 15,000 Cree and Ojibway people on thirty reserves in northern Ontario, and, with the late Drs Clare Brant and Jack Ward, I founded the Native Mental Health Association of Canada, a vibrant organization that is now entirely native-run. The intentional and inadvertent cultural genocide that Marie writes about is real. Among aboriginal peoples, dysfunctional communities and unsupported parents cannot properly take care of themselves or their children, and Marie's horrific statistics for aboriginal mental health, especially for children and adolescents, are the result.

This scholarly book accurately and eloquently articulates the parental experience with difficult children. It addresses the personal, interpersonal, and emotional struggle of parents with themselves and their children, the impact on the families, and the failure of systems mandated to help parents and children. These systems fail to carry out their mandate because of misunderstanding of the plight of parents with a child, biological or adopted, who suffers from conduct disorder. Rod and Marie's struggle was complicated by transracial adoption, but the struggle for all parents of children with conduct disorders is similar.

Marie's research reveals the feelings of parents as they lose normal healthy expectations for their children and then discover that their children cannot fulfil minimal requirements of living. She shares parental experiences sensitively and exquisitely. She identifies the hopeful and positive cognitive structures that parents build for themselves around their children and then painfully give up, replacing them with self–devaluing beliefs. She teaches us where and how these painful perceptions originate and how they are applied to parents, making it even harder for them. Her portrayal of "ideal-family memories" and "disruption memories" graphically presents the cognitive dissonance parents confront. The inevitable mourning is clearly and poignantly presented, along with the fundamental truth that this process is time–dependent and different for each person, and that it is never the same for mothers and fathers.

She explores the backgrounds of problem adoptees and demonstrates how the effects of failure of early nurturing combined with brutal trauma, though not obvious at first, make it impossible for unsupported parents to undo the damage to these children's ability to attach. Without special help, not available in most settings, there is a near certainty of painfully unsatisfactory results. This is emotionally and financially costly for the families, the children, and the state. She shows us that simply loving damaged children and giving them all that can be given is not enough. She demonstrates that the prospect of being loved is so frightening for these children that they recoil from it, convinced that it will mean only more of the brutal hurt and loss that they experienced in their previous attempts to attach.

The agonizing personal and public transformation of the mother's ideal role as a giver of love. nurturing, and support to that of a "criminal mother" of a criminal starkly confronts the reader. She shares these parents' painful drama and allows us to comprehend it without living through it. We are educated emotionally and intellectually by her powerful descriptions of what these children did with their lives and the fear and horror this caused for their parents.

Agencies fail these parents and their families, without having any awareness of their own inadequacies. They lack sufficient funds, staff, and training to understand and carry out their mandated roles effectively. Marie makes sensible recommendations about services and how they should evolve both for troubled children and for families in general and for adoptive children and families in particular, and especially for adoptions that cross race and culture. She tells us of the frustration felt by tragically unsupported adoptive families and adoptees, frustration that harms their relationships with each other, and with their other children, and takes a serious toll on their mental health. Marie describes the need to escape this distress temporarily though mental mechanisms, jobs, or recreation. Her description of the mourning such parents experience should be basic reading for all who come in contact with parents of difficult children.

I read with satisfaction that my parents' group had helped and that Marie had felt that the principles on which the groups are run make sense. Simultaneously, she outlines the harm and cost of society's failure to provide what is needed for these families pre- and post–adoption. There is hope, too, in the form of Barbara Tremetiere's Philadelphia program, which deserves emulation.

Finally, Marie recommends a variety of changes at the policy and research levels for parents who are struggling with difficult children. Her words are infinitely wise. They will enrich the understanding of policy makers, bureaucrats, and those agencies and professionals providing services to children. Students planning careers involving children and parents must read this book. Marie's advice will be precious to all parents. It is clear and authentic.

Marie, thank you for your courage and intelligence and for sharing your understanding. Your book will make the world a better place!

Preface

This book is another step in a long process of searching, understanding, and healing that began several years ago when our
adopted son, a boy of Cree ancestry, began to display bizarre and
frightening behaviour. When he left home at the age of twelve,
Tim, the little boy we had enjoyed and for whom we had such
great plans, ceased to exist except in our memories. Our Timmy,
the child who was in our heads and in our hearts, was not this
new and frightening adolescent. The Tim we loved was now
gone. We were not sure, but maybe in time we might come to like
and even love his replacement. Maybe things would turn out
okay. It was not to be.

After he left home, the difficulties we had been experiencing
with our son Tim continued. I felt guilty for feeling and thinking,
but never actually daring to verbalize, that Tim's leaving home
was as bad as or worse than his physical death. I remember more
than one conversation with my husband, Rod, in which we talked
about Tim's departure as a living death – worse than a cancer.
Unlike cancer, his self-destructive behaviour was not so black and
white – not so easily understood – not *really* understood by anyone.

Rod and I felt so alone. Most people – friends and relatives –
would not ask after Tim or about our torment, not because they
did not care, I believe, but because there was no easy way for
them to approach the subject. Then there were the comments of

well-meaning friends: "Forget him. He's no good." "You did what
you could." "He doesn't appreciate all you did for him." "He's a
dead-beat." "He has bad blood. Indians are like that." "Indians
are lazy." "I always knew he would be trouble … could tell by
the look in his eye." "Why bother?" Finally, some people implied
that we just hadn't been good enough as parents: "Maybe you
should have … He seemed all right at our house, with us …
Wonder why you couldn't …?"

When Tim was so unhappy at home, the tension created a big
black hole that spread through the whole family. But even after Tim
was gone, this big hole remained. How could we begin to understand the plethora of emotions we experienced – from anger to
grief, frustration to embarrassment? How were we to cope with the
realization that our family was not going to be what we had hoped?

At the beginning, there was very little professional help available for Tim. Throughout, there was virtually no help for us as
parents. Our grief went unrecognized, and, as far as society was
concerned, we were the sort of parents who had not quite made
it. The mental-health services and social agencies assessed us and
wanted to fix us and fix our family. Each agency had to deal with
Tim for a year or two before they would admit, "Oh, I know what
you mean, *now*." In each case, it seemed that the agency whose
help we were currently seeking would believe us only after the
honeymoon period was over and Tim had broken rules or threatened violence many times.

Our difficulties with Tim destroyed my clear and tidy image of
family. The shattering of my assumptions was a slow, insidious,
wearing-down process, like acid rain on tombstones. Over time,
and then, finally, with a quick, jarring, and devastating hurricane-
force wind, our world was torn apart and the pieces scattered
until no arrangement of them made sense to me. In order for
rebuilding to occur, we had first to acknowledge that our reality
was not what it seemed. The images that I had of Tim as my son
and of our family were no longer true. What I wanted and
thought I saw was not really there. Tim was no longer the person
I thought he was.

Searching for answers, I returned to university to study psychology. After graduating from York, I began a Master of Education degree at the Ontario Institute for Studies in Education (OISE)
in Toronto and eventually enrolled in a doctoral program. Then

a devastating series of events began to unfold. On 22 August 1992 Tim stumbled out of a Toronto bar, fell, and hit his head on the cement. This was not the first time that something like this had happened, so his friends carried him to a park bench thinking that he would sleep it off. He spent the night there and late the next day his friends still could not wake him. They called an ambulance that took him to St Michael's Hospital. His long-time social worker phoned us and that night, our family, all six of us, were together for the last time, as we gathered around Tim's bed to say goodbye to him. He spent five days in a deep coma before, on 26 August, his strong young heart finally stopped beating. His struggles were over. Ours were not. Why weren't we able to help him? And why had all the many agencies and well-qualified professionals failed him too? The questions were never-ending.

After Tim's death, I became more determined than ever to make some sense of what had happened. Some good had to come of this tragedy. My personal quest led me to begin work on a doctoral thesis focusing on adoption breakdown. Initially, I focused my research on Tim alone. I wanted to find out what made him act the way he did, why he experienced the difficulties he had, and why he rejected us and our values. Soon, however, I realized that a broader approach was necessary. I needed to talk to other parents who had had similar experiences. At that time, I personally knew of only one couple, but I was convinced that there were many others. And indeed there were. Eventually, I was able to incorporate extensive interviews with five other adoptive families in my thesis research. That thesis was completed in 1996 and, in revised form, is the basis of the present book.

It is my hope that this book will give adoptive parents a voice. In the past, our various experiences with government agencies, the legal system, and other social-service organizations did not provide us with the information we felt was the minimum we could expect. Thus, one of my goals is to influence the kind and quality of assistance one receives in adoptions. I also hope that my book will draw attention to the experiences of adoptive parents who, if not unwittingly at least naively, participated in a government policy that promoted the removal of native children and their subsequent adoptions into white homes, without adequate follow-up support. Social agencies, too, should find this book a useful resource in their attempts to offer the help adoptive parents seek: information, encouragement, reassurance, and concrete support. Lastly, I hope that my book will help improve attitudes and implement appropriate changes to guidelines and procedures for special-needs adoption, cross-cultural adoption, and the adoption of older children. These changes will help not only adoptive parents but also parents of children who do not fit the mould – children who have learning disabilities or who display behavioural problems.

I would not have been able to produce this book without the help of many people. It is impossible to name all of them: I thank each and every one. The following are some of those who merit special mention.

Working through the masters and doctoral programs and being one of the last graduates of OISE was a special experience for me. My teachers and, in particular, my thesis committee – David Hunt, Arda Cole, and Joel Weiss – willingly shared with me their professional knowledge and time. I benefited from their interest in my educational progress, as well as in my personal development. I extend special thanks to my thesis adviser, David Hunt, who, in his wonderfully quiet and patient manner, encouraged and guided my journey. He never for a moment doubted that I would complete it successfully. I would also like to extend special thanks to Ardra Cole, who accepted my struggle over Tim's death and gave me the space I needed to rebuild my life. Ardra also facilitated a thesis-support group that was like an oasis for apprehensive travellers. It was there that my colleagues and I shared our struggles, joys, and doubts, asked directions, and fortified our determination.

There were some travelling companions who gave their time, knowledge, and encouragement and who are now my friends. I thank Madeleine Trapedo-Dnarsky and her husband, Max, for taking us into their home and hearts. I thank Sharon Rappaport for the helpful suggestions along the way. And, I thank Robert Liv, who led the way and graduated before us.

I am grateful to Centennial College, where I now teach, for granting me a sabbatical so that I could complete my thesis. There were some special people at Centennial who made the journey easier: Francie Aspinall, who dropped off resource materials on my desk (I think I used every one); Lynn Sua, who edited my thesis during many of her lunch hours; and Robyn Knapp, for always being there. The work was also made easier by special people, like Nicole Calvert and Alousia Zubic, who contributed their time and talents, and Elspeth Ross, who kept me up to date with newspaper articles and videos on native adoptions.

I am grateful to our friends and relatives across Canada who recommended their friends and acquaintances for the project. Their responses and the abundance of possible participants served to reinforce the need for this research. There is no shortage of adoptive parents like us.

Dr Harvey Armstrong and the therapists at Parents for Youth offered me the opportunity to facilitate sessions for groups of parents who have troubled children. This experience has helped me put our own struggle into a different perspective.

Of course, there are no words to express my feelings to the participants. They shared their happiest and their darkest moments with Rod and me over endless cups of coffee, cookies, and soup, which filled our stomachs and, more important, nourished our spirits and warmed our souls. I am humbled by their generosity, moved by their stories, inspired by their continuing courage, and comforted by their kindness. I consider them our close friends.

Transforming the thesis into this book was accomplished under the guidance of two editors, first Chantal Carstens and then Curtis Fahey, whose conscientious attention to detail made the impossible possible. I particularly want to express how happy I was to find Curtis Fahey. His exceptional skills as a structural editor, as well as his dedication to the task, turned my work into what I dreamed it could become.

I wish to thank my family. I thank my mother and father for instilling in me the courage to try something new and the determination to follow it through to the end. My parents were my role models; I learned from them not to give up. With all my heart, I thank my wonderful children, Lorie, Jeff, and Melanie. Each has read pieces of my work, listened to my anguish, offered critiques, encouraged me, and rejoiced with me as I took each step in my research and writing. Each of them has his or her own memories of Tim, and each has experienced the joys, frustrations, and deep sadness in our family. Today, they are wonderful, caring, sensitive, and strong adults. It was their courage and love that sustained me.

Finally, this book would not have been possible if it had not been for my husband Rod's patience, support, and love. He participated in all the interviews, discussed ideas, withstood my impatience, and comforted and supported me when I faltered. He rubbed my shoulders, picked up supper, brought me many cups of coffee, and gave me the space I needed. He is my best friend.

Introduction

Most of the literature on adoption breakdown has focused on the supposed failings of parents. There has been little written on the effects of adoption difficulties on adoptive parents, or on the specific problems faced by non-native Canadians who adopt native children. Furthermore, there is precious little written on the topic of adoption breakdown. What literature there is does not address those situations experienced by parents whose children no longer live with their adoptive families and who have *not* gone back or been returned to the adoption agency. Nor does the literature include, as in our case, families who decide to continue to support and care for their adopted child (regardless of how bad the situation gets), even after the child leaves home and for many years after that. Finally, discrepancies in the definition both of adoption *breakdown* and of *successful* adoptions mean that statistics and supporting evidence must be interpreted cautiously.

The most detailed treatment of adoption breakdown is Richard Barth and Marianne Berry's *Adoption and Disruption: Rates, Risks and Responses* (1988). Barth and Berry conducted a four-year study of 120 adoptions of older children, about half of whom experienced adoption breakdown, which in their analysis is restricted to those instances where the adopted child moves away from the family, *without* family support, and where the family does not continue to view itself as including the child. The authors conclude that the problem of adoption breakdown must be viewed as a *family* problem. Accordingly, they are proponents of the family-system approach to adoption breakdown, an approach that locates the roots of the breakdown in the family as a whole. In this approach, the dynamics of adoption breakdown are best explored by placing the parties involved under the microscope, with experts observing interviews with distressed families through one-way mirrors and with the interviewers sometimes provoking conflict when there is none in order to examine the nature of the family pathology. This is a technique that our family and the others whose stories are told in this book experienced first-hand.

In theory, the family-systems approach intends not to apportion blame between the parents and the adopted child but to examine the dynamics of the breakdown within the family as a whole. Yet, in practice, while recognizing the role of outside parties (child-welfare agencies, social workers, governments) in the breakdown, and while not ignoring completely the responsibility of the adopted child, the family-system approach does tend to place most of the blame on the shoulders of the adoptive parents (Miall 1998). A number of family-systems studies have concluded that adoption breakdown occurs when adoptive parents suffer from a lack of self-esteem because of their inability to accept their infertility (Seglow et al. 1972: 31), when they are unable or unwilling to cope with the child's demands and behaviour, when they have unrealistic expectations for the adopted child (Brodzinsky and Schechter 1990: 216), or when there is a lack of fit between the child's strengths and the parents' hope for the child's future (Hornby 1986: 9). Parental expectations may be determined in part by the social class and educational level of the parents, particularly the mother: high achievers and upwardly mobile people have high expectations of themselves and of their children.

Even studies that do not explicitly take a family-systems approach, and that in many ways are sympathetic to the problems faced by adoptive parents, share the view that these parents play a central role in the process of adoption breakdown. According to Katharine Davis Fishman, for example, when adoptive families come to grief, it is often from a disparity in expectations: the parents expected something the child cannot deliver, or the child delivers something the parents did not expect. Parents failed to understand – and no one really helped them understand – what "accepting the child as he is," a pious platitude, would mean in daily life, and the professionals they encountered later seemed no better informed than the parents themselves (1992: 45). In short, the parents were ill-prepared for the adoption process, a shortcoming that was partly their fault and partly the fault of adoption agencies that did not bother to inform them of the child's history. Over the years, authorities have deliberately concealed from the adoptive parents particular details of the child's background that could, in the adolescent and teenage years, lead to anti-social behaviour. Instead, these children are promoted for adoption, but, in the end, many seem unable to bond with any adult. The child's failure in this regard is diagnosed officially as a treatable handicap, which causes turmoil and grief for everyone involved in the adoption.

The work of Miriam Reitz and Kenneth W. Watson (1992) illustrates a new and welcome application of the family-systems approach. Though they do explore the "characterological" deficits of adoptive parents – poor communication skills, inability to cope with stress, limited capacity for emotional attachment, and the like – their primary concern is the impact of adoption breakdown on each of the parties in the "adoption triangle," namely, birth parents, adopted children, and adoptive parents. They write: "Any family, regardless of type or level of functioning, can be struck by events (developmental or some other kind) that overwhelm its ability to operate by its usual rules. At such times of anxiety, the operations of a system often fluctuate, intensify, and/ or reach a crisis state. As members of such a system attempt to solve the situation, they may work their way through to more satisfactory operations, and perhaps to more open regulations. In other cases, family members redouble their efforts, so that the operations return to the prior arrangements or become more rigidly regulated. In still other cases, family members flail helplessly in all directions, with the result that regulation becomes looser" (28). Reitz and Watson further note that the children who account for the majority of adoptions generally come from minority groups, suffer from physical or mental difficulties, were abused or neglected before their adoption, and, as a result of all of this, display a profound confusion about their identity and a consequent lack of self-esteem. This being the case, they believe that it serves no useful purpose to assign blame. Everyone has shortcomings, and, in the case of parents, one of these shortcomings might well be the unrealistic expectations they hold for their adopted children. Blaming the parents for their expectations or inability to control the child's behavior, however, is no more productive than blaming the children for their lack of attachment or behavior. The objective should not be to assign blame but to understand the difficulties that adoptive families face and support them in their efforts to find new ways of viewing and of handling the unsatisfactory situation. Reitz and Watson stress the need for support services for adoptive parents and offer a number of useful suggestions for reforms to the adoption system. It is the responsibility of the social-service agencies, they maintain, to encourage and develop a culture of trust and respect – a climate of inclusion – for all members of the adoption triangle.

There have been some other encouraging trends in the literature on adoption recently. In a 1997 study focusing on the issue of sealed birth records, Katarina Wegar notes that from the 1960s on most adoption problems were blamed on the parents, who, it was thought, were the authors of their own misfortune through their lack of self-acceptance, their unrealistic expectations for the adopted child, and their latent hostility towards the adoptee; currently, however, there is a growing recognition of the role of the "adopted child syndrome" – involving behaviour such as lying, stealing, promiscuity, belligerence, and so on – in adoption breakdown (57). Similarly, in an edited collection on the adoption of special-needs children, published in 1997, Rosemary Avery emphasizes the large numbers of such children in the adoption system, the unique difficulties these adoptions represent, and the need for a wide variety of reforms to assist adoptive families, all the while demonstrating an awareness of the needs of the adoptive parents as well as those of the adopted child. Noting that "adoption is a lifelong process" (xiv), Avery stresses the impact of adoption "on all those it touches" and of the "grief and loss" that accompanies adoption difficulties and breakdown, and she underlines the wrongheadedness of the conventional view that the presence of a "loving, stable home" is enough to assure a successful adoption (11). There is no trace here of the parent blaming of the family-systems approach. In another essay in the same collection, Elizabeth S. Cole writes that adoptive parents are normal, healthy people who need assistance, not criticism; adoption "professionals" should spend less time investigating them and more time supporting them. She, too, highlights the multitude of problems in the existing system – lack of information, secrecy, bureaucratic inflexibility – and the pressing need for reform, particularly in the attitudes of professionals, who should start seeing their adoptive clients as colleagues rather than as victims of a pathological condition that needs to be cured, as good, caring people who need to be listened to, supported, and involved in whatever decisions are taken to address the problems they are facing. In addition, she suggests a number of policies to prevent adoption breakdown in the first place, including a more carefully thought-out recruitment strategy for adoptive parents, the sharing with these parents of background information on the child they are considering adopting as well as concrete advice on management of adopted children who display troublesome behaviour, and post-adoption services at the community level.

Another positive development in recent adoption literature is the growing understanding of the uniqueness of the "adoption situation." According to David Kirk (1981), adoptive families are not like other families; adopted children have needs different from those of biological children (for example, the feeling that they have been abandoned by their birth parents and anxiety over their lack of a tie to their adoptive parents), and adoptive parents face challenges unknown to birth parents. Crucial to the success of any adoption, he argues, is the acknowledgment of these differences on the part of adoptive families and child-welfare professionals alike. This view, to be sure, holds the potential for more parent blaming: adoptive parents who reject the uniqueness of their situation, preferring to see themselves as just ordinary mothers and fathers who can solve all problems with healthy doses of love, are sowing the seeds of trouble. Yet, in Kirk's hands, the "acknowledgment of differences" thesis is less a tool for apportioning blame than a vehicle for fostering understanding. It is one of the pieces of the puzzle that needs to be fully appreciated by child-welfare workers, who in turn should inform adoptive parents of its importance. Unfortunately, at the time when the families profiled in this book adopted, the "rejection of differences" was prevalent among adoptive families as well as child-welfare agencies and workers and was the deliberate goal of government advertising and policies. Kirk writes: "It is troubling to think that so much professional effort has been expended on regulating and controlling the legal and administrative procedures that lead to adoption, and that so little concern was shown for the internal and continuing process in adoptive kinship" (77). Adoptive parents who accept their differences from other parents, he concludes, can more easily bond with their adopted children; they can empathize more readily with the adopted child's feelings, listen with greater ease to the child's questions about his or her background, and answer these questions without discomfort.

It is generally recognized that adopted children are disproportionately represented among people treated for emotional problems (Ambert 1992; Senior and Himadi 1985; Lifshitz et al. 1975; Bohman 1971, cited in Brodzinsky and Schechter 1990). In the 1980s, children represented 9.8 per cent of psychiatric patients and adopted adolescents accounted for 15 per cent, compared to a base rate of 2 per cent in the general population (Kim et al., cited in Gelmych 1991; Brodzinsky and Schechter 1990; Sorosky 1984). During the same period, Parents for Youth in Toronto reported that 15 per cent of parents in their support groups had adopted children (Armstrong et al. 1994). Adoptees make up 4 to 5 per cent of outpatients in mental-health facilities (Kadushin 1970). Against this background, many of the studies on adoption breakdown focus on the adoptee's experience and behaviour before and after placement (Smith and Howard 1991). Children who have been sexually abused often blame themselves, not their abuser, and develop a deep-rooted negative sense of themselves that haunts them all of their lives, reducing their chances of achieving success at school, in the community, and in the workplace (Kellington 1993; Cole, cited in Avery 1997).

There has been an increase in the number of studies of adoptions of special-needs children. Among the factors addressed in these studies are the age of the child at the time of adoption, the child's emotional and behavioural problems and the nature of foster care, opposition to placement, the inability of the child to bond with the adoptive family, and parents' expectations and ambitions for the adopted child. Most of the research on the breakdown of these particular adoptions refers to adoptions that break down *before* the adoption is made legal by the signing of the final papers, rather than, as in the families profiled here, long *after* the adoption occurs. Still, research on the latter phenomenon is beginning to be done, a fine example being Rosemary Avery's edited collection, cited above, on the adoption of special-needs children. There is also evidence of a growing interest in the effects on parents of their adopted child's behavioural problems, but most of the literature continues to neglect this theme. Besides the Avery volume, again, exceptions are James Rosenthal and Victor Groze's *Special-Needs Adoptions: A Study of Intact Families* (1992), Anne-Marie Ambert's *The Effects of Children on Parents* (1992), and various articles by and about Harvey Armstrong (Armstrong et al. 1994; Petruccelli 1993; Carey 1989).

Studies done in the 1940s and 1950s generally presented a favourable picture (taken soon after the adoption was finalized) of the success of adoptions and, particularly, the positive effects of a good environment, which in most cases was taken to mean good, caring adoptive parents. Since then, new information on genetics and on the importance of pre- and post-natal care and of the first few hours, days, and months of the child's life have altered the perception of the child as a lump of clay that can be moulded by proper parenting. For example, pioneering research is currently being done on fetal alcohol syndrome (FAS), which refers to the collection of symptoms – brain damage, learning disabilities, behavioural problems – displayed by children born to alcoholic mothers. It is believed that FAS affects as many as one in every hundred children and has reached epidemic proportions among Canada's native peoples, and that it plays a role – perhaps the key role – in many if not most adoption breakdowns. One FAS expert, Albert Chudley, observes: "We've come from an era where the belief was that the environment makes the whole difference. The truth is that a lot of these kids have been in great environments, but they still turn out with difficulties." Fournier and Crey cite studies in British Columbia where it is believed that one in six aboriginal births are alcohol-damaged (178). In 1997 Chudley found that one of ten children on a Manitoba reserve were brain damaged as a result of FAS and that two or three times that number demonstrated behavioural and learning problems that could be directly tied to the same cause. "These kids have been robbed," he says (Wente 2000). On another front, research on the attachment process between parent and child is throwing serious doubt on the old idea that loving parents can make any adoption work. Attachment theory is nothing new, dating to the work of Melanie Klein and John Bowlby before and immediately after the Second

World War. Bowlby, particularly, believed that maternal deprivation through separation or death, as well as a mother's negative
attitude, could produce lasting emotional damage in a child if it
occurred after the age of six months – by which time bonding
usually occurred – and before the age of three (Karen 1990).
Bowlby's theories were rejected by the psychoanalytical community until the 1980s but gained broad acceptance in other circles
and were elaborated by a number of other researchers, notably,
James Robertson, Mary Ainsworth, Erik Erikson, Margaret Mahler,
Byron Egeland, and Mary Main and Donna Weston. The nature
versus nurture debate is still ongoing, but there is now a general
consensus that parent-child bonding in the first years of life is just
as important as heredity and environment in determining personality; there is also wide agreement that disruption of this bonding
can result in low self-esteem in the affected child, a problem that
in turn can lead to an "affectionless" character incapable of relating
well to others and prone to such behaviour as lying, aggression,
and even criminality (ibid.). Much of this was well documented
when Rod and I and the other couples in this study adopted, but,
incredibly enough, none of us encountered any trace of attachment theory in the adoption process as we were going through
it. Not a single child-welfare worker or family therapist once mentioned that the problems we were having with our adopted children might be at least partly rooted in the trauma caused by their
early separation from their birth parents.

   To turn to the subject of transracial adoption, there is abundant
American literature on the adoption of black children by white
parents, as well as on the adoption of American Indian children
by white parents. Such adoptions across racial lines have been,
for the most part, viewed positively or, at the very least, with
cautious optimism. In a 1972 study by David Fanshel, a group of
ninety-eight black transracially adopted children rated themselves positively, as far as self-esteem was concerned, but the girls
had lower scores than the boys did. As a form of substitute care,
adoption was viewed as a good alternative to a life of poverty.
The adoptive parents reported that they were happy and satisfied
with their children. Another scholar, Christopher Bagley (1993),
studied twenty-seven African-American and mixed-race (black/
white, Asian/white) adoptions over twelve years and concluded
that only 10 per cent of them were breaking down and that transracial adoption should be considered for all children who cannot

be placed with parents of the same colour. With regard to natives, however, Bagley took a much different view. In a study of native Canadian adoption breakdowns (September 1993), he found that the thirty-seven native children he followed were far more likely than other adopted children, including those adopted from other countries, to have behavioural and emotional problems. By the age of seventeen, nearly half of the native children studied had broken with their adoptive families. Adopted native children also carry a double burden: they absorb many of society's negative stereotypes of natives, and they are isolated from all of the positive aspects of aboriginal culture and values. Bagley concludes that native children, as members of a cultural group, should not be adopted outside their communities.

Suzanne Fournier and Ernie Crey, in *Stolen from Our Embrace*, describe the horrific assimilation policies of the Canadian government in partnership with the religious orders. They outline the policies that apprehended, from the poverty of reservations, young native children first for the residential schools and later for non-native foster and adoptive homes. The powerless and dispirited communities turned to alcohol to numb the pain. In the residential schools, the children were often subjected to physical and sexual abuse. When they returned to the reserves, they became abusers. "In the foster and adoptive care system, aboriginal children typically vanished with scarcely a trace, the vast majority of them placed until they were adults in non-aboriginal homes where their cultural identity, their legal Indian status, their knowledge of their own First Nation and even their birth names were erased, often forever" (Fournier and Crey 1997: 81). In 1930, 75 per cent of all Indian children between the ages of seven and fifteen were in residential schools (ibid: 178). In an effort to take control of their future, many aboriginal communities are striving to eliminate alcohol dependency and return to their traditional way of providing care for their children, many with fetal-alcohol syndrome, within their own communities.

In 1984 there were 8,273 foreign children adopted in the United States (Associated Press, 1986), and, according to a CBC Radio interview with Anne Westhues on 8 February 1994, about 2,000 children are adopted from outside Canada every year. This practice started in the 1970s with the adoption of children from Vietnam, Bangladesh, Korea, and Cambodia, and, more recently, adopted children have arrived from Romania and China. These adoptions were encouraged by church and community groups on the basis of humanitarianism, charity, and Christian duty. Westhues followed 126 children and their families. By and large, things have worked out quite well for them. The adoptees feel like they belong to the families, and, overall, appear to have a higher rate of self-esteem than the average population. The fact that the parents are above average in income and education, Westhues suggests, is the main reason why the adoptions have been successful: such families tend to have higher self-esteem. (Yet high income and high expectations, as we noted earlier, can also be cited as catalysts in high rates of adoption breakdown.) All in all, Westhues concludes that everyone benefits from such adoptions. She is aware of the argument that white families should not adopt non-white children, because the children will not develop a racial identity of their own. The alternative, however, seems to be to let the children die in poverty.

Some writers have attempted to explain the prevalence of black youths in Canada's Children's Aid Society system and in our detention centres. Their explanation includes two themes. The first relates to the early separation of black children from their mothers before the mothers came to Canada to work as domestic and child-care workers. The second refers to the reunification, a few years later, of the children with their mothers in Canada. The stresses associated with this switch often result in anti-social acts and family disruption (Brodzinsky and Schechter 1990). These black children are similar to native Canadian adoptees in that they were separated very early from their parents, and when they came to Canada they became part of a negatively stereotyped minority group.

Before 1960 native children made up only 1 per cent of children in the care of child-welfare services in Canada but afterwards the situation changed dramatically, with native children accounting for 30 to 40 per cent of all legal wards even though they represented only 4 per cent of the general population (Fournier and Crey 1997). This was a result of a government-sponsored campaign to encourage the adoption of native children by non-native parents. The results of the so-called Sixties Scoop and its aftermath were particularly apparent in Saskatchewan, the province with the largest native population. There, by 1978–79, 65 per cent of the children in care were native, compared to a range of

2–39 per cent for the other provinces (Wharf 1993); and by 1980–81, the proportion of native children in care had risen to 63.8 per cent (4.5 times the national rate) (Johnson 1983). In Canada as a whole, the number of native children in care reached 34.4 per 1,000 in the late 1960s and doubled to 62.9 per 1,000 in the course of the 1970s, and, by 1980–81, 8.1 per cent of native newborns were being placed in care (Wharf 1993: 147). The last figure had fallen to 3.9 per cent in 1988–89, but this is still five times higher than the rate in non-native communities. Canada, moreover, has a higher proportion of children in care than most Western countries, a distinction that is the direct result of the disproportionate number of native children being adopted or placed in foster homes (Armitage, cited in ibid.: 51).

The results have not been encouraging, to put it mildly. There are no precise numbers on the proportion of native adoptions that break down, but a documentary film on the subject cites a 95 per cent failure rate (*To Return: The John Walkus Story*). Whether this is accurate or not, there is no doubt that the rate is high and that adopted native children frequently demonstrate serious behavioural difficulties. Canadian and American social services estimate that 85 per cent of the native adoptions fail in adolescence (Fournier and Crey 1997). An 1996 study of three groups of adoptees (43 Vietnamese, 82 Koreans, and 46 native Canadian Indians) found that the Canadian Indians were the most likely to seek medical treatment (70 per cent), to be involved in the juvenile justice system (28 per cent), to engage in substance abuse (57 per cent) or to have had a background of substance abuse (93 per cent), to be a danger to self or others (46 per cent), to be prone to such conduct as lying (67 per cent), stealing (28 per cent), and running away (22 per cent), and to lack confidence (33 per cent). Only 54 per cent of the Indian children had developed successful attachments to their adoptive families, compared to 89 per cent for the Koreans and 95 per cent for the Vietnamese (Holtan and Tremitiere 1996).

Whereas native Canadians account for less than 2 per cent of Toronto's total population, a 1992 survey found that about 20 per cent of its 3,000 to 4,000 street youth had at least one parent of native descent. Ken Richard, executive director of Native Child and Family Services of Toronto, estimates that as many as eight in ten young natives on Toronto streets were adopted by non-native parents. He describes the typical street youth in downtown Toronto as an adopted native youth whose adoption broke down when he or she was eleven or twelve. These young people lack a sense of identity, have a deep-seated feeling of worthlessness, and are self-destructive and have their lives cut short (Westhues 1994). "They are looking for a sense of identity and belonging with other aboriginal street kids down there that they never got in their non-native home. Maybe eighty per cent of the girls and half of the boys have been sexually abused in care, but even the ones from good homes are on the run" (Fournier and Crey 1997: 90). Toronto's Aboriginal Legal Services reports that 43 per cent of its clients who face criminal charges have either been in foster care or were adopted. A 1990 survey of aboriginal prisoners in Prince Albert penitentiary found that over 95 per cent came from either a group home or a foster home (Fournier and Crey 1997).

In most cases, native adoptees, like their adoptive parents, have been told almost nothing about their backgrounds and are often thirsting for this information. Many native adoptees refer to themselves as red apples – they look like a native Canadian but identify with white society and have adopted its values. They feel, in fact, that they do not belong anywhere. Five native communities in central British Columbia tracked seventy-five children who had been adopted by non-native families. *None* of these children had been able to live successfully in their home communities again, although many had tried. A number ended up living on the streets of Vancouver. Some committed suicide either directly or indirectly (in the latter case, through self-destructive behaviour). In Manitoba, there is not one Indian person who has not been touched by the loss of these adoptees: "The tragic consequences of policy that placed thousands of Native children with white adoptive parents are evident today in urban homeless shelters, courtrooms and youth centres across Canada. Adoptive parents, unprepared for the racism and identity crises their Native children would experience, believed that a stable, loving home was all these youngsters needed. The odds were stacked against a happy outcome" (Sarick 1994: A4).

There are a few points to consider as we reflect on the results of studies of transracial adoptions. First, transracial studies are often confounded by the fact that many transracial adoptees are also special-needs children. In one study of 296 special-needs minority and mixed-race adoptions, 22 per cent were transracial (Worchel and Shebilski 1983). It is difficult to distinguish which of the factors are responsible for the majority of the problems. Transracial adoptees are often physically handicapped and have more often experienced sexual abuse, group-home or psychiatric placements, and adoption disruption prior to permanent placement. Secondly, the length of the study and the age of the child at the time the study was done need to be taken into account. If my husband and I had been part of a five-year study, or even a ten-year study, we would have been evaluated as wildly successful. At eleven years, however, the adoption had broken down. Finally, the factors contributing to breakdown of both special-needs and older children seem to overlap. They involve foster versus non-foster care, adoptive mother's education, presence of emotional problems, single versus dual placement, biological siblings in the adoptive home, and the response of family, friends, and neighbours to the presence of a non-white adoptee (Brodzinsky and Schechter 1990: 193).

One theory in particular has shaped my thinking on adoption breakdown and is critical to the analysis presented in this book. I refer to the paradigm of symbolic interactionism proposed by H. Blumer.

This paradigm has helped me understand that the environment our family provided for Tim was not the only determinant in his behaviour. The choices that Tim made in his life were also the result partly of his personal interpretation and assessment of his background and opportunities and partly of his background and genetic make-up. The symbolic interactionist paradigm, in short, considers the interaction of environment, background, personal make-up, and environment. It also emphasizes that the choices an individual makes have a strong role in defining who he or she is. As Blumer writes, "the individual must interpret in order to act ... He has to construct and guide his action instead of merely releasing it in response to factors playing on him or operating through him. He may do a miserable job in constructing his action, but he has to construct it" (Blumer 1969: 15).

Blumer's symbolic interactionism is not focused on the family, but it contains a wealth of ideas that can be applied to family life in general and adoption breakdown in particular. The first of these ideas, in my application of Blumer's theory, involves a person's view of family. In the case of our family, through the interaction Rod and I had with our environment and through our lived experiences, we formed our own picture, construct, or root image of family. Our picture of what a family is helped determine the desired shape of our own future family, as well as the roles for me, my husband, and each of our children. This picture was based on what each of us *noticed* and *interpreted*. When we adopted Tim, we were acting on our meanings of structure and function of a family, our roles in it, and the family's role in society. A second Blumer idea concerns *disruption*. Each one of us has learned through our personal experience, and through the actions or indications of others, what a chair is, what a star is, what a native is, and what or who each of us is. Each of these constructs can be altered by new experiences, interactions, and reflections. In our family, the shape of my family and my place in it were destroyed as a result of our difficulties with Tim. The images that I had of Tim as my son and of our family were no longer true. The painful essence of the disruption lies in the shattering of familiar patterns and roles and feelings that are meaningful to all of us. Our desire was for a close-knit family of achievers and contributors. This was incompatible with Tim's feelings of repressed anger and low self-worth. By the events surrounding the disruption process, we were unwillingly forced to redefine family and our roles within it.

The disruption was a process that forced a letting go and opening up. This leads to a third Blumer idea, namely, that we are not mere victims of circumstances but rather have the ability to make choices in reacting to those circumstances. For us, the adjustment process took place in two steps. The first was the acceptance that the old form was not viable, and the second was the devising of a new image. Three factors influenced the process: our ability to deal with our feelings of anger and hopelessness; our ability to be open to surprise and be flexible; and the new context (social-service agencies, courts, and so on) in which we found ourselves. The new definition of our images was drawn from the circumstances in which we were placed. It was a challenging and emotional exploration as each of us was required to redefine our son Tim, our family, and ourselves. For example, my roles of nurturing, caring, supporting, providing fun, sheltering, and comforting had changed to appearing in court, visiting hospitals, meeting with social workers, and participating in family-therapy sessions and parent groups.

Blumer's third idea suggests that meanings are modified by new encounters. Therefore, when we encountered unanticipated experiences or challenges that were not part of our root image or could not be dealt with in the expected way, we needed to reassess and alter the construct. These challenges caused further introspection, reflection, interpretation, and shaping. We modified our image as we encountered Tim's feelings and actions and as we met with social agencies.

Blumer describes an *interpretive process* used by a person when he or she reacts to his or her surroundings. This interpretive process has two steps. Initially, people indicate to themselves the meanings that things have for them. Then, through this communication with themselves, they interpret and react to these meanings. It is a formative process where meanings are used and revised as instruments for guidance and formation of future actions. The parents' group set up by Dr Armstrong was the key agent that helped Rod and me identify what Tim's struggles meant to us and then to see how we needed to revise and change our expectations. Further modifications resulted from our interaction not only with Tim and with agencies but also with each other in the family. Our acceptance lay both in redefining the role of the child who did not live up to or fit our earlier expectations and in reshaping our identities and roles as parents.

John P. Hewitt (1997) has elaborated Blumer's thesis, focusing not just on the role of individual choice but on the relationship between choice and personality. According to Hewitt, the symbolic interactionist paradigm explains the meanings people construct for themselves as they go about their daily lives, and how they construct them. The individual is not a mere puppet responding to the dictates of society or his or her own inner impulses; on the contrary, the individual is an active creature who constantly struggles for self-control and self-realization, sometimes following a course of action that runs counter to society's expectations and values, sometimes saying "no" to the impulses that demand a particular line of conduct. In this respect, symbolic interactionism is markedly different from behavioural and social-learning theory (which reduces human behaviour to stimulus and response), functionalism (which sees self-interest as the basis of all conduct), and psychoanalytical theory (which regards subconscious impulses as the primary force in determining conduct). Hewitt also argues, however, that our ability to reject impulses is not unconditional and limitless; it is determined by the extent to which we can see ourselves as objects, that is, viewing ourselves as others see us through the prism of their own expectations and values. This is the most fundamental of the meanings we construct for ourselves; it is the basis of each person's identity, of his or her sense of self-esteem, without which social interaction is difficult: we cannot respect others if we do not respect ourselves. Identity, self-esteem, and the construction of meaning, then, are all interrelated, for the way we view ourselves influences how we view others, how we interpret our experiences, and how we live our lives. A person's innate lack of self-esteem can dictate the choices he or she makes in life. Low self-esteem leads to anxiety and may make it difficult for an individual to feel well disposed towards others; high self-esteem, on the other hand, may make a person less sensitive to the judgments of others and thus less susceptible to social control. And so, in the end, no person is merely the product of his or her environment, just as no person entirely controls what shape his or her life may take. People are not that simple.

What this meant for Tim, as well as the other children profiled here, is complex. It is clear, first of all, that Tim's background resulted in low self-esteem and thereby may have seriously constrained his ability to respond freely and positively to the circumstances of his life. In short, Tim may not have been a mere creature of his background but his capacity to transcend that background was likely limited by the character traits he inherited at birth and developed in his early years. Some people are freer to adjust their outlook on themselves and their world than others. Yet it is also clear that a person's ability to make choices is seldom negated *completely* by his or her background; after all, many people with the most appalling pasts do manage to rise above their background and lead successful lives. It is plain as well that, by making the choices he did – whether these decisions were freely taken or not – Tim constructed an image of himself, or reinforced an existing one, that further limited his opportunities in society and his chances for a full and happy life. This was his tragedy, and ours. He, like the other adopted sons in this book, played a role in the events leading to adoption breakdown. Whether he was fully responsible for the choices he made, or whether those choices were influenced or even dictated by his background, is ultimately beside the point. The fact is that he made choices, just as we did, and that these choices had results. The adoption breakdown was not his fault alone, but neither was it ours.

The symbolic interactionist paradigm had concrete consequences not only for our family as we struggled to come to terms with our difficulties with Tim but also for the direction of my research into adoption breakdown. Specifically, by helping me to understand why we had wanted a particular type of family and why we had chosen to adopt, the Blumer paradigm led me to structure my interviews with other adoptive families in a certain way. The approach I would take in the interviews would be phenomenological, hermeneutical, and heuristic. Phenomenological, because my focus would be on the parents' experiences: their stories would recall experiences in a way that would give detailed meaning to the way they structured their lives. This kind of research, referred to as the human-science approach, is a systematic attempt to uncover or describe the internal meanings that structure lived experiences. It focuses on a particular phenomenon; here, it would focus on the meaning of the phenomenon of adoption breakdown. M. Van Manen describes phenomenological research as retrospective (1990: 10) and reflective on experience that has already been lived through. It uses specially practiced modes of questioning, reflecting, focusing, and intuiting. It is explicit and self-critical. A phenomenological description is always one interpretation, and no single interpretation of human experience will ever exhaust the possibility of yet another complementary, or even potentially *richer* or *deeper,* description.

My approach would also be hermeneutical, a word that refers to the theory and practice of interpretation (Van Manen 1990: 179). I wanted a rich description but I also wanted to understand what the experience meant to the parents. How did they interpret the breakdown of their family? How did they change? It was not my intention to stop with a description of the phenomenon of disruption; I wanted to make sense of it. I wanted to talk *with* other adoptive parents, to engage in conversation *with* them, in order

to understand the meaning of the disruption. Who we are today
has been formed by stories of our past, which help form our
personal constructs in the present. How did the disruption change
our parents' personal constructs and thus their experience as parents? By means of open, dynamic interviews, I wanted to discover
the meaning of the disruption. Hermeneutic phenomenology is
descriptive because it is attentive to how things appear and it
wants to let things speak for themselves; it is *interpretive* because
it claims that there are no such things as uninterpreted phenomena (ibid.: 180). Therefore, hermeneutic phenomenological research
is a search for the fullness of living; in the case of my study, I
searched for the ways my adoptive parents had experienced and
were experiencing their world (ibid.: 12).

Finally, my research was heuristic in the sense that the *search*
itself was critical. Clark Moustakas (1990) explains that "the root
meaning of *heuristic* comes from the Greek word *heuriskein*, meaning to discover or to find. It refers to a process of internal search
through which one discovers the nature and meaning of experience and develops methods and procedures for further investigation and analysis"(9). He further states that the researcher's
commitment to investigate personal experience propels him or
her to discover fundamental truths: "All heuristic inquiry begins
with the internal search to discover with an encompassing puz-
zlement, a passionate desire to know, a devotion and commitment
to pursue a question that is strongly connected to one's own
identity and selfhood. The awakening of such a question comes
through an inward clearing, and an intentional readiness and
determination to discover a fundamental truth regarding the
meaning and essence of one's own experience and that of others"
(41). Moustakas expands this inward inquiry to include others
who help one explore deeper meanings which are important to
the world generally: "The heuristic process is autobiographic, yet
with virtually every question that matters personally there is also
a social – and perhaps universal – significance. Heuristics is a way
of engaging in scientific search through methods and processes
aimed at discovery; a way of self-inquiry and dialogue with others
aimed at finding the underlying meanings of important human
experiences. The deepest currents of meaning and knowledge
take place within the individual through one's senses, perceptions,
beliefs, and judgements" (15).

This book exemplifies the intentions of heuristic research. By my own experience, I was motivated to do my research. With the participants, I hoped to discover the meaning of adoption breakdown. The understanding and knowledge acquired, I hoped, would lead to a reduction in the number of adoption breakdowns and a minimizing of their devastating effects.

What follows in Part One, the heart of this book, are separate chapters detailing our story and the stories of five other adoptive couples (to maintain the confidentiality both of the parents and of their adopted sons, names and places of residence have been changed). All these parents adopted their children between 1967 and 1973 – except for one boy, who was adopted in 1981. It was an idealistic time, and the adoptive parents profiled here felt that they were doing the right thing in helping a native child who, largely because of Canada's scandalous treatment of its aboriginal population, faced such a dismal future. Yet all of them have had their world turned upside down by the adoption's failure to meet their expectations. What they have in common now is sorrow over loss, anger towards a system that did not respect or help them, and doubt about their abilities as parents. What they had in common in the past was that they had each adopted an older native child, with the intention of sharing their bright and happy family lives and futures with a less fortunate child and, in so doing, to enrich their own family life as well. In the accounts presented here, in chapters 1 through 6, the parents tell of their reasons for adopting, their experiences with the child, the events that led up to the child leaving home, and their feelings about the dissolution of their adoptive relationship.

My criteria for the parents' participation in the study were that each of the couples had adopted at least one native child older than two years who had left home before the age of sixteen, after several years of conflict, to live in a government institution or on the streets; the child or children had to have been living in the home for at least five years; and the couples could not be separated or divorced. This profile would closely match our own. I asked the adoptive parents to select for the focus of our discussion one adopted child (if there was more than one) who met the criteria. Except for two children who are still not teenagers at this time, all the adopted children fit the criteria, since all had left home prematurely. The parents decided to focus on one of their adopted sons in each case, because they had been the most challenged by these sons' difficulties. That is not to say that the other children did not challenge their parents; they did but not to the same extent.

The first parents we interviewed were friends of ours. Another was made known to us through Parents for Youth, and the rest were contacted through friends and colleagues. I phoned each of them to explain the process and purpose. Every couple agreed to participate in three two-hour interviews. The first interview focused on their respective backgrounds and the initiation of the adoption process; the second interview summarized the adoption experience and the breakdown; the third interview highlighted the parents' personal struggles and their reflections. The sessions were informal and took place in our home and in the homes of the participants.

I decided at the outset that Rod would play an integral part in the research. Our adoption of Tim was a journey that we had undertaken together and its investigation would not be complete without his reflection and interpretation. I also felt that his male presence would make it possible to explore different gender interpretations. Another early decision was that the research would focus on the parents' experience. I wanted the participants to be retrospective and to remember, to tell their story, describe their feelings, and explain their understanding and reflections. I felt that Rod and I could provide a safe and comfortable environment for the participants, because we had experienced similar problems. I wanted all of us to look at the meaning of family, the experience of adoption breakdown, and the reconstruction of family.

The parents were asked in the first interview to focus on the pre-adoption events and early adoption experiences. They were asked to recall an event in their experiences with the adopted child that for them epitomized the family they had hoped for, wherein the adopted child seemed to be happy and completely integrated into the family. I identify these events as ideal-family memories. In the second interview, I asked the parents to recall the point in their relationship with their adopted child when they realized that the adoptive relationship had broken down irrevocably. This was usually a catastrophic and painful episode, a crisis, when the child suddenly appeared, not as their own child any more, but as a stranger. The realization that the child was forever lost to them was also the point at which the ideal-family construct was shattered and blown apart. I identify this sequence of events as the disruption memory. Each parent was not required to contribute both an ideal-family memory and a disruption memory (though some did); rather, though each *couple* supplied both memories, each *parent* was asked to give only one memory or the other.

The interview process provided all the participants with an opportunity to explain what the disruption had meant to them and how it had affected them. The conclusions we arrived at would help us gain an understanding of the trauma of adoption breakdown. Alone, each of us had tried to make sense of these events, to let go, to open up to other possibilities, and to accept new realities; together, we could discuss what had helped us understand the emotional difficulties involved in our gradual redefinition of the family construct. By looking backwards at our experiences, we would be able to increase our understanding; having increased our understanding, we could then more comfortably move forward.

Part Two of this book summarizes what I learned from the interview process about why people adopt (chapter 7) and about the process of adoption breakdown (chapter 8). The final two chapters draw general conclusions (chapter 9) and attempt to apply what I learned to specific issues in adoption and adoption breakdown (chapter 10). Further reflections along these lines are offered in the Epilogue, and concrete advice, in point form, to adoptive parents concludes the book.

PART ONE

Family Profiles

1 The Adams Family

Rod and I are both from Saskatchewan. Within the first five years of our married life, we enjoyed two beautiful, happy, well-adjusted children, Lorie and Jeff. At that time, there was publicity about the world population explosion and its dangers to the planet, as well as about children needing homes. And so in 1972 Rod and I applied to adopt. After we were interviewed several times over a three-month period, we saw a video of Tim, a two-and-a-half-year-old Cree boy living in Creighton, Saskatchewan. We were told that his mother was eighteen years old, had been in jail, and had other children. But only much later did we learn other details: Tim's first year and a half included many trips to the hospital for malnutrition and injuries; while his mother was in jail, his grandmother was left to look after five children; and, when she was charged with child abuse, Tim and his siblings were placed in the care of the Children's Aid Society. Tim's mother eventually committed suicide.

On Easter weekend 1973, the four of us drove for ten hours through a raging Saskatchewan blizzard to visit Tim and to decide if we wanted to bring him home. Of course, we very much wanted to adopt him. When we first arrived at his foster home, he was on a coffee table, screaming with wild abandon. I looked at Rod and told him that I would have the patience to raise him if he could control Tim's obvious physical energy. We did adopt him that

April, and six months later we adopted Melanie, a baby Metis girl, in Regina. Lorie was then six and Jeff four. I had just completed my four-year BEd degree and was staying at home to raise our family.

At the time, I had no doubts that I was up to the task of raising Tim, for I had grown up believing that, if I worked hard enough, I could make anything happen. I was born in 1945 in Gravelbourg, Saskatchewan. Both my parents were very determined people. Their attitude was that, if you are faced with a difficulty, you just go ahead and work through it. This is what each of them had done, and their spirit of determination and perseverance was embedded in me at early age.

My father's family had quite a tragic story. His father died in his forties from a heart attack. Then, a few years later, my father's older brother died from an accidental gunshot wound when he was sixteen. It was difficult for a young widow and four young children. Their house burned down because of a grease fire, and they lost everything. Shortly after, my grandmother married the hired hand. This also created difficulties, because he made sexual advances to my father's sisters, and each of them left the farm as soon as she could. When my father was in his later teens, his mother died of pneumonia. It seems that the doctors did not know that she had diabetes and they prescribed the wrong drug, further complicating her poor health. My father's stepfather later committed suicide. This meant that my father was on his own when he was twenty. He made his living by farming and working as a repairman for the telephone company.

My mother was born to a French-Canadian farming family, the Jeannottes, originally from southern Saskatchewan. She grew up a few miles from my father's home, and, although my father was eight years older than my mother, they attended the same school for a few years. My mother's father, who was an electrician, seemed to give up during the Depression, and her mother kept the family of six fed and clothed by maintaining a large garden, raising chickens, and doing hand-knitting. My mother is a wonderful cook, and she was cooking at a college for priests and brothers when she and my father decided to get married. About three years after they married, when I was six months old, we moved a few hundred miles north to the Ukrainian district of Meath Park, where my mother never really felt as though she fit in.

In this small town my father started up his own farm-machinery agency and garage. Both of my parents worked hard to make the business a success. My mother did the books for the business, cooked for the hired man, and raised the children (my brother was born when I was five). We did not have very much, but my mother was a real go-getter: she built her own kitchen cupboards and sewed from catalogue pictures. At the age of ten, I remember my mother asking me what I wanted for my birthday. I told her that I wanted a store-bought dress, something I had never had. So we went into town and bought a dress, which was not nearly as well made as the ones she made.

Ours was a strict family. Everyone did what he or she was supposed to do. Each of us understood the role we had to play, and we played it well. My father was the boss, my mother nurtured, comforted, and listened, and we children, of course, obeyed. Everything was black and white, and my parents never had to say anything more than once to me. Mealtimes were not much of a family time, because when we did sit down together we usually had a hired man boarding with us. My father and he would talk business and then go back to work. I know that my parents did not have an easy life together; in fact, I think that my mother really suffered emotional abuse from my father. No one could change him. (After Rod and I were married, we offered my mother a place to stay; if she wanted to leave, she could. She decided to stay.) Throughout his life, my father was a red-neck westerner and very set in his ways. He did not believe in luxuries of any kind. Our house was a small refurbished granary; we did not even have a coffee table until we were given one as a going-away gift. My father was always working in his garage, and the few occasions we had fun together as a family – usually at the lake – stand out in my memory because they were so rare. I also have fond memories of school, which I was good at. I started by skipping grade one, and so I was always the youngest in my class. I also took piano and swimming lessons. I was twelve when we moved to Saskatoon, and there I attended the convent as a day-student. I started Teacher's College the day I turned seventeen, and one year later I began teaching subjects in grades nine to twelve.

My husband's background is quite different. Rod came from a large extended family. His mother was the second-oldest in a family with nine children. They were quite poor and lived on a farm near

Cudworth, Saskatchewan. Rod's mother and her sister did not
have the opportunity to get much education, because they had so
many responsibilities raising the younger children; later, when
they had to sell the farm and move to Prince Albert, his grandmother took in boarders. On the other side of his family, Rod's
father was second in a family with four children. He had a happy
childhood living in a rented house in the small town of Sceptre,
where Rod's grandfather drove a school bus. At an early age,
he worked in lumber camps and later joined the army where he
learned mechanics. Soon after he met the woman who was to
become Rod's mother, the army transferred him to a base in
Ontario. Then, after a short three-month courtship, Rod's mother
travelled to Hamilton so they could get married. But six months
later, when Rod's mother was pregnant with him, his father was
transferred overseas. His mother then returned to live with her
in-laws and later with her parents. Within the year, she became
quite ill, and Rod was cared for by his aunts and uncles. In this
environment, Rod's mother struggled with her lack of independence. When Rod's father returned after the war, Rod was almost
three years old, and bonding was difficult. It was also a stressful
time, as the family moved across Canada, and then back again to
Saskatchewan, trying to get established. His sister was born
shortly after; she is four years younger. Rod also has a brother –
an "accident" – fourteen years younger.

His father owned a small service station near Prince Albert and
struggled financially during the years Rod was at school. At this
time, Rod became very interested and successful in sports. His
uncle was his role model. Rod was forced to be self-reliant and
independent. He says, "I adopted the traditional male values.
I don't think I ever had a curfew as long as I can remember."
When Rod was twenty years old, he graduated from high school
and began work with the company of which he was to become
president. Financially, Rod says, "we weren't spoiled; we came out
of families that had nothing. It was easy to aspire to have more."
About his growing up, he observes, "I have a large extended
family. I think that through that process there are always a lot of
differences of opinion, a lot of 'ups and downs,' and a lot of fights,
or whatever you want to call it. I think, for the most part, there
was still that real central feeling that you were still a family. You
could share and lean on each other."

When Rod and I got married, he was twenty and I was eighteen. Our daughter Lorie was born three years later, and Jeff was born two years after that. We had often talked about having a larger family. Rod would have been quite happy with two, but I was the one who pushed to adopt two more. I said, "If I am going to stay home, I'd like to be busy, and I don't think I'm going to be busy enough with two, who will soon be in school ... and there are so many kids needing homes, why should we have more of our own?" When we requested a child, we were willing to accept a child with a physical disability, such as a club foot or cleft palate – anything that could be corrected. We also specifically asked to have a fair-skinned child, because we did not want people to come into our home and say, "Whose kid is *that*?" Our children were both very fair, and we thought it would be awkward for the adopted child if he or she looked too dissimilar. This was a consideration we set aside once we saw Tim. At that time, native children needing homes were pictured daily in the newspaper. In general, natives were not well thought of, especially in northern Saskatchewan. We would hear that there was a lot of alcohol abuse and fighting, on and off reserves. Rod remembers, "Every time I saw a native, he or she was almost always stone-drunk. So, it was a conditioning process [for us]. From my perspective, ninety-five per cent of the Indian population had a problem with alcohol. And in sports, I saw a lot of negativity." However, when asked, Rod can explain why he agreed to adopt a native child. "I guess I was convinced that it was environment. We believed that if a child was raised in a good and loving environment, he or she could overcome whatever problems he or she had inherited or had faced before the adoption." Commenting that everyone benefits in an adoption, Rod adds, "The reason [we] adopted [was] not to be wonderful people. [We] adopted because [we] wanted to share that experience [of family] and gain from it ... It was a sharing experience."

There were a few things about Tim that stood out from the start. He was terrified of men in white coats. This was probably due to the fact that, when his foster parents took Tim to the doctor after he cut himself, the doctor stitched the wound without a local anaesthetic, just holding him down. Tim ate everything he was given, and this included an entire apple core. The agency told us that he had very good teeth. As it turned out, all of his back teeth were soft so we had to have them capped. As well, his baby teeth were stained. This was because his mother had been prescribed tetracycline when she was pregnant with him.

Tim did not seem to bond with us. He never cried for his foster parents, with whom he had lived for over a year. He also did not particularly like to be hugged or cuddled. Because he never cried, there were few opportunities to console him. When we brought him home, his vocabulary was limited to "dump truck" and "ski-doo." One thing was quite frustrating: he would not say what he wanted. He simply repeated the end of the question. For example, when we asked him, "Do you want cereal or toast for breakfast?" he would say toast. If we asked, "Do you want toast or cereal?" he would say cereal. He never said no to anything for the first year he was with us. Never. He did not seem to have a mind of his own. It was a memorable moment when the family, sitting around the table, heard Tim say no. We saw this as a big step forward.

Tim had some trouble finding his niche in the family. Lorie was so bright, and Jeff was bigger and stronger. Melanie was always cute and small. However, Tim really liked the outdoors. We used to do a lot of outdoor things: camping, hiking, and swimming. At those times – whether we were diving off the edge of the pool, canoeing, or hiking – Tim stood out, because he was so relaxed in the setting and he would notice things that no one else would notice: a bird in a tree, a concealed footprint. He never got sick and never, ever complained about being cold. He could go outside in the winter with just his shirt on and not complain. He never asked for anything.

As he grew up, Tim had a good sense of humour and enjoyed life, as long as there were not too many restrictions. He was popular with his peer group and was considered a leader. Tim was also an excellent hockey player. Rod remembers: "I spent a lot of time with Tim coaching his hockey team. I don't think there was that real sense of father-son or family. We had the physical thing, but there wasn't any real tie-in, not emotionally, not spiritually, so to speak. He didn't demonstrate many emotions. He learned to hug and give a kiss, but he wasn't spontaneous and didn't seek them out. When prompted, he would give a bear hug, but it was playful and seemed devoid of emotion. Even when he was nineteen, he would give one of us a hug, but a light hug."

Still, our family's early years in Saskatchewan and British Columbia were fun-filled and very good. Our serious difficulties began only when we moved to Alberta and Tim started school. In school, Tim was an underachiever and often got into trouble. He chose to lie every time he thought he was in trouble. At home, he behaved the same way. For example, he would steal a chocolate bar or a coke, and Rod or I would say, "Tim, did you take it?" He would reply, "No." It was so frustrating. I would say, "We won't punish you if you tell us the truth. Did you take it?" or "Why are you lying?" Then he would always respond, "I don't know." The opportunity to build trust was not there. It seemed that every time you would give him the benefit of the doubt he would take advantage of it. He would lie constantly. We tried disciplining with time-outs, lost allowances, and limiting television, but nothing worked.

In 1980, when Tim was eleven, we moved to Toronto because of Rod's job. We wanted to find a culturally diverse neighbourhood. So, when we began to shop for a house, we drove around the city to look at the kids as they were going home for lunch. We moved into a neighbourhood where there were Canadians of Asian, East Indian, Italian, Filipino, and other backgrounds. For a short time afterwards, all our children did well. There were a lot of happy moments. We had some great times swimming in the backyard and also travelling across Canada. We even took a trip to Walt Disney World in Florida. Tim seemed so happy. He was strong physically, a great swimmer and hockey player. He was witty, with a quick grin. I can remember often looking around and thinking that life was just about perfect. The children were growing up and doing so well. Rod was successful at his job, and I had started a teaching job, which I really enjoyed.

But the good times did not last, for Tim's troubles became more severe. When he was eleven, Rod and I arranged for him to visit a psychiatrist. This doctor played chess with him. Even though this did not seem to be the best tactic to use with Tim, who was so active, the psychiatrist was friendly and conscientious. He told us that Tim was a time-bomb and, thus, potentially dangerous. Once he called us to his office late at night and advised us to cancel a weekend trip – a respite for me – because he was worried. Tim had told him that he was going to harm his younger sister if we left. As time went on, we had more concerns. Rod remembers the "sick smile, almost like he was saying, 'I don't care what you do.' He used to get this funny grin on his face that used to disturb us so much. His eyes would glaze over. You could never find the 'hot button' with Tim. It was so frustrating."

Then the real trouble began. That second summer after we moved, Tim started lighting fires in the neighbourhood. He lit fires on lawns and once burned down an attached garage. When we found out, we turned him in to the police. In response to the arson charge (to which Tim was to plead guilty), we hired a lawyer, Monty Harris, who in turn elicited the services of Dr Harvey Armstrong, a psychiatrist at the Family Court Clinic, to interview our family and to write an assessment for the court. At this time, Dr Armstrong was piloting a support group for parents who, like Rod and me, were distraught over their children's severe behavioural problems. After resisting for many months – probably because of my shame and embarrassment – we joined a group, which met once a week. We stayed with it for more than two years. This experience lessened my guilt and helped Rod and me to accept what was happening to our family, as well as to be more realistic about our expectations of Tim and of ourselves. However, the group did not explain *how* something that had seemed so right could turn out so wrong. As well, we were faced with life's normal crises: a change of residence and business locations, job responsibilities, my father's death from cancer, and, in my case, a crippling back problem.

Meanwhile, Tim continued to spiral out of control. He stole pornographic books, a bike, canaries, and money. He would sneak out of the house many nights, and he ran away a couple of times. He had a kind of funny obsession with animals. He had stolen a hamster, and we found it in his bed. He would steal the girls' panties and other things like tools and knives. His room began to smell; the wall behind his captain's bed was coated with semen and urine. Finally, he stole some music tapes from a nearby store, and when he was taken to the police station, he repeated what he had often said: "I don't wanna live with you." He would say this in a very snarly way. We broke down and said, finally, "Okay, you win!" Of course, at that time, we thought that he would soon want to come back home.

After Tim left at age twelve, Rod says, "I ... was just happy by the end of the day – you could feel the tension leaving our house – because he was turning our house upside down." But for me, it was a very different experience. When he did not come home, I walked in the house, and it was so still, so calm. For about one year before that, the air had been so thick that you could have cut it with a knife. When people came to visit, they commented on the tense atmosphere. The day he left, this calmness made me realize that it was over. It just hit me and I screamed. I thought I was all alone, and I just screamed and cried and cried. It hurt so much. And then Jeff came downstairs and said, "Mom, what's the matter?" I thought I had a private moment when I could let all the hurt out alone, and now my son was witnessing my agony. I felt terrible. After that, I felt a heavy, heavy sadness, and there was a long mourning period. But Tim was at least still alive then, and when I look at this period now, there was still hope that maybe some day he would be okay.

Soon after he left home, Tim went to Thistletown, a home for children who have severe emotional difficulties. While he was in the lock-up facility there, he was given medication to sedate him. Then he started running away, and he again got into trouble with the law. He overdosed a couple of times; once, it was alcohol poisoning. He just drank until he dropped. Each time, we visited him in the hospital. He also had some needle marks, but he said he really was not into the hard drugs. Many times over the next few years, one of us went out looking for him, driving around the city, looking in all those horrible areas downtown. Tim just seemed to be far too young to be on the streets.

By now, Tim, who had just entered puberty, was starting to display anger towards women. He was angry with me. The agencies would team up a female worker with a male worker for him. At this time, as well, Tim often voiced his anger with us for adopting him. He said that he had learned the white man's values and the white man's culture but did not fit into either native or white society. He called himself an apple Indian (the white values inside, covered by red skin). Sometimes, when he was coming off drugs, he would phone and yell, "Your f...ing grandmothers killed my f...ing grandmother." He phoned me often when he was either on drugs or coming off drugs. He was angry with me for a long time.

I would try to explain, "You're mad at your biological mother and grandmother because they hurt you so much, but you're taking it out on me."A couple of times over the first three years, we were called to the Youthdale Crisis Centre, an institution to which Tim had been brought from a group home. Once, he was in a strait-jacket and verbally abusive with everyone. He rolled on the floor and tried to shove into people. It was so difficult for us to watch our son writhing in a straitjacket, yelling obscenities.

After two years of treatment centres, which cost the govern-ment some three or four hundred dollars a day, we were told to take him home or we would have to start paying the costs. Rod and I signed a release form that in effect gave him back to the Children's Aid Society. This was one of the hardest things we ever had to do, but I do not think that any of us looked at our rela-tionship with Tim any differently. He was still our son, even though we knew that legally he was no longer ours. Six years later, we were responsible for his funeral, but only because we asked to be.

He was in constant trouble with the law over those years. Until he was sixteen, Rod and I phoned and/or visited him in detention centres; afterwards, he was usually the one who initiated the visits. He had charges against him for break-and-enter, assault, aggravated assault, drug possession, and prostitution. Once, on a TV documentary, he was interviewed as the most popular boy prostitute in "Boys Town" (the area for young male prostitutes in downtown Toronto). When Tim was in jail, he also had a difficult time. Rod says, "He would often comment on the hatred between the blacks and the native Indians in jail. He felt that the native Indians were one step above the blacks." One time, when the police were looking for him, Tim phoned us and said he wanted to see us. Rod recalls, "I drove down to the subway station to meet him. Just after he got off the phone, a couple of police cars had gone by the subway station, and so he ran. Later, he phoned us so angry, because he said we had called the police." After he turned sixteen, Tim started to phone us more often. It seemed that he phoned when he wanted something to eat and when he was coming off drugs or just before his birthday. Meanwhile, our commitment to Tim meant that Rod and I had many meetings and visits with his social workers. It also meant that the family attended special family-therapy sessions. These were stressful and frustrating, because it was difficult for all of us to attend and, sometimes, Tim, who was living on the premises, would not show up. Tim's siblings resented these sessions.

There were times when Tim seemed to make some progress. He would be in a detoxification centre for a while and would get through the program, but after a week or so he would be back drinking again. There was one new program with a theatrical group that he seemed to enjoy for two or three months, but he did not quite finish it because he hit the bottle again and returned to the streets. He worked at Select Sandwiches for a while, as part of another program, and then with Anishnawbe and Native Child and Family Services. He never came back home to stay. The longest visit took place after he had been released from prison, when he was nineteen; he stayed for two weeks, and it was a good visit. By this time, he was able to talk about his feelings and his problems. He seemed to want to make a fresh start. His social worker helped him find an apartment, and then, as Rod says, "We moved him down there, set up his apartment, gave him a bunch of stuff, paid his first and last month's rent ... He never did make another payment on the rent. He ended up getting kicked out, and all his stuff was dumped outside in the backyard."

Once, when he was fourteen, I read a description of the sociopathic personality. I was horrified. It seemed to be a description of Tim. He manipulated people. He could be charming – socially, Tim was very good, even when we had company for dinner – but then he would break the rules of the house, the legal limits, or would assault someone. He never acknowledged his guilt and never really apologized for anything. And soon he would be doing it again. He did not seem to have any remorse or conscience. At the same time, Tim always seemed to get hooked up with somebody who was just as badly off as he was. They would end up pulling each other down instead of helping each other. He had a native girlfriend for three years who also had a problem with alcohol. One time, they assaulted someone who would not give them a cigarette. She was a prostitute and had been in jail a few times. During the five days before Tim died, however, she was always by his bed. Two years later, she, too, died tragically in downtown Toronto.

That last year, in January, when Rod was away in Florida, Tim phoned me and wanted to come for a visit. I was worried about meeting him at home alone, so I arranged to meet him in a restaurant. We had a chance to talk seriously. He told me that he was not really that badly off. He was not sleeping over warm air-vents, because he usually had a place to stay. I am glad I had those two hours with him. I suppose that, through all those years, we always had hope.

IDEAL-FAMILY MEMORY

My ideal-family memory takes us back to Big White Ski Resort in the Rocky Mountains. There was fresh powder, and we were skiing near the top of the mountain. The sun was shining, the sky was blue, and the snow was piled high on the trees. No one else was in sight, just us: the four kids, Rod, and I. Tim was sort of giggling and laughing without restraint, being himself. Nobody was doing anything wrong, there were no interruptions, no hassles: it was an unblemished and relaxed time. There was no competition; we were together, in harmony, separate from the rest of the world. There were no rules, and the hierarchy of family structure seemed absent. Tim was in his element. This occasion was so special for me, because, as a child, I had experienced only a few carefree times in my family. Rod says that he would have picked another kind of memory: "There were times that I would take Tim and Jeff to hockey. They play their hockey, and we might stop at McDonald's [Restaurant], or something, afterwards. There seemed to be an atmosphere. I felt that Tim was really part of the family." Rod says that this memory is significant for him, because his father had never attended any of Rod's sports events when he was a child.

DISRUPTION MEMORY

The occasion that signified for Rod the point at which he realized that Tim was not going to be an integral part of the family took place when Tim was twelve years old:

It was very vivid to me. It was in the kitchen, and it happened at dinner time. It was after a period of time when we had been experiencing a lot of difficulty with Tim walking at night and going out of the house, and, trying to guard

against that there was a good deal of tension and pressure
within the home. Something came up through that particular
meal, where Tim's behaviour became extremely negative.
And, as a result, I was trying to discipline him in terms of the
situation. As I think about that time, it is almost like, when
I relate to it, all of a sudden, everyone disappeared, everyone
was gone. And there was just Tim and me. I don't even know
if that's what it was, but that's the way I always remember.
It was just Tim and me, and everyone just kind of gone. And
I forget what I said to Tim, I was extremely angry. And I said
to him, "Your attitude, if you want to continue that way,
I am going to beat the crap out of you," or something like
that. I was really right at my ... and he just gave me this
real, sick kind of smile. He said, "Do whatever you want.
I don't care what you do." And, this whole sense of, I guess,
hopelessness just washed over me. I mean, it just washed
over me, I mean, it was just unbelievable, in the sense that
[there] was absolutely nothing that I was gonna be able to do
that was going to really impact this kid. It just wasn't there.

Rod says that for him this was the end of what he had dreamt of:
Tim fitting into the family environment, no matter how difficult
things got:

I just knew, or felt, [that] there was no elasticity. There was
no getting angry on his part and coming back as family.
There was nothing there, just *nothing*. And that was the point
that I felt [it]. I guess because it stood out so clearly in my
mind as being a breaking [point], especially for me. And I
consider myself fairly optimistic and the optimism left with
Tim at that particular time. And when you just isolate the
situation, it seems like a very small item, but for me it was
a very ... I guess, a turning point. There was just something
there that ...well ... hopelessness, everything seemed so
hopeless. That's always been the point. That stood out of my
mind as being the one [occasion] where I really felt that. It
just wasn't going to work with Tim, not in a traditional sense.
You know you may be going through difficulty but there was
still the hope that, you know, we make some inroads, so that
you can influence him somehow. But, I really sensed that,

he was … certainly walking to a different beat of the drum.
[There] was just no way that it was going to happen. There
was a tremendous amount of anger. But once that had sub-
sided, and I was dealing with this kind of shell of [a] person.
I guess I felt sad, and I felt … almost beaten, somehow, like
I just … frustration, all of those things. And I think I just kind
of walked away from it.

The effect Tim had on our family was widespread. Although Rod
never blamed me for what happened – I would have been devastated if he had – he was often exasperated with my feelings of
responsibility and sadness. I would frequently cry and want to
talk about Tim, but Rod would ask me to drop the subject for a
while. Rod recalls that "the guilt trip used to drive me nuts. She
resorts to crying. I can't get into all these emotions. [She had]
become a much more serious person. I think those are things that
I hate[d] to see go away, because that's an important part of life,
being able to laugh, and that's where I [saw] the difference in
[Marie]. I think it's hard to be totally honest with your partner,
too, because you don't want to hurt them any more. They're
struggling, and you know sometimes you're fighting some of
those feelings. And that can be stressful in itself."

Rod says that he did not share my feelings of responsibility. He
knew that there was not much more that could have been done
for Tim. He expresses it this way: "I feel sorry, but I don't share
any guilt. I am not going back saying, 'God, if I would have been
at home at 5:30 instead of 6:00 three days a week, this never
would have happened.' I don't say those words." But when he is
pushed on the subject of guilt, Rod says that any guilt he felt
would have been focused on the other children and the effect that
Tim had on them.

We were angry at the effect Tim had on the other members of
the family. Because our home was often filled with tension and
because we deferred to Tim on so many occasions, the other children probably suffered from a lack of attention from us and from
the absence of the stability of a normally functioning family. Even
ordinary things, like a happy supper together, were marred by
tension and tears, with the children not wanting to be at the table
when things got out of hand. So often we felt that we were not
carrying on with our usual responsibilities towards the other

children. Tim, in fact, took up more space and time in the family, and, as a result, the other children were probably deprived of a lot of things. One daughter suffered from an eating disorder, and she was terrified that Tim would break in and hurt her. For many years, she had nightmares of him holding a knife over her, and our son now admits that he slept with a knife in the door – to keep it closed or locked.

Except for one special couple, our family and friends were essentially unsupportive, and, for some, Tim did not seem to really exist. Inquiries would be made about our other children but not about Tim. We also worried about the effects of Tim's criminal activities on our neighbourhood. The time he set fire to a neighbour's garage made us realize that Tim might be capable of much worse, even of killing someone. We felt anger and frustration that there was so little help for Tim or for us as parents. I did go back to the Children's Aid Society two years later, but they were not particularly interested in helping us: it was *our* problem by then. We were made to feel as though we were at fault as a family. Consequently, we were told, the family needed fixing. To put it in Rod's words, "It's a square peg in a round hole, and they wanted to change us. When you do try to force that, it cracks, the family cracks, we *all* did crack."

We came to realize gradually that we were wrong to think that Tim could fit into our family. As a result, both Rod and I adjusted our levels of expectations. Rod admits, "I don't expect such high standards from people." And I certainly experienced a change in my self-image and in my level of confidence through our experiences with Tim: I wasn't the wonderful person I thought I was, and I am not entirely sure if my confidence will ever be fully restored.

Throughout these years, we found solace and refuge in work and sport and in our other children. For me, the physical separation from home when I was at work helped me to forget for a few hours the unpleasantness of what the family was going through. Work was like an island refuge. Relief came, too, when Tim was in jail, for then we could breathe more easily, knowing that he was in the care of others for a time and would be safer incarcerated than he would be living on the streets. We also found support in Dr Armstrong's group and in his counsel. What he once told us relieved a lot of the anxiety about Tim's behaviour and about what was going to happen next: "Imagine the worst," he told us, "whatever the worst is, it will happen. Whatever it is, prepare for that." This bit of advice gave us a sense of control: we were prepared.

And so, when Tim reached the end of his life in August 1992, we were devastated but not surprised. The street workers considered Tim's death, and others like it, a form of passive suicide, a result of a high-risk lifestyle. Tim had said many times to us, "I'm not going to live 'til I'm old; I'm going to die young." It was terrible for the workers and for us to see him destroying his life. The risk-taking was somewhat similar to someone with lung cancer continuing to smoke and turning down treatment. Tim was so young. We were prepared for his early death; we just didn't know what form it would take – drugs, violence, AIDS? For us, his death was not that of the wonderful little boy who had lived with us; rather, it was the death of the person whom we would sometimes see and who would sometimes come to our house for a Sunday visit. When he died physically, the hope that he would finally turn his life around and be able to accept and trust himself, look forward to the future, and perhaps be able to contribute to society evaporated. We saw his death as an end to his unhappiness, but it was also a loss of opportunity for him to live and enjoy life. There was a real sadness that his life seemed to have been for naught.

Tim's death was not considered a terrible tragedy by others in our family. When he died, not one relative offered to come to the memorial service. Perhaps they viewed our relationship with Tim as an artificial arrangement over which we should not be too upset, because Tim had been such a problem and, after all, he was "only" adopted. They did not seem to think about the emotional investment that we had made over the eighteen years that we knew Tim. And if they did not see his death as a loss, how could they see our need for their support?

Fortunately, others did rally around us. The native community invited us to join his street friends and workers in a sweetgrass ceremony in a downtown Toronto park. We shared the ritual of the smoke, and we knew that all those present shared our deep sorrow. A couple of days afterwards, many of our friends and associates, as well as social workers and friends who had known Tim on the streets, attended a memorial service; it was a tremendous gathering of over two hundred people, and a Roman

Catholic priest and a native leader were co-officiants. The service was not really for Tim; it was for us, the living. His death served to bring all of us together. For our own family, this memorial was also a recognition of the loss we had felt so poignantly ten years before when Tim had left our home. I had been mourning him for all those years before his death.

There was such an outpouring of sympathy at the service. And I kept thinking that I had needed some of this sympathy years ago. I did not need it so much now; I no longer had any hope. It was back then that I would have liked people to have said, "It's okay. We're here for you. We want to help you." But I understood that it was not anybody's fault. They would have been there, if they had known what to do or what to say.

In the fall of 1993, our family laid Tim's ashes to rest near a pond, under a young maple tree, while a lone heron circled high in the blue sky. According to Indian legend, this was an auspicious sign.

2 The Roethler Family

The story of the Roethler family is a complicated one. Alison and Georg Roethler did not have any of their own children and adopted together three older native children – siblings – each of whom presented a particular challenge.

Alison Michaels grew up in Reading, Massachusetts, in a middle-class family. She had an older sister and a younger brother, and both her parents were professionals. Although her father worked every day, her mother, a landscape architect, stayed home when the children were growing up. The family reflected the typical family structure of the times. Father worked hard and long hours, a stern, distant, and quiet man who read to his children but never played with them. Alison regrets not having had the opportunity to get to know him any better. Her mother, although a quiet woman in her own right, was supportive of her children and went to their school events and hockey games. She influenced the children in her own particular way. Although Alison's parents were not overly strict, the children respected the control and authority their parents wielded; the mere threat of punishment was effective discipline. This was the way most families seemed to operate.

Alison had a Quaker education, even though the family was not religious. This schooling instilled a particular set of values, and the weekly services and community projects that were part of the curriculum gave her a strong moral foundation. After university, in the late 1950s, she went with a friend to Germany, where she worked in a laundry and in a pharmacy before she started teaching. She met Georg, a German, in England while she was on holiday, and the two went back to Germany together. They were both twenty-four when they got married, and they lived in Germany for four years before immigrating to Canada. Alison's family was horrified that she had married a foreigner, and her sister was not happy with having a person of another nationality in the family. For their part, Georg's parents were not thrilled with the marriage either and in particular with the prospect of Georg and his new bride moving to Canada.

During the war, Georg's grandfather had been a member of the Nazi Party, while his grandmother demonstrated against it. Georg's father was part of a large family, and his father's brother's family had eight children before six more children were adopted. Georg speculates that these children were probably intended to be used as cheap labour. Georg's mother was his father's second wife, the first having died in childbirth. His father, an inventory supervisor, was a fairly quiet yet outgoing and happy-go-lucky type; his mother was the boss and spent a few years supporting the family by working away from home. Georg had three younger siblings and a half-sister, who died during the war.

Towards the end of the war, the family was evacuated to southern Germany and lived on a small farm. They went on holidays together and enjoyed hiking. Georg liked going on long bicycle rides on his own and hiking with his buddies. Because the educational system in Germany streamed students into different programs after grade eight, Georg started college in a commercial apprenticeship program and worked hard to earn his high-school diploma at night. In the 1960s he was active in the anti-war movement.

When he and Alison came to Toronto, Alison got a job at a girls' school and earned her teaching degree over a few summers. Georg also eventually entered the teaching profession. Together, they talked a lot about having a family. Having just acquired a teaching position, Alison was reluctant to take time away to have a family. In any case, she loved her teaching job too much to give it up. Upon her insistence, they decided that they would adopt instead. They decided on two children and were not particular about whether they should request infants or older children. "We didn't care whether they were infants, because we thought it wouldn't make a big difference. We thought we should take hard-to-place children, because that was just our idea of what was personally right about adopting for us," recalls Alison. All the Roethlers knew was that they should request children who had experienced difficulty in finding a home, although they did not think that their active family lifestyle would be easy on a child with a physical handicap. They knew that children of colour and older children were in the hard-to-place category. Soon after reading an article in the "Today's Child" column in the newspaper about children looking for a home, Alison contacted the Children's Aid Society.

The Roethlers were put under the care of Sally, a social worker with an excellent reputation. One day while Sally was away on holidays, another social worker phoned the Roethlers about three cute and active siblings who were currently living on a small farm in Kenora. They were in need of immediate adoption, because their foster mother was not well. The timing could not have been more perfect. The year was 1972, and since it was July and both Georg and Alison were off from teaching for the summer, they were able to fly out on a Friday to meet the children: Donald, seven, born in 1965; Rebecca, four, born in 1967; and Jimmy, three, born in 1968. By the following Monday, the children were in their new home, only nine months after Alison had contacted the Children's Aid Society.

All that Georg and Alison knew about their children, apart from a basic medical history, was that they were native and had been born at Blue Lake, in northern Ontario, of an alcoholic mother, who had been in and out of jail. They had the same father, who, at the time of the adoption, was in a jail in Manitoba. The children were in a poor state and had suffered from neglect, so they were eventually removed from their birth mother by the police. For the next two years, the children lived together in several different foster homes. One of the foster families could not cope with the three children and shipped them back by plane. In the last foster home, the parents had been particularly abusive and meted out cruel punishments that included holding the children's heads under water. The foster parents even warned the Roethlers against taking Jimmy because, they said, he was evil.

Once home with their instant family, Georg and Alison's nightmarish struggle to cope with their children began. Although the children played well together, their behaviour was strange.

Of the three, Donald was the only one who really spoke, so he became the interpreter for the other two. The three siblings were a tight little unit and would go off and busy themselves. They played inventive games and liked lots of pencil-and-paper activities. However, they hoarded things such as food. They were resilient children who could tolerate cold and injuries without complaint. Sally, their social worker, advised the Roethlers not to finalize the adoption so that they could have access to support services, if they needed them. Sally knew that this adoption would be difficult, and she spent the next two years working closely with the Roethlers and offered them all the support she could.

Life over the next few years was a fragile existence that depended on regular routine. If anything threatened to disrupt this routine, such as taking a trip, the children would get frightened and would act in a bizarre manner. When times were difficult, Georg and Alison discussed the possibility of sending the children back, but they knew that if they opted for this choice, the children's lives would be ruined completely. The prospect of having the children possibly split up and bounced from one foster home to another made the Roethlers realize that the children's best chances lay with them. As time went by, Georg and Alison became even more determined not to give up. These were *their own* kids; it did not matter that they carried the genes of another couple. They speculated that perhaps their own biological children might have been difficult to raise, too. Bonding with the children took more than five years.

When the children started school in the fall, a babysitter came in for the afternoons; she was good with them. Even Sally came to babysit occasionally, perhaps because she felt pity for the Roethlers' precarious situation. The Roethlers deliberately sent the children to a racially mixed school so that they could fit in more easily. But even there, when Alison came to pick them up at the end of the day, other children would ask them in disbelief, "Is *that* your mother?" The parents tried to involve the children in the local native centre, but it was disappointing to find nobody there. Alison understood the children's need to identify with their aboriginal roots and traditions while coming to terms with the white society in which they found themselves.

During these years, Georg and Alison found solace in their teaching jobs. Having a career, especially for Alison, gave her a sense of accomplishment and success, and it helped her realize that not everything in her life was fraught with failure. She took up playing the clarinet, which made her forget for a while the nightmare that had become their life. Still, in this atmosphere and because of their focus on their children, the Roethlers found it hard to maintain friendships and to make new friends. There was a certain shame in having such troubled children, and they were convinced that other people would not understand that the problems their children were having with the law, for example, were not the result of a lack of parental love. Besides, Georg and Alison did not particularly want to face astonished looks when they admitted that they still stood by these children, still had faith in them, and still loved them. In any case, the children could not be left in the care of a sitter for long, because they were so hard to handle. It seemed that any time Georg and Alison planned a special evening for themselves, something would happen with one of the children to put a stop to the arrangements.

There were, however, some enjoyable times. All the children were quite musical and took lessons. The family enjoyed the outdoors and went hiking, cross-country skiing, canoeing, and swimming together, and they often went to conservation areas for picnics. When they were still young, Georg took Rebecca and Jimmy to Germany, where he still had an uncle. The uncle's house – a sort of fundamentalist inn – was located right in the Alps. The children met their cousins and spent the entire summer playing together. There were other highlights for the family over the next few years, but, more often than not, the family did not seem complete, because one of the children was in trouble or missing. Social workers came and went, but they only seemed to make matters a little bit worse. One by one, the children slipped from their parents' reach, as each struggled with inner turmoil.

One of the first things Alison remembers teaching Jimmy was not to crawl under cars. He was a curious little boy and extremely active. His liveliness and quick wit and humour were entertaining during the day, but at bedtime he would be still bouncing up and down, eyes wide open, and destroying his surroundings. In order to get Jimmy to lie quietly, one parent had to lie with him. It sometimes took two hours for him to fall asleep. A scrawny, skinny little boy, with a potbelly and pipe-stem arms and legs, he suffered from terrible nightmares, chronic nosebleeds, bedwetting, and ear infections, and, like his brother and sister, he eventually needed a tonsillectomy and glasses. In the beginning, all Jimmy could say was "yellow submarine."

From the start, Jimmy was deeply attached to the family cat, and his mother worried that when the cat died, Jimmy would lose a little piece of himself. He loved Lego building blocks and took great pride in whatever he built. Like his siblings, he enjoyed drawing. He could occupy himself for long periods of time, but he could not sit down and play board games nor could he fit in with team sports. After he got over his initial dread of water, he joined a swim club in senior public school and was quite a good swimmer. He asked a lot of "why" questions and was extremely curious, but without the normal inhibitions one would expect in a child. The Roethlers were forced to put padlocks on the main doors, from the inside, because Jimmy would get up early in the morning and go outside. One time, he fearlessly entered another family's house and, with lipstick from a make-up kit, marked up the walls.

In school, Jimmy was a teacher's worst nightmare. Although the older children would tolerate his presence, they never included him in their activities. In his desperation to fit in and to belong to a group, Jimmy would make up weird stories. At one point, a doctor prescribed the drug Ritalin to control his hyperactivity, but he became such a zombie that the medication was discontinued. There was nothing that Georg and Alison could hold up as a carrot to motivate him. His behaviour fluctuated between moderate and extreme expressions of rage. His parents could tell when trouble was about to erupt when Jimmy drew an extraordinary number of skulls, death symbols, and Nazi swastikas. He was never well behaved for any length of time, and he always managed to disrupt significant family occasions such as birthdays and Mother's Day.

In his early teens, Jimmy's behaviour became even more erratic and bizarre. He did not eat properly and got run down. He was still very hyperactive and, in his search for an identity, he experimented with different persona: the ninja dressed in black and lurking in the dark, the punk, the skinhead, the motorcycle gang member, the cult member, the Satanist. Even his speech became monotone and robotic. He lost all sense of language. It was "fuck this" and "fuck that," says Alison. His parents could not have a proper conversation with him; everything was negative. He marched to his own drummer. He shoplifted and was also accused of going in a parking garage, getting into people's cars, and rifling through their glove compartments. Georg and Alison were even told once that Jimmy had sexually assaulted a boy. The police were often involved. A psychiatrist said that Jimmy suffered from an identity disorder.

Jimmy wanted to have a weapon, and his mother found missing kitchen knives under his mattress, as well as a pellet gun and chains which he had hidden under his clothes. Alison remembers, "I smashed more than one pellet gun in my life, and we had to throw away a lot of knives." Jimmy was eventually charged with carrying a concealed weapon. His parents felt that the boy they had come to know was now a different person: his behaviour was bizarre and his personality not his own.

By the time that Jimmy was fifteen, he began to run away, and many times his parents went to the Eaton Centre to find him and bring him home. Jimmy was put on different medications, but he would never stick to it, and then he would be off again. He lived on the streets and, according to his parents, hung out with the worst scum – criminals. However, they also realized that he had found his little community of outcasts: thieves, street kids, drug addicts, and bag ladies. By seventeen, Jimmy's criminal activities had escalated to breaking and entering private property. When he broke into his own home, smashing the front door into a thousand pieces, his mother began to fear being at home alone. Georg and Alison started fortifying their home, feeling under siege under their own roof.

The Roethlers despaired at the obvious pain and loneliness their youngest son was experiencing. They could clearly see that his difficulties were not of his own doing, but also that there was simply nothing that they or anyone could do to help him. This helplessness was their biggest frustration. When they ran out of ideas on their own, Georg and Alison enlisted outside help. They contacted many agencies, but most of them had long waiting lists. Later, Jimmy was considered too old or too severe a problem. Finally they found an organization, Dalewood, that took him in, reluctantly; most agencies would not consider a dangerous sixteen- or seventeen-year-old youth. Jimmy soon ran off from an outdoor camp and broke into a cabin and stole a truck, whereupon he was charged with property damage, possession of stolen goods, and theft. During his jaunts away from Dalewood, he would adopt his ninja mode and frighten the staff. Later, he ran away to Kingston where he committed another break-and-enter offence and stole guns. For these offences he spent three months in a detention centre. While he was at Dalewood, he was away from the influence of the streets and had to get used to a highly regimented system. He was also involved in a wilderness-survival program.

The Dalewood camp program had a pilot mothers' group where Alison found some support among the other mothers. Meeting other parents made Alison feel better: "You met the other parents, and it was nice to look around and think, 'I'm not a freak; everybody here is pretty normal.'" Before this point, Alison could exchange her stories only with her sister, who also had two adopted children. She now realized that she and Georg were not alone in this mess; in fact, family-therapy sessions sometimes revealed that some of the other troubled children were worse than their own. Still, they resented attending these weekly sessions, especially after a hard day at work and all of the other concerns of their lives. They did not at all feel comfortable with the way the agencies regarded them. They were often made to feel that they had failed their children. Georg recalls, "They didn't like parents who challenged them. We were really not considered valid, somehow our opinions didn't count. Jimmy was considered [only] because he was sixteen. They didn't like the idea that he had been involved with guns. In the system, there is a tremendous gap; there aren't many places to go if the kid is sixteen or seventeen."

It was this resentment that finally led Georg to the conclusion that Jimmy should sort out his own problems. "We had put in so many hours and we were trying to get our own life together and to carry on with our work or whatever. And then we'd have to go down to these meetings all the time. I think that's when I started thinking, it's not our problem, it's his problem, or it's their problem, and why should we be involved anymore?" They had done their very best for Jimmy, and they had given him everything they could. Perhaps that would be enough to sustain him as he sought help on his own.

Government agencies, social organizations, and the courts had not provided the Roethlers with the help that they had expected. Indeed, their view of the system was negative, because it was abusive to their children and themselves. They did not have a choice as to what doctors and social workers would be assigned to their case. As a result, they often got less-than-satisfactory help. Sometimes they had to wait for Jimmy to break the law before they received any assistance. Even then, when Jimmy once asked if he could remain in a prison he felt happy in, he was transferred to another one. Alison felt that Jimmy could not get the help he needed, because he was incapable of communicating with those who could best help him.

The Roethlers were drained of all their strength and vitality; they had been defeated too many times. Their energy for other pastimes and each other flagged, and they often found that they had no emotional energy left for anything else. Their circumstances were not conducive to a happy marriage. As each felt more and more despondent over their difficulties, the energy to support the other spouse slowly disappeared; worse, they sometimes found cause to attack each other. When Alison wanted to cry, for example, Georg would become upset and impatient with her and was incapable of showing much compassion. Alison recalls, "Sometimes, I needed to cry, but [he'd] say, 'Don't cry.' I would want to cry, and if I cried, I knew it would upset him, so I tried not to cry. I mean, I found this hard." And when Georg decided to take a tougher stance with Jimmy, Alison did not always agree with her husband or stand by him. Conflicts over what to do with Jimmy were frequent. "Those were pretty big disagreements because you tended to ignore things – damn it – you have to deal with things," says Georg.

Alison went to see Jimmy in the hospital after a horrifying incident in which he was thrown off a moving train. She recounts that, as soon as he was discharged, the police took him directly from the hospital to jail. "They wouldn't let me take him home from the hospital, they marched in the hospital as soon as he was discharged and took him over and charged him and threw him into jail, right from the hospital. It was disgusting. I was irate and powerless, and I was screaming and sobbing in the police station for two hours, yelling at them. It was awful. It was horrible."

When Jimmy was thirteen or fourteen, Georg and Alison were paying a lawyer who helped them work out a plan of action. They negotiated with a childcare worker to have Jimmy come and live with him for a year. After this stable time, Jimmy returned home and had a job with a roofing company. But things quickly started to fall apart once more. Jimmy again went into his skinhead mode, and even in his new circles he felt rejected. Alison says, "It was ironic, because here was this boy of colour trying to fit in with skinheads who didn't want anything to do with him. He got beaten up really badly. We'd bring him home from the hospital, but he'd run off again the next day." When Jimmy was about seventeen, Georg and Alison wanted to be able to support their son in any efforts he was going to make, but they decided they were not going to pay for more lawyers. At one point, however, Jimmy was lucky to find a good legal-aid lawyer.

As for the other children, they were also experiencing difficulties. Jimmy's sister, Rebecca, was a shy and withdrawn little girl when she came to live with the Roethlers. Her whole body was hunched up and she made a lot of animal-like noises and giggled a lot. Alison recalls, "Rebecca had the worst tantrums; she was very hard to reach. I never had a hug from Rebecca." Rebecca was good in school and enjoyed drawing, at which she was quite good. The most musical of the three, she took music courses, sang in the choir, and played the piano. She joined Brownies, but she did not make any friends. Still, she was not any trouble until she hit puberty at just over twelve years old. "She could, and still can, give a silent treatment like no person in the world can," says her mother. "For punishment, we used to put them into the corner, but this didn't work for Rebecca. She stood there for hours."As Jimmy's problems increased, Rebecca became even more withdrawn and went downhill quickly. Alison feels that, with Jimmy taking up so much of their time, she and George inadvertently neglected Rebecca.

By the time she was eighteen and in grade thirteen, Rebecca started to act out sexually; she began sleeping around, once had a very abusive boyfriend, and hung around with people who were heavy drug-users. "She screwed everything up," says her mother, and then ran away. She lived in utter squalor and would not accept any help from her parents, who worked hard at keeping in touch with her. She lived a life of heavy drinking and promiscuity. She even had a baby that was taken away by the Children's Aid Society, because it was not being cared for. During those desperate years, Rebecca had contact with native people, some of whom were in college or university. One fellow, whom

Georg and Alison quite liked, was in college and very involved with native traditions. He even carried a little medicine bag.

As for Donald, Georg and Alison's oldest child, he was an outgoing and physically active youngster, but he did not do well at school. He could not focus on anything for long, and even though he was in Cubs for one year, he could not make or keep friends. Because of his passive–aggressive behaviour, Alison and George arranged for play therapy when he was eight. His therapy focused on his lack of male identity. Donald was fixated on the character of Mary Poppins and on Julie Andrews, and when he played, he often dressed up and played the role of mother. By the time he was eleven, he had entered a stage of isolation. He did not seem to feel that he fit in with his family. He took to lying, cheating, and stealing. He denounced the family and called his mother Mrs Roethler. He fixed a sign to his bedroom door: No Whites. His rejection of the family generally made life miserable for himself and everyone else. His unhappiness quickly spread to his brother and sister.

Donald was about thirteen when he was referred to Dr Harvey Armstrong at the Family Court Clinic. He was so wild at the time that he often tore Dr Armstrong's office apart. Afterwards, because he was diagnosed as needing strict rules and a highly regimented lifestyle, it was suggested that Donald live at a Youthdale residence. He stayed at Youthdale five years. Armstrong again met with Donald and his family and concluded that living at the youth residence was Donald's best chance. Although Rebecca and Jimmy were angry with their parents for sending Donald away, Alison and Georg knew that there was no alternative, if the whole family was to keep from breaking completely apart. Separating the children by sending Donald away and keeping Rebecca and Jimmy home was, ironically, the only way the Roethlers felt they could keep the family whole. Rebecca and Jimmy were unable to articulate their resentment at this new arrangement.

The couple endured therapy sessions for all three children, but they always came out feeling rotten. Although they knew that Youthdale was Donald's best hope for rehabilitation, his parents doubted the effectiveness of some of the staff members: it was quite clear from their comments that they did not know what was going on with the residents. Some specialists, however, like the Family Court doctor, never made Alison feel small or stupid or that she was to be blamed or that she had done the wrong things as a mother, and a few Youthdale workers did seem to benefit Donald. Yet, despite some improvement in his behaviour, Donald never came back home to live permanently. After Youthdale, Donald lived in several other hostels, and everyone suspected that he was making a living through prostitution. Eventually he entered a get-off-the-street program. Over the years, he did some volunteer work, caring for others and doing odd jobs. However, he continued to be manipulative and had a knack for aggravating everyone with whom he came into contact, especially Jimmy.

IDEAL-FAMILY MEMORY

Georg recounts a particularly enjoyable time with the children. This was the moment which for him most closely captured his picture of the ideal family. It was one of the few times they were all together. The family had rented two canoes and was travelling through the Everglades in southern Florida. They were enjoying looking at things and poking around; everyone was relaxed and no one felt any pressure. They were at peace in this idyllic setting, removed from the cares of the world and happy to be together. It reminded Georg of his childhood experiences of camping and canoeing. Life's pleasures could not get much better than this. "It was like being in a jungle. We were all sort of on the same level," Georg says. Sadly, it was also one of the last trips they would ever make together.

DISRUPTION MEMORY

Only three days after he had stolen Alison's clarinet and pawned it, Jimmy stole two sets of car keys. That night, when Jimmy tried to steal the Roethlers' two cars, was for Alison her lowest point, the point at which she was the most frightened of Jimmy.

The couple was getting ready for bed that night, and while they sat in their bedroom, they fully expected Jimmy to return to steal the cars. The moon was full, so they had a clear view of the driveway below their bedroom window. Georg had disconnected the cars' distributor caps so that the engines could not be started. Rigid with fear, Alison says that she waited for the crunching sound of the gravel in their driveway that would indicate Jimmy was about to make his move. When the crunching sound finally came, Alison rose to see that Jimmy was dressed in black paratrooper pants with a black T-shirt, and that he was not alone. In her terror, she wondered what Jimmy would do when he discovered he could not start the car. What if he was carrying a gun? Alison did not want to have to phone the police on their own son, but this time she felt that she had no choice. Not wanting Jimmy to hear her on the phone – the windows were open – she dialled 911 and spoke softly. Meanwhile, when Jimmy and his accomplice realized they could not get the first car started, they rolled it out of the way in order to get at the second car. When Alison mentioned to the dispatcher that the thief was probably their son, the matter was not treated seriously. Fearing for their lives if Jimmy were to realize that the two cars had been rigged, she insisted that police be sent round. Alison went to hide in a cubbyhole, because she was sure Jimmy would come crashing through the front door, as he had done in the past, to kill them both. The police took an eternity to arrive, it seemed. Georg went outside in his pyjamas to meet them and told the police to charge their son with attempted theft. In the past, Georg had felt that the presence of police only made crises worse. That night was not an exception. He was struck by how nervous the young policewoman appeared when it was clear that Jimmy was carrying a gun – a pellet gun. Georg remembers, "Both of the police had their guns drawn. I thought that they were going to shoot him right there on the front lawn. They were out of control – so hyper – they were scared."

For Alison and Georg, the entire incident had played itself out like a scene in a bad movie. This could not be happening to them! In hindsight, the Roethlers admit that this was the very worst incident Jimmy or any of the other children ever put them through. Alison says, "He was our *son*, but he was a total *stranger*. And to see him come, as a stranger, was just awful for me, just horrible. I really felt that I didn't know this person. I did, but I didn't. He was our son, but he was a total stranger, almost like an alien, and I had no idea whether we meant anything to him." It was not knowing how Jimmy was going to react that instilled a fear of their child that neither parent had known before – or could ever imagine feeling. Georg had always said that he, personally, would never call the police on Jimmy, but that night the person trying to steal their car was not their son.

For Alison, the tragedy was that she could see that Jimmy was slipping from them. Everything they had done for him, everything they had worked so hard to build up, was gone. There was nothing left in their relationship with Jimmy. The dissolution of their relationship was like a personal attack on them as parents. They began to wonder what had ever possessed them twenty years ago to think they had the capacity to succeed as good parents. Did good parents not produce good children? What had given them the idea that theirs would be the picture of a happy, functional family?

Today, the children are quite close to each other. Donald and Rebecca remember to phone their parents on birthdays, and when Jimmy comes home, they all get together. Donald and Rebecca each have a drinking problem, and Rebecca often needs money and has to come home to do laundry. Jimmy has attended some special college programs, but he has not yet earned any credits. He is artistic and likes to draw. Georg and Alison still support him. He phones almost every night, reversing the long-distance charges. When he comes home for short periods to work on odd jobs, problems arise, because he stays out until 3 A.M.

The children, like the others in this book, see themselves as "apple Indians." The most positive thing that has happened – the light in all this darkness – is that all the children have met their biological mother. Alison says that their children's alienation from their native culture and from their family had not been deliberate, but for the children the effect was the same: loss of identity. The contact the children have re-established with their family up north has done wonders for them. For Jimmy, making a connection with his Indian roots has made him proud. A friend of his birth mother made him a choker, which he wears all the time, and he has learned about the sweetgrass ceremony. It is obvious that Jimmy wants to be Indian. He has participated in a healing circle and has belonged to the Native Brotherhood. Their biological aunt, Josephine, visited the Roethlers and made them a gift of their family cradle board, and she has sent them quilts she has made. The parents felt honoured by these gifts and have enjoyed their contact with their children's relatives.

Georg and Alison had always hoped to fulfil their vision of one big, happy family enjoying each other's company. Those times were rare. Slowly, the ideal-family image was painfully chipped away, as their perceptions of the possibilities constantly changed and as their standards lowered. They resigned themselves to the fact that theirs was a dysfunctional family, not for lack of love and effort, but because the odds were stacked against them from the beginning. It had not occurred to them that an infinite amount of love still could not make a difference for their damaged children. It was as if they had been bystanders in their children's lives, watching as, one by one, each child struggled. On the other hand, Georg and Alison also know that, precisely *because* they never relinquished their love or the hope that things sooner or later had to stabilize, the children were able to stay together and are today close to each other. Furthermore, their re-establishing of contact with their native family has been of benefit to them and to their self-esteem, and it has also given Georg and Alison a new appreciation of their children and of the task they undertook twenty years ago. Raising these children has been far more problematic and far more complex than either parent would have thought possible. Their new outlook has also affected their work: Alison has worked with children who have learning disabilities, and Georg has successfully promoted special school programs for aboriginal students.

3 The Brooks Family

Arnold and Mary Brooks had four healthy and happy children – Donna, thirteen; Von, twelve; Allan, eleven; and Kelly, six – when they adopted Jon, who was at the time five years old. Six years later, they adopted Jamey when she was one and a half years old.

Mary initiated the talk about adoption because she had always wanted a large happy family, something that, as an only child, she did not have but yearned for. Her family background and her upbringing were unusual. Her father, James Reagan, came from a proper, staid, and religious family, and when he was old enough he joined the navy. It was shortly thereafter that he met Mary's mother, Gloria. Gloria was unlike anyone James had ever met: he found her interesting and attractive, with a great zest for life. In fact, eighteen-year-old Gloria had been leading a chaotic life, had no father, and had a mother who had been divorced several times, which was quite out of the ordinary for the times. James's mother disapproved of his plans to marry Gloria, but Gloria and her mother set it up so that the minute James turned twenty-one, they married and moved away. Mary's father always regretted not telling his mother and still shakes his head when talking about Gloria's mother's forceful personality.

Mary was born in Victoria about nine months after her parents' marriage. Her father was soon sent overseas, however, and she was brought up by her mother and grandmother, who partied a lot and left Mary in the care of other people for long periods of time. Mary had no father figure during the time they spent with their natural mother: "We had no supervision, and my uncle put me through all kinds of ridiculous things for a three-year-old. Then we went to live in a store, and he sexually abused me until I was eight." Mary feels that being sexually abused "doesn't make you promiscuous. It doesn't make you bad. It is also something that you can turn away from. A lot of it is choice, and you decide for yourself." When her father returned from the war, Mary felt that neither of her parents really wanted to take on a child. Her parents later divorced, and when her father remarried and Gloria asked him to take Mary, he did. Mary lived with her father and stepmother for about three years. Then, she went back and forth between her natural mother's family and her father's family.

As Mary got older, her natural mother continued to live a free and easy sort of life. Mary describes her visits home when she was twelve and thirteen: "Every time I would go to visit her, it was 'party-time.' She was a young mother, and therefore she wanted a daughter who was more like a sister, and so I would be dressed up in high heels, wearing lipstick, the whole bit." Eventually, she had only sporadic contact with her natural mother. While living with her stepmother, Mary had to take on a whole different persona. Her father was quite rigid, and Mary was made to feel terrible if she made a mistake. Her father and stepmother seemed to equate love with living up to their particular standards, and Mary found it difficult to do so. She found them so critical of everything.

Mary feels that neither of her mothers was a good mother; she says that "I knew exactly how it felt to be unloved." She attended eleven schools and "was always lonely." She never seemed to fit in. When she went to other people's houses, she would see that there was a lot of laughter, and she longed to be part of those happy situations. During that time, she poked holes in photographs of herself and cut herself out of group pictures. She recalls her feelings at the time: "The emotion I had when I did it was absolute anger. I don't know why I took myself out. I think it was that I didn't want to belong. I didn't want to be in that situation."

Mary also attended different churches. When she was really small, she went to a "Holy Roller" church with her mother. And when she went to live with her father and stepmother, the three of them went to the United Church, but only at Easter and Christmas.

However, Mary went to church on her own until she was about seventeen or eighteen years old. It was at that point that Mary began to think about what she wanted in life. She realized that having all that freedom at her mother's was not a particularly good thing. She got a job at a bank and then applied for training as an airline stewardess. Out of the 200 applicants, Mary was one of the two chosen. She completed the program, and it was while she was a stewardess that she met Arnold. Of the impact he had on her life, she says: "He turned my life around. He was extremely stable, and it gave me everything that I wanted: a stable home and all the things that went with it, and encouragement." Arnold's mother was also a big influence on Mary. "She was a fantastic person. Because they were such good Christians, even when she talked about one of her sons who drank and [had] done a lot of pretty awful things to them, her answer would be, 'He needs me more than the others do now. The others are all well, have all done fine, but this son needs us now.'"

As for Mary's relationship with her father and stepmother, they have worked out all kinds of things over the years and her parents have enjoyed Mary and Arnold's children. Yet, while her relationship with her parents is fine now, there were times when, as a teenager, Mary just wanted to kill herself. She says, "There were times that I walked out, but I had nowhere to go, and I had to go back, and I had to work it out. There was nowhere to go." Just recently, Mary's father said to her, "Well, you know, I realize we called you stupid all the time, and I had no concept that that was a bad thing to say."

Arnold came from an average family, to use his words. Born in Prince Albert, Saskatchewan, to German emigrant parents, he had four older brothers and four older sisters. His parents, who were very close, had had a rough time when they had begun home-steading, just after the turn of the century. There had been a lot of physical work to be done, and all the children had to contribute their labour to the family farm. "The women had to work from dawn to dusk; the men had to work their ass[es] off just to keep things going on the mixed farm." At home, Arnold's parents ran a tight ship but not a harsh one: "I guess the rules were set down from the oldest down to the youngest. If there was any repri-manding, I probably didn't get it from Mom and Dad as much as I did from other members of the family. I think that you are always stricter with the older ones, and so my older brothers and sisters probably remember my mom and dad differently than I did. I think, basically, that the rules we live by were set down by virtue of the church and by your parents."

His family was Catholic and always went to church, and Arnold remains an observant Catholic today. As he says, "You go [to church] because either you believe in God, or you feel that you have a destiny with the Maker somewhere down the line." The stability offered by the church has been important to Arnold, because it helped set guidelines for his parents and for himself. He does not think, however, that his religion had any bearing on his decision to adopt.

Arnold says that he learned from the experience of stable parents and so many sisters and brothers, each with his or her strengths and weaknesses. He says: "I was the last of nine and that was good for me. There were goods and bads. I guess that's all part and parcel of a family. You can't gloss over the things that went on with the nine different personalities. I basically didn't cause any problems. I just did basically what I wanted to, as long as I didn't get into trouble. There were minimal educational standards. I came and went as I wanted to, *when* I wanted to, and, of course, always showed up at the meal table on time."

As the years progressed, Arnold's parents had more time for themselves and for him. He feels that his parents probably spoiled him. When he was younger, he had lots of brothers and sisters milling around, and there was a lot of activity. It was only later, during his teen years, that he really had any time with his parents. Then, when his parents got older, Arnold helped them and bought a house for them: "I was able to do it, and all they had was enough money to pay for the taxes and so forth. The house was always open. There were various brothers and sisters that came back with the kids and stayed from two months or more." Arnold recalls one time when one of his brothers and his family had been living with his parents in the house Arnold had bought. His mother's nerves got so bad that Arnold finally had to tell his brother and family to get out within one month or he would sell the house. They moved out.

Arnold believes that his parents raised their nine children well, and that the children, in turn, all had good marriages, with varying degrees of happiness. He says, "I would say one of the things that I always liked about our family is that they could get together, even after some of these altercations. We could have a few drinks and so forth and not get down to the bitter disputes. We didn't lower ourselves into acting like goofs."

On the subject of adoption, Mary is quite clear on why she wanted to adopt:

The adoption was very essential, because I knew how awful it felt not to belong. I was always lonely and I never fit in, and I knew how it felt and that's why I wanted to adopt. I'd read about or seen stuff like that, and it always touched the child in me or whatever. I had four of my own, I would have perhaps had more of my own as well as adopting. It was just that I knew that for as many children that you have, there's other children that need a home. My stepmother and my dad had a good marriage, so I wasn't going to prove that I could have the ultimate marriage, but I was going to prove that I could be a really good mom. When I met Arnold and his family, I was impressed because I thought that this is the one thing that maybe I can do, is to be a mom. And I thought the one thing that maybe I can do is to somehow take a child and give it a home. I just thought there's a lot of kids out there. That was my career. It's fulfilling me. This is what I wanted to do; I always wanted to adopt.

Arnold's reasons for adopting were different. He explains: "I think you're trying to give something back. You can equate that to a feeling of religion or whatever. But I didn't really want to adopt any children unless I got them adopted at birth." He was worried about a child's ability to bond after two years old: "Getting them at five, you're high risk, and with sexually and mentally abused and physically abused, you're walking a tightrope." Arnold felt that if he could get the child involved in sports or in the family, it would help, but he knew that a person can go only so far in creating an environment that will encourage the child to feel as though he or she belongs.

Mary and Arnold were living in Vancouver when they adopted five-year-old Jon. Little was known about him, and little was revealed by the adoption agency. The only official information was that his mother was Ukrainian and that his father was Metis.

When Mary asked for more information, the agency told her that Jon's mother and father were drug addicts in Regina. They said that his mother had had five sons before Jon, and that another boy was born after Jon. Mary and Arnold also learned that, while Jon's father was in prison, his mother had been out on the street prostituting. This is when she was arrested and sent to prison.

Jon had been in and out of the hospital at least two times: when he was six months old, he was admitted for malnutrition, and when he was a little bit older he was admitted for a concussion. As well, Mary later learned that when Jon was three years old, he had been left in the care of a twelve-year-old boy for over a week. During this time, Jon suffered horrendous abuse: "The boy tore Jon's hair out, burned him with cigarettes, scratched his face right down to the bone, hung him over balconies, stuck his head in toilet bowls and ended up shaving and ripping his hair off – actually tearing out parts of his scalp ... burning him badly, including his penis." As Jon grew more comfortable with his adoptive parents, he asked them, "Is it bad to go visit old men in their hotel rooms?"

When they first brought Jon home, they were appalled both at his lack of coordination, on the one hand, and at his verbal dexterity, on the other. Arnold says, "He couldn't even ride a tricycle. That's how bad his motor skills were. We were always impressed with how much he would keep trying." And, although he was very verbal, Mary and Arnold characterize his speech patterns as cocktail speech. "He never said anything original, only polite things that he knew people wanted to hear or that he had heard someone say a few minutes before." Jon was able to bond with his younger sister Kelly and a little to Allan, but he was not able to bond with his adoptive parents. Jon constantly rejected Mary. She remembers "how it was like a game with us. It was like, we would say, 'I'm going to make you love us,' and he'd say, 'No.' It seemed that his greatest enjoyment was seeing us embarrassed."

Arnold and Mary changed Jon's middle name because they wanted to give him some of their identity. Yet they had a difficult time getting to know him. It appeared that he was whatever person they wanted him to be. Mary says, "There was no Jon and I knew that. Because of his chameleon capabilities, he was capable of taking on other people's personalities. He knew how to push all the right buttons. I never saw Jon angry. If you grounded him, he wouldn't even swear; he wouldn't even stamp his feet, he wouldn't do anything. I used to say to him, 'Scream and yell. Tell me I'm an asshole, tell me what you think. Don't just sit there and look at me. Give me some feedback.'"

The only time his parents can remember Jon showing his temper was when he became angry with his younger sister and tried to choke her. Jon seemed to have a tremendous amount of anger although he appeared calm. Mary describes Jon's appearance in this way: "He would just look at you and his eyes were dead. He just smiled at everyone [but the smile] never reached his eyes. There were times when I thought that Jon could've killed us in cold blood." If his parents ever felt that they were reaching Jon emotionally, it seemed to frighten him and he would lash out. Mary and Arnold have trouble coming up with good memories, because Jon quickly destroyed them.

Jon also liked to control a situation. He was the type of person who let other people hurt him, and he seemed to enjoy being hurt. Once, when he was still a little boy, Arnold and Mary had a confrontation with him. Mary recalls, "It seemed like he wanted us to hit him. Then one time, I did go after him and I knew what I was doing. It was like he enjoyed it, saying 'Hit me. Hit me.' He was still controlling the situation by causing me to hit him." At that point, Mary decided never to discipline him physically again. She also remembers when Jon once said that he loved the theatre because of the power over people it gave the actor. The feeling of power, he told Mary, was tremendous.

On one occasion, when Jon was fourteen, he and his four siblings were travelling on a ferry to visit their grandparents. His sister Donna could not find the money she was sure she had on her. A little later, Jon asked for some money so he could play video games. All his siblings pooled together to give him money to play these games. Mary explains, "Well, of course, the story was that he had ripped his sister off for all this money. Then he came back and made them all give him more money." Jon was quite good with his younger adopted sister Jamey, until he reached puberty. Then he began to play mean games on her. Although Mary says that these games were not so terrible, she was watchful, given her own history of sexual abuse, to make sure that these games did not escalate into something more serious.

At school, Jon was a poor student. Mary says that he had a learning problem and that he could not put his thoughts on paper. His school, however, just put him through the system, even though he was not academically ready to move on. Mary arranged for him to visit psychologists and psychiatrists, but Jon was not at all cooperative: "He played mind games with all those people. We had a brain scan done on him and a CAT scan to see if there had been some trauma to his brain." They did not find anything conclusive. One psychiatrist told them that Jon was the type of child who would probably do well in a military college, away from home, because the closeness of family life was stifling him. In the classroom, Jon acted like Mr Macho, which caused distractions, and when the teacher said something, Mary says, "He would act up. It was just a cop out – mind games." Jon did play some sport, but not for very long. If his parents remarked on his skill or how well he was playing a sport, Jon would quit instantly. Jon seemed to be a total loner, and he often cut himself out of his school pictures.

It was difficult to discipline Jon, and he never seem to learn from his mistakes. Arnold and Mary found this frustrating. There were one or two fights between Jon and his father. Once Arnold grabbed Jon and threw him up against the wall. It did not seem to make any impression on the boy. One time, when Jon had broken curfew again, he was grounded for two weeks. The first night the curfew was over, he came in at three o'clock. When asked why, he responded, "Well, I didn't particularly want to do anything for those last two weeks. Tonight, I've had a really good time. So now you can ground me for two weeks again."

The year before Jon left was a busy one for the family: two older sisters got married, one in the fall and the other in the spring. The Brooks also had to move to another house, and Mary felt that this had an effect on Jon: "The old one [house] was great 'cause we had a pool, and he had a good room and everything was fine. Then we moved, and the new home wasn't as good. He was sort of stuck in this little room." It was at this time, too, that Jon reached puberty. He started smoking pot, and his room was disgusting. He also started staring at his younger sister and then, at other times, at Mary: "It just unnerved his younger sister, because he would be angry with her, he would go up and like stand and stare at her. When the kids had finally left home, that's what he started doing to me, he would sit in an armchair and stare at me for hours on end. [It would] unnerve me, I would think to myself, I'm not going to let it get to me; he's only looking at me … a mind game."

In high school, Jon ran for student council on a ticket that totally opposed everything that the school stood for. Then he got involved with a girl who was manipulative and clever. Jon was attracted to her and was excited about taking her to the school dance. As it turned out, she absolutely hated her father, and so she talked Jon and another girl into moving into an apartment with her. At this time, Jon had a job at a service station. One day, Jon came home with the two girls and announced he was leaving home. He had signed up for an apartment and had moved his belongings in, unbeknownst to his parents. Mary remembers her feelings: "He'd keep playing this head game, and I wasn't going to let him win. At the same time, I was relieved and so sort of gave him his two garbage bags and said, 'Fine.'" Jon later told his parents that the two girls were lesbians and that their sexual relationship was a *ménage à trois*.

To keep the communication going after Jon left, Arnold and Mary would invite him for family events. But soon he ended up as a male prostitute (by now he had decided that he was bisexual) in the downtown core. One day, Mary got a call from someone with Social Services, and they said that they were concerned about Jon. An old, really scary person had befriended him and was waiting outside for him when he picked up his welfare cheques. Arnold and Mary did not go down to get him, because they said that Jon knew that he could phone them if he wanted to. Not long after that he went back to Regina, where he had been born, to live on social assistance and by begging. Friends phoned Mary when Jon was seen in a TV documentary. He was interviewed as he sat on street corner begging, with a rat on his shoulder.

IDEAL-FAMILY MEMORY

For Arnold, the ideal-family memory involving Jon takes place in the family room of the house. A fire is burning in the fireplace, and Arnold, Mary, and Jon – just the three of them – are sitting around, talking and eating popcorn. For Arnold, this scene was reminiscent of the times he had enjoyed alone with his parents after his siblings had left home.

No interruptions, a chance to really dig in … direct conversation, sharing, talking, doing things and getting feedback. He was making an effort to be part of the family. He was giving of himself for a change. He had finally opened up. He looked animated; his eyes were shining, relaxed, he was being natural. He acted like he was happy being in our company. There's hope for him. It looks like he's finally opening up. He felt like our son. We made contact with our child. He felt touched. He enjoyed the evening too. He likes us. We all felt this. He felt it. Just a good feeling with him on a one-to-one basis as compared to always being involved in a family situation.

DISRUPTION MEMORY

Not long after Jon was seen on television, he was picked up for stealing a carton of cigarettes. It was the only illegal thing Jon was ever charged with. But, for his mother, the scene that was to unfold shortly thereafter was the moment during which she realized that the Jon she had raised had been replaced by a gruesome stranger. The setting was the steps of the courthouse where Jon was to appear on the charge of theft. Mary recalls the event vividly:

We got a call one day from the police saying Jon had been picked up for stealing a carton of cigarettes. We went to pick him up for court because he had slept in. Arnold went and picked him up and didn't even notice he had a ring in his nose. Jon showed up in a black overcoat and big shoes and earrings, his head shaved and that's when I broke down. He looked terrible, he had shaved his head, pierced his nose, he had thrown up on his shirt, it's all ripped … he's wearing an old trench coat and it was all saggy, he had no socks on, his shoes are all torn and dishevelled. He was very, very pale … scars on his head from when he was a child all showed. He had just had his nose pierced and that day before he knew he was to appear in court, knowing that he was going into court so it was all swollen. And he said, "I was gonna get my nipples done and a chain put in but it would've hurt too much." And I went outside and started to cry. I'm so angry, I'm shaking. I'm totally devastated. And I'm looking at him and I'm thinking, my son is dead, the person standing here beside me, I don't even know him, my son is dead. I'm thinking my son is dead. Because I looked at him and

I didn't know him any more. I didn't know this person. There was nothing left, there was nothing of what I suppose ...

Maybe what I was seeing was Jon, maybe for the first time in my life I actually was seeing Jon, and I saw him as so devastating. 'Cause the Jon that I had known or the Jon that I had thought I knew was standing in front of me and I didn't know him. So far as I was concerned, my son was dead and I didn't know who that person was. I just looked at him and I honestly knew that the person was not anything like the person that I had raised, that for some strange reason, that he had gone, as far as I was concerned he had died. And he looked so terrible that it flashed through my mind that he needed a collar and a chain on him, he needed to be led. He looked like some kind of sick, perverted person. He just looked that terrible. He looked like somebody that could be used for evil purposes, he looked like a vessel of evilment [sic], that's what he looked like. He didn't look like he had the power to be evil himself, he looked like he was waiting for perversion to enter him, looked like an empty vessel, like an empty shell of some person. I walked to the car and I start to scream [pounding] the steering wheel and I kept yelling, "He's dead."

I'm here with my son. Arnold is here. Arnold cared about this kid and he's mocking every single thing that we've held up for him. And we're not talking education. We never pressured him, we never asked him to accept our values, but I didn't ask for him to turn out to be a vessel for a pervert and that's the feeling I had when I saw him when he said, "I was thinking about having my nipples pierced."

Later, Jon moved into a friend's home, and he managed to get a job as a waiter. He still did not seem to have settled down, because he said then that acid was his drug of choice. As far as Mary was concerned, she chose to pretend that there was nothing left of Jon. She had decided that she no longer wanted him in her life: "I couldn't relate any more at that point, I shut down ... I couldn't stand to be rejected; he couldn't handle being touched."

Jon never returned home to live. He completed his grade twelve and took a few college courses. He found these difficult because of his learning disability, but he saw education as a way to gain respect. For the first few years after he moved out, he would phone and talk about himself. He admits that he hit the streets to find his Indian heritage, but, since he did not get the respect he wanted there, he decided to give up on his Indian heritage. He seemed to have little interest in what the other family members were doing. Occasionally, he came home for family celebrations and weddings. Two years ago, he moved back to the west coast where he worked in a fast food restaurant and took acting courses, which he loved. He began seeing a psychologist. Then he returned to Regina, where the only family member to see him was Kelly. He married but was soon divorced. He then moved to Ontario where he took a job in a large health-care facility. He is an excellent worker and maintains regular contact with Mary and Arnold through phone calls and the occasional visit.

Today, Arnold and Mary are busy with their other five children and their grandchildren. Mary realizes now that her expectations for being the kind of mother who could overcome the difficulties inherent in adopting an older child were too high. Although she had envisioned a large happy family and motherhood as a fulfilling career, the problems she and Arnold experienced with Jon dramatically altered her expectations: "I didn't prove myself to be this wondrous Pollyanna that I thought I was, which was good for me, the humbling experience ... I just screwed up royally."

From the outset, as already noted, Arnold had not been wholly in favour of adopting an older child. Mary was disappointed that Arnold did not entirely support her desire for a large family, and, for his part, he often sounds angry and bitter when he talks about the adoption experience: "She just steamrolled over me and that's what I object to ... if there had been any time in our married life that I would've considered leaving her, that would have been it." Their adoption of Jon, therefore, was and is a source of tension between the two of them. The difficulties they had with Jon affected their relationship with each other. It irked Mary that Arnold could dissociate himself from the tension in the household; she grieved and wanted to talk about Jon twenty-four hours a day. She said that she needed, but did not receive, her husband's support during the painful episode after Jon left home. She recalls her obsession: "It became a bit of a compulsive sickness with me. I wanted to talk about him all the time, any time I found somebody. I would say, for a good two or three years, he became the focus of my thoughts all the time. I didn't like [Jon], and I was busy telling people I [didn't] like him, that I no longer wanted him in my life, that my son [was] dead."

Mary and Arnold are happy that Jon is able to support himself and that he lives some distance from them. Mary thinks that she can speak to Jon on the phone because by so doing she can dissociate herself totally from him and because Jon probably realizes that, with her being so far away, he cannot hurt her anymore. Sometimes, what Jon is able to say is a comfort to her. Jon once said, "If it hadn't been for you guys, I'd be dead right now." Arnold is also satisfied that he and his wife did the best they could for Jon, although he, too, feels extreme disappointment that things did not turn out differently. But today, Arnold tells his son that he is proud of him: "I said [to Jon], 'If you can do what you're doing and get by, I'll be very proud of you. You're a self-made man. I'm very proud of you.' I grabbed his hand and I told him I was proud of him."

If Jon feels that there is a little bit of goodness in life, then Arnold feels that he and his wife have done the right thing for him. Arnold hopes that others will evaluate the way in which he lived his life not by his wealth or accomplishments but by the degree to which he was able to raise a family of happy and well-adjusted individuals: "The only thing that I'll be judged on, at the end of my life, will be what I leave behind in terms of my family. And so, to me, [that will be] the essence of what Jon thinks now and [how our adopted daughter] Jamey feels."

4 The Graves Family

John and Ella Graves had three healthy and happy children when they decided to adopt Ken and Grace. Although their first three children had been easy to raise, the Graves's experience with Ken and Grace was fraught with difficulties. The strained relationship the couple had with their two adopted children was like nothing John or Ella had ever known in their own families or with their first three children.

Ella was born in a small town in northwestern Ontario to Mary and Philip Graham. She had only one younger sister but was surrounded by a large extended family. Although the family was somewhat poor, her parents were both loving and good towards her and her sister, and she has wonderful memories of being taken to a local Indian reserve where they could swim and fish. For Ella, the happiest times were definitely at the lake. Because of the shortage of money and her frayed clothing, Ella thought that she had been brought up during the Depression. However, when she once expressed openly to her parents, just before a school trip, her wish that money in the family not always be in such short supply, her mother produced a five dollar bill for her to take along. She cherishes this memory as an example of her mother's love and goodness. Ella suspects that her mother married her father on the rebound and that, as a result, her mother perhaps feels she married beneath her social status. Ella says that her father is aware of her mother's feelings. Ella attributes the family's financial hardships to the fact that her father was somewhat lazy and perhaps a bit unmotivated to look for work beyond that which a friend offered him at a rate lower than minimum wage. He drove a truck and then became a mechanic. Ella remembers that, although her father was gruff and harsh and not terribly fatherly, he was a good father who never punished his children.

When she finished school, Ella worked in a restaurant, then in the telephone office, and finally in a beauty parlour. At twenty, she met John in Kingston. He also came from a family of modest means. Although his mother aspired to have wealth and status, he says she felt that she, like Ella's mother, had married beneath her social status. While his brother excelled at school, John did not. He played basketball and golf but did not like hockey. When he got out of school, he had a choice of five or six different jobs. There is no question in his mind that his generation lived in prosperous times, when jobs were plentiful and self-confidence was high. He chose to work for the same utility company in Kingston that his father worked for – a job he really liked – and now his son works there too.

John met Ella when he was twenty-one, and they were soon married in a big wedding. Because of her job at the beauty parlour, where the elite of the town were said to go, Ella was the one who was able to pay for most things when they were first married. (She was even able to pay for a speeding ticket John was issued.) The plan was for them to take turns paying for things, but, in the end, Ella bought the furniture while John paid for the car. Ella continued to work after they were transferred because of John's job. With promotions, the family moved often. Soon, money ceased to be a concern, and they could do what they wanted. For example, they were able to save and buy rural property. Within three months of acquiring the land, they began to build their own home.

The couple had three children: one boy and two girls. Ella continued to work up to a point, but after one of their moves, she decided to stay home with them full time. Though her pregnancies were good, each baby was born early because of Ella's diabetic condition. As a result of serious complications with the last baby, Ella decided that although she would like more children, she should not undergo another pregnancy and risk her health and that of the child's. She and John had had such an easy time raising their three children that it was an easy decision to adopt more. "We adopted kids because we wanted more, but we also adopted likely 'cause we had such an easy time with our own. So, you're in this element. It's quite comfortable and easy-going and no big shake-ups ... Honestly, anything negative the system would've said, I wouldn't have believed." Ella remembers reading an article that described the important role of the environment when raising children. Her philosophy was that a mother could nurture her children until they were in their early teen years, after which time she would become their good friend. This relationship, she determined, resulted in the contented children she and her husband had raised.

Initially, Ella and John wanted to adopt a baby, but just when they were scheduled to receive a child from the Children's Aid Society, John was transferred to Hamilton. There, they were told that adopting a baby was a near impossibility, but that a couple held a better chance of adopting if they agreed to consider children with learning disabilities. To this proposal they said no, because their son had learning disabilities and a hearing impairment, and Ella knew the difficulties the parents of such a child encounter.

Finally, in 1973, the agency called with the offer of a brother and sister from Saskatchewan – Ken and Grace – who were of Metis-Cree ancestry. Ken was five and Grace was four. The children had been abandoned by their mother when they were babies: Ken was a year and a half and Grace was a few months old. Their mother dropped them off at the local Children's Aid Society. Since the agency was not able to locate her, their father had to sign the papers that formalized the agency's custodianship. The children became wards and were placed in a foster home where they experienced difficulties. Ken was locked out in the cold for long periods of time and he had to sleep in a crib because he wet the bed.

Ella and John were given pictures of Ken and Grace. The social workers said to them, "You have to be ready if you're going to take them; you have to be ready to stay there until they're ready to go." So John went to his boss and said, "I'm going to be home tomorrow, or I'm going to be home in two weeks. See you later." Then Ella and John flew out to Saskatoon and drove to a small town, where they checked into a hotel. John explains his reaction to being driven by the Children's Aid Society representative to the place where Ken and Grace were staying:

> God, it was awful! This Children's Aid lady comes along and drives on and on down these old gravel roads to this house with umpteen hundred kids … [at least] six or seven. You had to kind of make up your mind 'cause you didn't have a chance to get to know them … You either liked them or you didn't. They're all over the place … [even] upside down.
> So I just turned to them [Ken and Grace] and says, "You kids want to go home with us?" They said, "Sure," and so I said, "Okay fine. So we all come back in the car." So, back we go. We have broken hockey sticks and crap by the ton. Ella had said to them, "Pack everything, even what's broken. I don't wanna hear about some stuffed toy that you left behind." So we threw everything in a cardboard box. They had nothing really.

Each child came with a piece of paper, a questionnaire that had been given to the foster parents about the children's habits and characteristics.

They went back to Saskatoon the next day. When they went out for supper, they noticed that the other restaurant patrons were whispering about the fact that the parents were white but that the children were clearly Indian in ancestry. John says, "It was brutal. I really didn't realize it and I really got my eyes opened in that restaurant."

Ella had decorated the children's room in such a way as to attempt to make them feel comfortable. She hung prints of Indian children and so on, but in hindsight she does not think that it made much difference to Ken and Grace. Their first impressions of their new children suggested that they might adjust to their new home. They called their new parents Mom and Dad, and they readily kissed them good night. In fact, the children *expected* to be kissed just before bedtime. To Ella and John, these signs were normal and encouraging. The children seemed to be eager to please their parents, because they did not want to have to move again. They asked their parents for this reassurance often. Ken took to the family dog in a serious way. He also enjoyed playing with Lego toys and was good at drawing. He was, however, nervous and always agitated, moving from place to place, unlike his sister, who seemed more relaxed. Neither of the children spoke much, and Ken could not laugh at himself. He was a bed-wetter until he was twelve and often had nightmares during which he would cry out. Both children needed eyeglasses, and Ken had to have his tonsils removed.

Over the years, the family had great times horseback riding, fishing, and snowmobiling. Ken was an excellent, if daredevil, skier. They did a lot as a family, but usually as two groups: first, the older children were taken on an outing, and then, sometime later, Ken and Grace were taken on a similar outing. This gave Ella and John a chance to spend time with Ken and Grace by themselves. John remembers that, as a youngster, Ken was skilled with his hands, and, when he was shown how to do things, he learned quickly. John enjoyed watching Ken learn a new task and then excel at it: "Ken was a quick learner. He'd take parts off the other kid's bikes and put them on his. After I showed him how to change a tire, he practised about fourteen times after school. He could take a tire and that tube apart faster than I could and put it back together. *He* had to show *me*." Ella remembers how Ken loved books and how he was a reader from an early age. He also did well in school, bringing home As and Bs on his report cards. His grade eight report card said that he was a quiet and cooperative student. This made Ella feel that they had succeeded with Ken. He passed his beginner's swimming test and was on the championship baseball team and in Cubs, all in the same year.

Ella and John did have serious concerns about Ken, however. They found that he was often immature. In the sandbox or at school, he seemed to enjoy playing games that were too juvenile for his age. And, according to his teachers, he seemed always ready to pick a fight. Ella tried to reassure Ken that the children only wanted to be his friend, but Ken did not seem to know how to act. Before he became proficient at baseball, if Ken struck out, he would dissolve into tears right on the spot. He also loved to torment his sister Grace, with whom he was not close.

As time went on, Ella and John's concerns about Ken's behaviour increased. He did not like to be told what to do – and still doesn't. He took to lying and was somewhat destructive of things. His parents also caught him carrying a knife when he was still quite young. Although, like Grace, he was never truant in public school, in high school he left the school property, as many of the other kids did, to go play video games. Ken never did bring home his grades nine and ten report cards. Ella also remembers many confrontations when he was a teenager; she hated to get into arguments with him. Once, when she asked Ken to take the garbage out, he deliberately threw out a favourite planter she had. She decided then, "Shoot, I'm not going to get into this one ... I just hated those confrontations."

When he was only twelve, Ken took Grace and a little four-year-old boy to visit a friend at a cottage down the beach from the Graves's own cottage. As it turned out, the friends were not home, so the children proceeded to break all the windows in the cottage. They went into the house and threw sugar all over the floor. Although the Graves's insurance paid for the damage, they were horribly embarrassed about the incident. Ella says, "It was more than I could fathom; [it was] malicious, really down deep mad."

Ella contacted and pleaded with her family doctor, and he arranged for the children to see a psychiatrist. The psychiatrist reported that Ken was full of anger and said, "You know Indian children being adopted by white families hardly ever worked." But, he noticed, "this *is* working . Ken does not have the anger that he had." Over time, Ella and John grew dissatisfied with this psychiatrist, because they felt he did not really know how to probe Ken further. Apart from telling Ken that he, as an Indian, would not be able to drink alcohol (because Indians were said not to have the necessary enzymes), the psychiatrist did not do much for Ken.

When Ken got older, around fifteen, confrontations over his behaviour became more of a challenge. Although Ella did try to cope by appealing to reason, John's tactic with Ken was to come on strong and honest so that Ken would back down. Down deep, John surmised, Ken was a big chicken. At about the same time, during Ken's early teen years, Ella and John started to be concerned about his interest in liquor and how it changed his lifestyle and behaviour. Ken began stealing liquor from neighbours and from his parent's stock and replacing what he had consumed with water. Once, they came home and found Ken in the kitchen blabbering away, drunk. Ella recalls, "I didn't know how to handle this." She also began doubting herself as a mother, "I don't know what made me think I could be a mother." John says that they were a long time in catching on to Ken's stealing and drinking, because their first three children never did this sort of thing. Ella found that her relationship with her neighbours suffered as a result of Ken's actions: "One neighbour, I had her key. That's how he got into her house. He said he threw her key back in the bush. I said, 'You better hope you know where you threw it or you're going to have to pay for brand new locks.' It wasn't too long till he found it. I never kept her key again."

Thefts were not confined to liquor and beer. Once, before Ken was sixteen, John and Ella's son Will called them at the family cottage: there was trouble with Ken. John knew that it was serious, so he and Ella headed home. When they got there, they found some stolen chocolate bars and a cash box from the nearby ski lodge. This was a lodge near their home, where all the kids had worked. The family was well known there and respected. They also discovered that Ken's girlfriend had spent the night in their house. John, feeling that this was *the last straw*, phoned the police and turned his son in, hoping that an encounter with the law would change him. A trial date was set.

During the trial, after centencing Ken to probation, the judge asked John, "Do you want to say something?" "Yeah," John replied, "It's now time [for] you guys to turn the screws down on this guy, and you're letting him off … I don't understand … We really don't want to flush him down the toilet, yet. We need help!" John had even told the lawyer he had hired to represent his son that he should ensure that a guilty verdict was reached and that the full weight of its consequences was applied: "Here's this kid that should be at least slapped on the wrist or something, and the judge more or less says to me, 'Well, what do you want me to do about it?' I said, 'It's time to do something about this.'" John was frustrated and disappointed because Ken's sentence was only probation. However, the lawyer did get in touch with a group home that was willing to accept Ken for two weeks. When he left, his parents caught up on their sleep. John warned Ken that the next time he would have to face the law on his own. Ken eventually finished grade twelve.

Until Ken was in his later teens, there was not much trouble at home, because Ken did everything away from home. But, later, they found that Ken was getting into even worse trouble. John admits, "Then, it wasn't pleasant here. He was getting out his bedroom window. People weren't home when he broke into houses and cars. Twice he's taken the car. Once we found tire marks all over the yard. He and another guy took our old truck and goofed around. He mucked up Will's truck. [That time], he was sixteen and was driving too fast, spun out and put it in the ditch. I covered for him that time."

For Ken's last six or eight months at home, life for the Graves family was very difficult. John says, "Ken was greasing the skids to get out. He stayed out overnight a couple of times without permission. He showed anger, [would] go into the room and play music, never socialized, never watched TV until we'd go to bed, and then he'd come out of his room and watch TV. Yeah, he was a very bitter boy at that time, very bitter." Ella remembers reading an article about teens who, when they cannot handle things, go to their rooms to play their music. They show up to eat and then disappear again. They do not watch television with their parents, but when the parents go to bed, the teens come out of their rooms to watch it. Although the article told her that these were signs of a rebellious teenager – something she didn't need to be told – it did help her know what could be done to reach Ken.

John was often away on business, and the rest of the family felt threatened by Ken's verbal abuse, his stupid behaviour, and the generally awful mood pervading the house. Ella remembers how she felt powerless to help her son, who clearly was very unhappy. Furthermore, she and John were prisoners in their own home, not daring to leave Ken alone. They could not trust him. Even Grace, who got on reasonably well with him, was having trouble. She could not stand him and his behaviour.

Once, when Ken was on the phone, he began bad-mouthing John to his friend. Older brother Will, who was home visiting with his baby, told Ken to quit. Ken dropped the phone and went and grabbed Will's head and held it in a headlock. John heard the commotion and describes the scene: "I got hold of Ken, gave him that knuckle burn thing in the head. Ella grabbed the baby. I said, 'We just don't need you around here anymore. Ken, you've been really aching to get out of here, and now, if you want out, is a good time to go.' He packed and he had a smile like you wouldn't believe. He went down to stay with a neighbour, a bachelor."

Ken returned to the house a couple of times after that, and during those times, Ken took their car twice and had a girl and friends over, all of them drinking and carrying on. There was a lot of tension. The time John and Ella were waiting for the news of the birth of another grandchild, they instead got a call from the police saying that Ken was in jail. He had taken cassettes out of cars and had stolen a car. He was eighteen then. After that, Ken was on the street for a while. He and his friends would sleep under the evergreen trees in the park and even on some of the rooftops in the city.

In her last few difficult months at home, Grace went to school every day. She did well and had a boyfriend who had his own apartment and whose parents lived a couple of hours away. Ella could see that Grace would inevitably end up pregnant if some boundaries were not set. In the end, Grace did become pregnant and left home and school as a result – six weeks before graduating. Grace got pregnant at the same time as Ken announced that his girlfriend was pregnant. "I told them both to get abortions," Ella remembers. This was a particularly stressful time for the family. Two of her older children had married and also left home – all within two years.

IDEAL-FAMILY MEMORY

Ella says that her ideal-family memory is set at the family cottage, on a summer night, with the children and neighbours all enjoying a fire, some roasted wieners and marshmallows, and some favourite campfire songs. The older children were helping the smaller ones, and all seemed right with the world: "It's just happy … because I feel it all over. Wood snapping, waves flapping, bark flying. The kids, just happy; our older kids happy, even grumpy-happy. They're interacting all the time, looking after each other, loving to sing. Freedom and no schedules and water and sun and company." Ella had spent many happy moments at the lake as a child.

DISRUPTION MEMORY

John recalls the occasion that for him spelled the breaking point in their relationship with Ken. The scene was the one where John came home from the cottage after receiving a call from Will telling him that there had been some trouble with Ken. John recounts the episode:

We went up to the cottage to get away from this for a while and to open up the cottage. In the morning, we got the call. You always think the worst. Will really didn't say a whole lot other than he thought there was something wrong and we should come home. Well, by the tone of Will's voice, I said I'd be right there. I was tense because Ken had been instructed not to have anybody in the house. I knew it was Ken. I don't even recall the ride home.

When we got home, we went upstairs and found a number of chocolate bars there. We went into the attic and we found this cash box. Ella and I went back downstairs and I asked Ken, "Where did all these chocolate bars come from?" He didn't admit to anything. Through this whole thing, he didn't say anything. He never said a thing. He looked just blank. He had his head down a little bit. I believed him to be very tired, basically he had no energy left. He was zonked, he had nothing to offer. He knew he was wrong and he wasn't going to fight.

I phoned the police and we waited for forty to forty-five minutes for them to get here. During this time, I think I marched around a little bit. I never left the room, I stayed with him the whole period. We never really said very much.

It was a sullenness ... and frustrating, even to the point where I thought, I'm going to show control here to see if I can get him upset, to see whether he will react, and I was hoping that he would tell me all about it. But he didn't, so I finally said, "Come on, Ken, you know, we've been together long enough, you can tell me. I'm going to find out anyway, you know I am. You know you've really done this." And before the police came, he said, "Yes, I have done it! Okay?" After the police arrived, the constable took him outside, and the sergeant and I were alone in the house for fifteen minutes.

Ken never did come back to the house after that. I went out to the outside of the car and I said, "You know, Ken, I'm really sorry this has happened. I hope you learn from this." I can't recall what he said. I was somewhat set back.

John remembers how determined he had been to make sure that, from a legal point of view, everything possible would be done. At that stage, he and his wife had done everything else they could think of. John thought that, by ensuring that the full force of the law was applied to Ken, it would do his son some good at this stage. They certainly could not sit back and accept what he had done.

For the last few years, Ken has been living in Saskatchewan. John says that "he is living with a girl, and when they get mad, they beat each other up. She has charged him. One time, she was on cocaine and she had a fire in her apartment. A child she was babysitting died, and her own children have been taken away from them." Ken has kept in touch with John and Ella by phoning regularly (Ella and John have given him "Call Me" cards). He has managed to get work, mostly outdoors, painting and repairing, and has become an excellent artist; however, he has not managed to save any money. He has visited the reservation where he was born and a few months ago reconnected with his brothers. Together, they visited their mother who is now residing in Manitoba. Although there was a lot of drinking, the visit went well for everyone except Ken; his mother accused him of being "just like his father" and this hurt him and made him angry. His father had been an abusive man whom the family had feared. Ken has a problem with alcohol. He has suggested that he would like to come home and visit with Ella and John, something he has not done for a long time. This is fine with them as long as he promises not to drink. Their children are still angry with Ken. Grace will not speak with him; on the other hand, she does not want to speak with her biological mother either.

Grace lives near Ella and John with her husband and two daughters. Ella describes her as having a close and loving family. She is a hard worker and pays back everything that she borrows. She wants to take part in family get-togethers, although Ella feels that Grace does not think she fits in with the rest of the family. She seems uncomfortable and plays with the children more than she talks with the adults. Ella says, "It's almost as if she doesn't belong." Ella's relationship with Grace, she says, is not a satisfactory one. Grace phones and visits with her sisters occasionally.

During the interviews, when John described his disruption memory, he did not speak of his own emotions but through statements made in the second person. Ella makes it clear that she would not consider adopting again and that her own children would never adopt. She also admits that she would not have kicked Ken out if she thought he would never return. During the interviews, Ella and John found out that their biological children had been quite worried about them, and their daughter Cindy even came by the house to check on her parents while we were talking.

Ella and John emphatically state that their greatest source of strength and comfort is their grandchildren. These children are responding well to the same routines and expectations that Ella and John had for their biological children. This reaffirms for Ella that her approach to childrearing and her abilities as a mother were indeed sound: "You say to yourself, what did you do wrong? But once you start dealing with your grandkids, I convinced myself I didn't do anything wrong. 'Cause you kind of go through this again with your grandkids and you see what they're doing and their response. You look back to those times when things weren't so great around here, but really in my mind, I don't think we did anything wrong. We tried very hard. I didn't do anything different then than I do now so … We have these kids that have done very well for themselves."

Ella had wanted to adopt because raising her own children had been so easy, but the difficulties they encountered with Ken and Grace left her feeling damaged and lacking in self-confidence. "When you are exposed, you change … When it hurts, you build walls around your heart. You have to protect yourself. Something inside me hardened. Even the family was damaged … I know we caused them a lot of anguish … [but the other children] hated [Ken] for what he did to us." About her level of confidence she says, "I don't know what ever made me … I thought I could be a mother … I don't think I was great parent … I often have thought, if I hadn't taken them, would they have been better off with somebody else? …" She and her husband feel that they lost Ken: "[It was like] a cancer that lasted three years before it finally took him … He was like a different person, [with] bizarre behaviour." She is also deeply hurt by Ken's rejection of them: "I really get almost bitter about the lack of gift-giving. He's giving friends and friends' families gifts off me, and I don't even get a card."

Ella and John, like the other parents in this book, felt a tremendous sense of helplessness. John says that he tried to stay in control, to see whether Ken would react and talk to him. But when Ken's behaviour was more than could be tolerated, John says, "We just couldn't have him around anymore at that time ... he had done enough damage around here and ... he had to leave, smarten up or leave ... When you're exposed to something like this, you change, in terms of being more of a disciplinarian than I really wanted to be."

On the lack of support from friends and family, Ella reports that her sister-in-law made it clear that she thought Ella and John were poor parents: "My brother's wife thought we really screwed up with these two. She thought we did it all wrong, that we were the worst parents." Ella and John also felt abandoned by their immediate community. There was no help forthcoming from family and friends (instead there was fear and rejection), no empathy and understanding (instead there was blame), and no support and sympathy (instead there was alienation). John says, "I remember going back to work and feeling so dirtied, the secretary saying, 'You're not the person I know.'"

The parents also felt abandoned by the social welfare/medical community when things became desperate: "Every time we went for help, we got help. When we needed the cops we got them. When we needed a psychiatrist, we got one, but there should be more help when you are in *trouble*," John states. He says that he felt he had been led somewhat astray by the psychiatrist: "So then he kept on with Ken for two years and after two years, he came back and said, 'I think you guys are going to be A-okay,' and that was kind of the end of it." Ella turned to the Tough Love support group for help: "We were there a year anyway. That was a big help. You found out you weren't the only one. Like the first time I went, I was in tears at the meeting. It was awful. Then you just get used to it. And then you think it isn't your fault. They were really emphatic that this was our house and that we don't have to put up with things like that in our house. I don't know if their methods are absolutely one-hundred-per-cent right, but, boy, you do get support! You aren't alone in the world when you go there. It was pretty eye-opening. We had a lot to learn."

5 The Verdan Family

Edward and Elaine Verdan already had two of their own children – Diane, five, and Jim, three – when they decided to adopt Gerald. A third child, Mathew, was born when Gerald was eight. The Verdans had difficulty discussing their story because their adopted son had sexually abused Mathew. Gerald was thirteen or fourteen at the time of the abuse and was removed from the family within a few days of its discovery. During this time and after, Edward and Elaine did not talk to each other very much and seemed to have repressed their feelings about their experiences with Gerald. At the time of the interviews, their children were still concerned about them.

Although she was determined to have a lot of children when she was married, as a young girl, Elaine had grown up essentially on her own. Living in Toronto, she was six years old when her mother almost died giving birth to a second child. This child did not live. Two years later, Elaine told her mother about a tiny foster baby she had seen at a friend's house. Shortly after, Elaine's parents adopted this same six-week-old baby girl. Elaine was fascinated with her new baby sister. The adoption was excellent, and the little girl's adjustment went well. Elaine's father did not seem to care if they had another child; it was Elaine's mother who wanted more children.

Elaine says that, in some ways, her adopted sister seemed to be closer to her parents and more fun than she was. Elaine remembers herself as being the serious one. She enjoyed school and did very well. The public school she attended allowed her to skip two grades. Success in academic work came easily to her. In high school, however, her teachers pointed out to her, as they did with many young women at the time, that the commercial stream was probably a more practical choice of courses, since she would inevitably work only a short time before marrying and raising a family: "I liked the academic part, but it was suggested to me [since] I was probably going to get married and have children some day anyway [that, instead of university, which my parents couldn't afford] I should just think of a nice commercial course." Elaine left part way through grade twelve and got a job. She hated the work and planned to go back to school but never got around to it. She really did not get much encouragement from her family to return to academic studies. Even when Elaine did go to university as a mature student, her mother reminded her that people who went to university often had funny ideas. Her mother had worked in a factory right until she married. She had to quit, because married women could not work in the factory during the Depression. Her father had started out working as a floor boy and was promoted to the level of manager.

Edward, who has two younger brothers, describes the family he came from as normal. His parents were immigrants from England. His mother came over as a domestic, and his parents met in Toronto and got married. Edward's father had a variety of jobs: bread salesman, milkman (with a horse-drawn cart), a Toronto Transit Commission worker, and an elevator mechanic's assistant. The family did not have much money. He says that his mother was tolerant of his father's adventures and absences; during the First World War, his father served overseas as a drummer, and he did not come back until Edward was almost nine. When he was ten, Edward deliberately set a couple of fires in the neighbourhood, burning down a double garage and a house under construction. He is not really sure why he did this, but he says it was probably because he wanted to see the fire trucks in action.

Edward also had plenty of fun skipping school, but this behaviour, together with his difficult relationship with his parents, led him eventually to drop out of school. He was anxious to leave home and just could not see eye-to-eye with his parents. For example, while Edward was taking lessons to get his pilot's licence, he bought a car. He fell out with his parents who, being strict, wanted him home with his car by eleven o'clock. Eventually, he grew tired of arguing with his parents and told them to keep the car. A few years later, Edward went to college and graduated from two certificate programs. He began to work with a major utility company, where he stayed for thirty years.

Edward and Elaine lived only two blocks apart in Toronto, but they did not get to know each other until later when they went to the same church. Edward explains that he became a Sunday school teacher there, following Elaine's example. The couple married from their own homes. Edward was twenty-one, and Elaine was eighteen. Elaine describes their first years of marriage: "Edward set about to work as much overtime as he could. And we saved. Two years to the day after we got married, we signed the papers for our first house. I had quit my job. The nursery was all ready for the baby, and I had a miscarriage. Then after we had been married a couple of years, we had a full-term stillbirth. I was in labour several days. It was really tough. And we had done everything according to the rule. And if there was any generation that ever believed rules worked, I think, it would have been ours. So, yeah, it was hard." Elaine became pregnant again, and she says that "that pregnancy was really good. I'm not really a religious person. But I prayed that this one would live. I believed it would be okay, but Edward, he was just awful; he had migraines and was sick to his stomach." Their first child, Diane, was born. Elaine says, "I was pretty determined to have a lot of kids. Anybody that I knew that had a large family seemed happy; it just seems like a nice way to grow up." Their second child, Jim, was born two years later.

There were many factors that influenced the Verdans' decision to adopt. First, Edward and Elaine had been warned on several occasions by doctors and by her mother to stop with the baby business. Also, as Edward and Elaine knew, "there were all these children [who needed] homes, and we're working towards zero-population [growth]. So, it just didn't seem right to keep on having your own children when there were children that needed homes." Finally, both Elaine and Edward enjoyed being around kids, and they both liked the idea of having many children. In fact, they had hoped to run a group home. Edward remembers,

"Our dream was to get a big house and get six kids." Elaine also described a popular television program, *Today's Child*, in which children needing homes were featured: "There would be a living room ... and the foster moms would be in there and the kids would be playing. Of course, the camera would go on to the child, and there'd be sort of a voice-over ... talking about the child. At the beginning and the end of the show, they would play the music, *All You Need is Love* ... The marketing concept is obscene when you think about that ... it's kind of 'pie-in-the-sky' stuff."

The couple planned the adoption carefully. Edward had worked at a home for children with problems, so he knew the work involved in raising a child with behavioural difficulties. He wanted to adopt a child at a young-enough age so that his or her development could be influenced by the kind of parenting he and Elaine could provide. They thought that adopting a boy close to the age of their second child, Jim, would be a good idea, because, as Elaine hoped, "When they were grown, they'd think of supporting each other." Although Elaine and Edward did not begin by specifically asking to adopt a native child, they eventually considered it seriously. Edward explained, "We knew they were farming native kids over to the States; in Canada, they couldn't find a home for them then. We didn't view being a Canadian Indian as a handicap." In preparation, the couple joined the Indian Eskimo Association.

The Verdans were pleased that the adoption process took only three months, instead of the usual three years or more. Gerald, who was two when he came to live with his new family, was born off-reserve in northern Ontario. It was reported that his mother was Ojibwa and his father was Cree, but, years later, Gerald found this to be incorrect. Since his parents were not married when Gerald was born, and, probably because he was born to a woman who lived off-reserve, he was not officially registered as an Indian. Beyond being told how tall Gerald's parents were and that neither parent went to school after grade four, the Verdans knew little about Gerald's background or his early years. All they knew was that Gerald was offered for adoption at age three months, and no one could tell them why he had been relinquished by his parents. When he was older, Gerald managed to find out, with the help of the Native Brotherhood, that he had seven siblings and that they had all been abandoned. He also found out that his parents had had problems with drinking. His father was believed to be dead, and his mother had stopped drinking and was living on a reserve. Gerald still wanted to find his brothers and sisters.

There was a delay when Edward and Elaine went to pick up Gerald from the agency: he had chickenpox. The entire Verdan family was disappointed and Elaine cried. When they finally picked him up, Gerald sat on Elaine's lap and cried all the way home in the car. In his last foster home, Gerald had become too difficult to handle. When the Verdans collected him, his clothing was covered in nail polish. Their first impression of their new son suggested that Gerald must have had a difficult time as a baby. His baby teeth were decayed (although his adult teeth were healthy when they emerged), he was still wearing diapers, having had little or no toilet training, and he had a serious sinus infection and a nose that bled at the slightest provocation (which Gerald triggered when he wanted to cause a sensation). He did not yet speak, although he was almost two and a half (to indicate he wanted something, he would point and take), and he was a tremendous eater, with the capacity to consume soft drinks until he was sick. These patterns alarmed his new parents. When going to sleep at night, Gerald would carry on a kind of humming and would roll back and forth, as if to soothe himself. Sometimes, however, the rocking was quite violent, and his whole body lurched back and forth. Elaine would often sit in a chair next to the crib, and, with her hand on his chest and his hands on top of hers, he would calm down.

Gerald was also a little destructive with clothing, especially where buttons were concerned, and with upholstery and vinyl coverings, especially if there was a little hole to begin with. His violent behaviour with other children was often frightening, particularly if someone had something he wanted: he would hit the other child and simply take what he or she was holding. This meant that Elaine was reluctant to leave Gerald unattended, even for a short time. She remembers what happened the first time she left him for a few moments: "He did go hysterical right from the beginning. The first time I walked down the stairs to get the mail, he just went ballistic. I had to get the mail when he was sleeping or after Edward got home. Our schedule was that I probably never went out." In those early years, Edward worked six days a week. He would have some time on Sundays to spend with Gerald and the other children. This gave Elaine a chance to sleep in.

Elaine and Gerald did a lot of things together. They went to Story Time at the local library and to Moms and Tots swimming. Elaine was a volunteer for the Children's Aid Society, and Gerald would accompany her on home visits. Gerald had many interests while he was growing up. He enjoyed having stories read to him and seemed quite musical, being able to pick out tunes on a little organ. Physically, he could do anything. He could outrun his older brother, was an excellent swimmer, and could dive backwards off the dock: "He was fearless. I've never seen him frightened by anything," recalls Elaine. Yet, as much as Gerald seemed to enjoy things the way any other child would, his parents realized that his responses were not quite normal. They remember, "He was saddened. He seemed to close his eyes not with his eyelids [but] with a veil or something. They were dark, and they closed off a lot of times. He was probably angry at us [sometimes, but] he didn't lash out. He didn't respond normally." Gerald was petrified of Edward's shop coat. If Edward wore it, Gerald would freeze and cry. One time, when he was three years old, he took Diane's pet guinea pig out of its cage, put it on the window sill, and hit it with a shampoo bottle; the pet died on the way to the vet's office. Gerald seemed to enjoy being in the outdoors and looking for wild animals. He could spot things that no one else would notice, and he would bring home all kinds of creatures. The other children would look up to him, because he seemed to be an interesting person, who could find things to do that were more fun than anything the children could do alone.

Over the next few years, Elaine and Edward's concerns about Gerald's strange behaviour increased. He would sleepwalk around the house, and he urinated everywhere he went. He lied and began stealing: first, small things taken from the other children; and, later, larger items taken from the house, especially tools. Once, when he stayed over at Elaine's sister's house, he stole an entire suitcase-full of her sister's children's toys. Elaine says that she received more and more negative I-told-you-so comments from her sister's family. Only a few members of Elaine's family would agree to look after her children. Elaine's mother had discouraged the adoption. She thought that two children was the optimal number and told Elaine, "If you choose to have more children, I won't mind them." Elaine was discouraged by the lack of help from friends and relatives: "As far as the rest of the family was concerned, the extended family, it was like they didn't care, they didn't wish to discuss it." Edward comments on the lack of sympathy they still feel today: "They don't want to believe that kind of crap they see on TV exists in the closets of their own family. Only one person asks how he is. It's like he never existed."

When Gerald was eight, the Verdans moved into a new house in an ideal location for children. There was a park-setting all the way to school. However, by the time he was eleven, Gerald started to get into other people's backyards and steal. Elaine and Edward were unable to get through to Gerald: "He was like a blank wall." In fact, they felt that they were never able even to have a good conversation with him. As a result of these concerns, Elaine and Edward sought help, and Gerald was placed in play therapy when he was eight or nine. Edward did not find the sessions particularly helpful. He explains, "The psychiatrist, with the beard and clipboard, said, 'Oh yeah, he is a little disturbed, emotionally disturbed, but aren't we all?' They also said, 'It took him a long time to get like that, so it's gonna take a long time for him to get over it all.' I was so mad!" The Verdans' friends and neighbours also made their own statements about Gerald. One of Edward's fellow-workers, who was part Indian, reminded Edward that adoptions of Indians by white people never worked. The mother of one of the children's friends helpfully pointed out, "There's something very strange about Gerald, and I don't know what it is."

One of the biggest problems was over incidents that took place at the cottage. Gerald had a horrific habit of finding frogs, which were plentiful about the place, and squeezing them until their innards were forced out. Edward remarked that Gerald seemed to lack emotion, guilt, remorse, and any kind of a conscience. This made enforcing discipline difficult, even from a very early age. Elaine describes how they struggled with discipline issues: when he was aged four, she said, "I was mildly uneasy. If you could spend a couple of hours, you could get a confession out of him, by bugging him, scaring him and shaking him up. But, basically, he would sit there with his head down and the tears rolling and [he would] sniff. My question was 'Why?' and his favourite response was 'I dunno.' We depriving [him], confining [him] to his room, or to the property. It was just so hopeless. One time, afterwards, I thought, 'Oh, my God!' because I [was] out of control."Another frustrating aspect of Gerald's behaviour was the way he treated his eyeglasses. Every time he was asked about their disappearance, he would simply answer "I dunno." Invariably, they would turn up broken. Elaine believes that it was a way of him being aggressive without being "aggressive"; he would break his glasses on purpose, he would stomp on them.

At school, Gerald was an average student. Teachers tried hard to encourage him, and Elaine and Edward were surprised that he did as well as he did with the little effort that he put into his school work. Of course, there were times when he came home and was upset. These were times when the other children had called him names like Chinky Chinaman. When one of the parents was reported to have explained to his children that Gerald was not Chinese but Indian, it seemed to worsen the situation: "Well, of course, he was still a bad guy – cowboys and Indians!" For Gerald, there seemed to be no pride in being an Indian. He was not interested in the local Indian Centre or in youth groups. When he did join a youth group, he ended up being expelled from it.

Then, in grade five, Gerald began to run away. He was truant from school and would hang out in a large storm sewer or in the woods. Elaine remembers one particular occasion: "He took swimming lessons. I'd drop him off. One time, he didn't come home. He was picked up by the police the next night. He said that he had come out of the pool and two men forced him in a car, and drove him to the nuclear power station. He eventually got away and traced the [telephone] line home. The police noticed that he didn't have any blisters. He had played in the valley, built a fire, eaten the food some workers had stashed and, when he felt it was time, came home. That kind of thing happened four or five times." A couple of years later, Gerald phoned the police and said that he had found a bicycle. Edward describes what happened next: "Meanwhile, he had found another moped and ridden the thing until it had run out of gas. Then, he hid it. The police came and I asked Gerald, 'Where is the bike so they can be on their way?' He didn't know. I grabbed him and shook him … [I] knew damned well that he did take it. Eventually, he showed me where it was."

The couple's relationship with Gerald was stressful and frustrating. They felt increasingly helpless. Elaine explains that they were grasping at anything. The family began attending counselling sessions at the Family Court Clinic, with a psychiatrist. The sessions were distasteful to the other children, who were feeling increasingly resentful towards Gerald – he seemed to be the only one who did not mind going. At one point, everyone thought that the therapist was picking on Edward, and the children became upset. Eventually, they refused to keep going. If the Family Court Clinic was unhelpful, court itself was not any better. When Edward asked to recite passages from a concise history of the family's difficulties with Gerald, the court appointed the couple to be Gerald's probation officers. The Verdans thought that this suggestion was ludicrous. Edward says that they lost all hope that anyone could help them: "It just got worse and worse. I couldn't get answers. You go to different sessions and these characters, they stroke their beard and smoke a pipe … We wasted all this time."

The most frightening aspect of Gerald's behaviour was that which involved younger boys. One day a neighbour came to the house. Elaine remembers, "[She said], 'I really hate to bother you, but the boys came home and were talking to me about Gerald.'" He had taken them into the woods and been involved in sexual activities with them. Later, another neighbour, aware that his children had been taken into the woods by Gerald, flew into a rage every time he saw him. The Verdans were never sure of the details of these incidents involving this neighbour's children. But they soon had their own cause for worry. On Saturday mornings, Gerald used to watch cartoons with the youngest of the Verdan children, Mathew. Apparently, Gerald had been fooling around sexually with the dog and with Mathew. Gerald told Mathew that his mother would be angry if Mathew told her what they had been doing, so Mathew did not tell. When it happened again, Mathew didn't want the dog to get hurt so he decided to tell his mother: "We talked about it, and I thought, 'Oh my God! He's only four!' I panicked absolutely!" That very day, Elaine phoned the Children's Aid Society and told them what had happened, to which their response was, "What do you see us doing?" For Elaine, this time Gerald had gone too far; she knew that Edward's reaction would be one of outrage.

Mathew was not physically or, evidently, psychologically hurt by the incident, which, from what Mathew reported, Elaine knew to involve oral sex. She and Edward spoke to the psychiatrist who said that, although Mathew appeared to have emerged unscathed, Gerald could not continue to stay home, because he was endangering the health of the whole family. Even the family dog, who had been in the family well before the first child was born, was afraid of Gerald. The dog's reaction gave Elaine further evidence that there was something terribly wrong with Gerald. Although she could not name the problem, she felt helpless in the face of it. Today, she says, "In my heart, I feel guilty for what I brought on everyone … I felt responsible to make it right."

The stress of Gerald's behaviour was beginning to affect Edward's health. He went into hospital. He had lost weight, and, according to Elaine, was fading away: "Ed started feeling sick, almost like a flu, coughing up blood. He had chest pains and was put on IV for a week, and surgery was scheduled." Elaine worried that the stress was ultimately going to kill Edward or, alternatively, that he would lose his temper to the point where he would do something he would later regret. Their daughter, Diane, was also starting to react to the tension in the house. One Saturday morning, the day before Mother's Day, Diane packed her bags and left home and went to stay with friends for six weeks. Elaine was devastated by this turn of events – Diane had appeared to be coping with the stress that Gerald's behaviour inflicted on the family. That afternoon, shortly after Elaine brought Edward home from the hospital, the couple sat together in the backyard, crying about their daughter leaving home. Elaine recalls, "I was just very sad it had happened. It was just absolutely not like anything you expected to have ever happen to your family … Not so much to yourself, but to the family." During Diane's absence from home, Elaine was able to meet with her to discuss the family's concerns with Gerald. Diane eventually returned home.

To add to the Verdans' difficulties, Edward's father was also very sick. While Edward was away in another city on business, Elaine and Edward's brother comforted Edward's mother. Elaine felt anger and frustration at Gerald's apparent lack of sensitivity towards these other family members: "We had a lot of illness within the older people in our family and I watched him throw his life away while other people were in pain and dying. I started to get angry with him. Something hardened more in me." By December of that year, Elaine and Edward were at their wits' end: "Finally, it just all fell apart, along with the other things that happened. All of a sudden, the light just went out for me. I was starting to lose control," Elaine remembers. She recalls Edward saying, "It's either him or me. One of us has to go, because I can't take this." And Edward also recalls saying to Gerald, "You're going to have to go. I can't cope. We're all going down the pike ..."

They finally made the difficult decision to place Gerald, who was now fourteen, with the Children's Aid Society. He was made a crown ward and placed in a treatment centre. Still, Elaine and Edward felt that nothing in their relationship with Gerald had or would change: he was still their son. Although he never came back to the house to live and was in jail several times, he did visit on occasion, and he is still included in the couple's will. Elaine says that, while the rest of the family felt relief when Gerald was no longer in the house, she felt terrible about his absence: "I didn't feel relieved at all. I felt terrible. And underlining it all, I was probably angry that everyone felt better, in a way, after he left home."

IDEAL-FAMILY MEMORY

The setting of Elaine's ideal-family memory is the family room. Edward is in his workshop next to the family room, and Elaine is coming down the stairs. Gerald has just mastered something that neither Diane nor Jim was able to do: back a tricycle into a corner: "The kids were really happy. They were encouraging and were really proud that he could do this. They were so proud of him. He was so proud of himself. He just smiled ... it was his face and their faces. I was happy. This is the way it should be. It was really working. His eyes were open, not veiled. He seemed free. He just seemed released from whatever burdened him. They were really supportive, not contrived. They were sharing ... [to] see them together, feeling successful. I thought, they will always be there for each other." For Elaine, who had been an only child until the age of eight, the sight of these children happily playing together represented the epitome of what families should look like.

DISRUPTION MEMORY

Edward's disruption memory focuses on the time Gerald escaped from custody and was on the run for a few days:

We hadn't seen Gerald for months. He had been taken from the jail in a van for a court appearance. The two guys with him had wanted to escape. He didn't want to but when they broke out, he had to run too. He spent three days and three nights downtown, and then he phoned us. He said he was afraid to surrender ... Elaine made suggestions, but Gerald always said he had to surrender. He hung up a few times, but the last time he called, he finally said he would [surrender]. Elaine said she couldn't meet him, but she said that I would. I called the place where I was going to meet him and told them not to call the police, and they agreed.

It was a miserable day, grey, wet. I couldn't find the place. Finally, I got there, but I was there only three or four minutes when these guys came in through the door: plain-clothed cops. They flashed a badge. They handcuffed him and started to take him away. I tried to intervene. There were three other cars outside, more cops surrounding the building. There was nothing I could do that time. I wanted to spend some time with him. The police had to do what they had to do; that's their job, but one person had snitched. These other people [who snitched] didn't have to. I knew it would be a long time before we saw him again.

From [Gerald's] point of view, it could have been seen as a trap. It was like they were arresting Al Capone or something because of his previous record. This wasn't kid stuff anymore. I saw it all as totally unnecessary. I figured he'd be hungry, we'd go have a meal or something somewhere. Now you see them handcuffing your own. Previously, you form a mental picture about what happens to him. I just anticipated it as being one of the very few opportunities to talk to him. It would be one hell of a long time before I saw him again, if ever. He seemed to show some remorse, some emotion.

He was afraid to go back to prison, afraid to stay on the streets, afraid of being caught. He seemed so vulnerable at that one particular time. He was seventeen. It just felt like a chance to be close for at least two hours, but it didn't work.

Today, Gerald is out of jail and living in southern Ontario. He was married to a woman who had children from a previous relationship, but he was abusive towards his wife and the marriage did not last. The children are now in foster homes. Elaine and Edward correspond regularly with Gerald's stepdaughter, and she sometimes visits them. Gerald moves from job to job every few weeks and is still struggling with alcohol abuse. He has little contact with the Verdans, but he does phone or write them two or three times a year. This past year, he came home to stay for a week. The visit went very well, although the other children will not have anything to do with him at this time. While Gerald was in jail, native artists went to talk to him and encouraged him to pursue his own interest in art. He took their advice and for a while found much enjoyment in painting; however, he has not done much painting in recent years. Earlier, his parents had sent him money occasionally in order to help him with his art supplies.

Although the Verdans know little about why Gerald's life developed as it did, they now have some insight into the effects their difficult years with Gerald had on them as individuals, parents, spouses, and members of their community. Elaine says that "I am a different person when he is not on my mind. You can put [the reality of] it in a box somewhere and live your life, but once the lid comes off, it's kind of scary ... I feel damaged." She continues to have confidence in the power of prayer to guide her and maintain her strength. Edward still feels the frustration of not having been able to do anything for Gerald at the time: "I try to figure out why he does do these things, and I get nowhere. I never did figure out what the hell his problem was. Look where he is today, and I am not his problem ... I am not affecting his life now." As parents, both Elaine and Edward felt a degree of guilt. Edward says, "I had a lot of guilt. I felt I had failed. I was relieved and quite glad that someone else was having this problem with him. It wasn't just me."

The Verdans are also aware that their relationship with each other suffered in the midst of the turmoil, that they each coped individually by repressing their feelings. When asked about the change in their relationship, Elaine said to Edward, "That became an issue for us, the more frustrated I am, the quieter I get ... I think if we'd talked more ... if I had listened and encouraged you to talk about what you really wanted ... We should have talked more, with the three children, [to] deal with what was going on." Edward added, "I felt she responded too quickly to his requests. I could have blocked it out but she can't. There has to be some end to it." The lack of support and help from the community, Elaine says, made them feel rejected and lonely.

Elaine has since gone back to school in order to gain some understanding of the underlying causes of Gerald's behaviour.

And Edward says, "I didn't know about this fetal alcohol syndrome, of course. If that were true, it's like trying to climb the mountain with running shoes ... Look at all the things I did wrong (when I was young), and I figured that I grew out of that. So, I had hope that Gerald would grow out of it." Both Elaine and Edward now realize that the profound sadness they felt about Gerald was grief. Elaine explains that she did not have a word for how she felt after Gerald left home: "You just knew, and that person died at a particular time in your experience with the individual: it's grieving for this child [who] might have been."

As far as the Verdans are concerned, one of the main causes of the rupture of their relationship with Gerald was the adoption system itself. Quite apart from the obscenity of the marketing of native children, as Elaine put it, if the agencies were aware of all the inherent problems of adopting older native children, they should have prepared prospective adoptive parents for the undertaking. Edward feels bitterness towards this system: "If they knew what was going on, they could have made it easier ... I kept telling myself I was given defective goods right from the beginning, but I didn't have any recourse to go back. You have nothing to learn from ... you have no built-in knowledge. There is no rule. There is no guideline. There is nothing in society that has any support for it." Edward also expresses a sense of betrayal: "Society has done an 'about-face.' When I hear 'scooping' [native children from their homes to place them for adoption in white homes], that changes the whole picture. These kids were never considered special by the agencies ... I saw it all as totally unnecessary, and I was angry with this agency."

6 The Pelligrini Family

Initially, Victoria and Lou Pelligrini did not want to have children of their own. But after two years of marriage, Victoria suggested that perhaps they should adopt. The Pelligrinis were then living in western Canada and they often heard stories of native children living in dire straits. Vincent was five when he came to live with the Pelligrinis.

Both Victoria and Lou came from working-class families of Italian background. Victoria's parents, Tony and Maria Romano, were born in Italy. Her father emigrated to Toronto three years ahead of his wife, who already had a three-year-old boy and was pregnant with Victoria when he left Italy. Although her parents learned to speak English, Italian was the language spoken in the home. Her mother worked in a factory, while her father worked in construction. Victoria remembers that there was not much communication between her and her father. He was often away at a job site, and when he was home, he was very quiet. He developed an alcohol problem and could be very abusive when drunk. When Victoria became serious about Lou, her father's alcoholism increased. Her mother was piously stoic about her husband's drinking. Despite these difficulties, the family was a good Catholic one and attended Mass on Sundays.

Her parents appear to have held Old World ideas about proper behaviour, especially for women. Her mother told Victoria not to draw attention to herself, because, as an Italian, she said, there would be much prejudice against her. Her parents, she remembers, were very strict – her mother more than her father – and they also enforced a strict curfew. Even when she was twenty-five years old and engaged to Lou, she still had to be home before midnight. Although her father usually showed his disapproval by giving Victoria the silent treatment, she remembers that, once, when she was twenty-four years old and came home later than her curfew, her father struck her. This was how he expressed his outrage. Still, she did not expect to be treated otherwise: in those days, all parents seemed to be strict and could exercise a good deal of control over their children.

She describes her parents as hard-working people who expected nothing less from their son and daughter. Because her parents wanted things to be better for their children and knew that education was the route to success, the same discipline of hard work and achievement was applied to school. Unfortunately, Victoria did not excel in school, unlike her brother, whom she describes as gifted. Her marks averaged in the sixties and seventies, while his averaged in the high nineties. As a result, Victoria's parents did not think that she would go very far in higher education. She did, however, complete four years of university and one year at teacher's college. (Both she and her brother paid for their own education, she by working as a cashier at Miracle Food Mart.) After university, her brother went to Africa with the Canadian Universities Service Overseas (CUSO) for two years, but he said that he hated the experience because he had no patience for lazy people. She says that he still has little tolerance for black people, and there is nothing that will change his mind on the subject.

Lou also comes from a family with working-class Italian roots. He remembers his grandfather Dino (his paternal grandfather) as a tough little kind of guy who hustled pool. His father, born in Montreal, was on his own by the age of thirteen or fourteen. He had little education. He married a French-Canadian girl when still a young man. The couple had two children: Lou and his older sister. When Lou was only eighteen months old, his father left his wife and moved with the children to Toronto. The father never spoke of the separation, and Lou never pursued the matter, out of respect, he thinks. Lou does not even remember what his mother looked like. He believes that his sister, however, keeps in touch with their mother.

By the time Lou was six years old, his father began living with the woman who would become Lou's stepmother. Now, in addition to his older sister, he had a stepsister. He says that the three children got on well enough. Their father worked in construction as a superintendent. Lou describes him: "My Dad had natural intelligence, you know. He was running million-dollar jobs, under budget. Considering he had a grade three education, he had a lot of street smarts. There's no doubt about it. He wasn't a tall man but had pretty big muscles. Yeah, he was a pretty solid guy; his biceps were probably fifteen inches [around] at one time." His father had boxed as a youngster, and Lou says that this aggressive, controlling side of him came to the surface if someone bad-mouthed him on the street. His father thought nothing of physically pounding the offender. This sort of discipline was also expressed in the home. Lou remembers, "I'd get my butt warmed once in a while. One time, I took a new pair of socks and went and played hockey and got them soiled. When I walked in the house, my Dad just open-handed me one. I hid in the garage for an hour and cried. But I've never been beaten to a pulp or anything."

In spite of his father's nature, his stepmother exercised the authority in the household. Since Lou's father was moved all over the province by his company, she took over the running of the household from the time Lou was eight. He describes how things worked with his mother: "I was given a fair bit of leeway. My mom told me to make decisions on my own. She's never questioned me. Instead, she would say, 'Well, that's up to you. You know what you gotta do around the house.' I had to fend for myself in some ways. I still had my chores to do and I had to shovel snow and cut grass, and I didn't do a very good job of either, but I did it. I mean, I wanted to play hockey and the hell with all the other shit, you know. I played hockey 'till I was twenty-eight or twenty-nine years old and was a referee for ten years as well. So sports [were] really good to me." He would also play hockey with his father. He remembers with fondness one particular time when he and his father were playing hockey down in the basement and put about three holes in his mother's cold-cellar door.

School was a challenge for Lou, and he had only mediocre academic success. When he was moved from Catholic school to public school, he failed grade three. In grade eight, he was so borderline that he was given a choice of repeating the grade and staying in an academic program or going into grade nine on trial while in a technical program. He opted to take the technical stream and did well, with first-class honours. As for his Catholic education, he had to continue these studies on weekends, but he says that he hated them: "They made no sense to me." Although he did not bother going to church, later, when he lived in western Canada, he played guitar in folk masses.

By the time he was in grade eleven, his family had been moved to Thunder Bay. Living in such a remote part of the province for Lou was not a hardship. He loved it. He was able to play hockey and go ice fishing, snowmobiling, and water skiing. He also worked for the same construction company his father worked for and made a lot of money. Of this time, he says: "I was a pretty solid kid. I played hockey and I chased the girls, and it was pretty much normal sort of stuff, you know." For a year, the family lived on the local Indian reserve, where the company had placed mobile homes they had purchased for their workers, and Lou went by bus to school in town, along with all the native children. He enjoyed this time: "Oh, sure, I was the butt of some of their jokes, and you'd get drinking scenarios from time to time. They also hosted some pow-wows."

Victoria and Lou came to know each other in high school, after his family had moved back to Toronto from Thunder Bay. When Victoria was in grade thirteen, Lou was in grade nine. He describes their relationship: "Victoria would walk by, and I'd say hello, and the next thing we'd know, we'd be sitting on the front lawn (I'm supposed to be cutting the grass), and we would talk for hours, and talk and talk and talk." When they decided to get married, Victoria shocked her parents, particularly her poor mother, when she said that *she* was buying Lou a ring and that they would be doing their own planning for the wedding. Victoria says, "Our parents were three doors away only, but they didn't know each other. I guess they met the night of the rehearsal before the wedding. At the wedding, Lou's parents were over here and mine were over there [indicating that the two families were on separate sides of the hall and did not readily mix]. And since then, which is seventeen years ago, they haven't met a great deal, maybe twice." The tacit understanding when Lou and Victoria married was that they would not have children. "Getting married was just to be with each other. I mean, Victoria and I, yeah, we fit," says Lou.

After they had been married for a year, Victoria was laid off from her teaching job, along with many other teachers. A job-research grant helped her find a job in rural Alberta. Victoria remembers, "We were still on our honeymoon. We truly had no idea what we were doing. I was teaching an all grade-two class, and I kept hearing horrible stories about native kids' home lives, etc. So, I said to Lou, 'You know, Lou, we ... don't have children of our own, and we probably never will choose to have our own. Maybe we should adopt.' Next, the social worker at school started talking to us. So I bulldozed Lou into thinking, well, this might be a good idea." Lou had mentioned that he wanted a boy with whom he could play. Neither he nor Victoria ever considered that the fact the child they were going to adopt was native would be a potential problem. All they were concerned about was that this child needed a home, and they were a couple who wanted a child. When they went to their parish priest to ask for a reference for the adoption agency, however, the priest refused to give them one. Victoria remembers the priest saying something like, "Mixed relationships don't work. How dare [you] think that [you] can adopt ... a native child and [that] it will work. He'll go back to his people."

The boy the Pelligrinis eventually adopted – Vincent – was five years old when the adoption process began and he came to live with them. He was nine when the adoption was finalized. All the couple knew about their new son was that he had been a victim of alcohol abuse and that he had four teeth missing. The agency wanted him to be in a home where there were no other children, because it said that he would need a lot of attention. The adoption worker brought Vincent to the school where Victoria was teaching so she could bring him home with her. The boy was carrying two green garbage bags: one had clothes, which turned out to be too small for him; and the other had broken toys and an old tattered bible. He was also carrying a little hamster, which, Victoria says, her cat killed two weeks later. In the absence of his pet hamster, Vincent took to the family yellow Labrador Retriever dog, Roxanne. This dog became Vincent's, and she often went to bed with him.

The first night with the Pelligrinis, Vincent was tearful. In order to calm and reassure him, Lou and Victoria decided to call up the family from which he had come so that he could say hello to them. Victoria was shocked, however, when one of Vincent's foster parents said, "He's crazy ... and good luck to you!" Among Vincent's behavioural patterns that soon came to concern Lou and Victoria were bedwetting, frequent and easily provoked bloody noses, keeping food under his bed, and eating as though he had never eaten before. Further, Victoria reports, "He'd either be talking in his sleep or he'd have this look on his face. Oh, torment beyond belief. He would toss and turn and he'd fall out of bed. But, then, there'd be times he'd just wake up and walk into the room and start yelling, when he was in the middle of a dream and he'd sleepwalk." She also remembers that Vincent did not talk about his feelings at all, but "on the occasion that we would go for walks, he would talk a little bit about stuff ... I believe that he [had] bonded very well to us, but we got too close to him and he very much all the time had his guard up. He needed a lot of space." Another peculiar habit Vincent had was defecating in his bath. Victoria says, "He'd have a bath, and there'd be little globs of stool. Right from day one, right until he left home at sixteen. I would say to him, 'Fine, here's the Ajax, here's the towel. Afterwards, I want that bathtub cleaned.'"

Vincent did not seem to believe that he was going to stay with the Pelligrinis permanently. Every June, when school ended, says Victoria, "he was almost ready to go ... [he would start] packing his stuff [and say], 'Thanks, gotta go to my new foster home.' In June, every year, he had to move, like clockwork." Once, when he was ten, Vincent took home a bad report card. He had been sent home before his parents had arrived home from work. Lou describes what happened: "He's home. [Victoria's] not there. Clothes are strewn around the bedroom. His knapsack's gone. He packed some extra underwear and some hot dogs. And I found him walking down by the airport in the town where we lived. He was always very worried about doing the right things. Because our expectations, I guess, were very high." During those days, Vincent had only one good friend, Sam, who lived across the street. When Sam moved away, Vincent found his friend's absence difficult to take.

Although Vincent seemed to be a loner, he needed a lot of attention, which Lou and Victoria gave him. Both tried to be the ideal parent and to give him all the quality time they could. Victoria took Vincent to the library – he loved books – and the two of them enjoyed doing arts and crafts at the gallery. Lou engaged Vincent in play activities. When the three of them would go to Calgary, Victoria says, "I [would] let the guys out at the toy store, and they'd be out there playing with dump trucks and stuff. 'Okay boys' – I would call them 'the boys' all the time." Vincent got involved with hockey for a couple of years and scored some goals. Lou recalls, "He could've been a really good hockey player, given his tenacity and his natural strength. His athletic abilities could've been limitless, but he just didn't have that drive, I guess." But he and Lou did have some good times: "It was like the Wild West. We used to go for picnics on the riverbank … If there was another vehicle there, we'd drive across the river, park on the other side of the river and have a picnic. Vincent would bring his trucks out. The dogs'd rip up and down, and the shotgun sat on the hood, just in case bears came by. I used to load it with one-ounce slugs, you know. We had the whole thing. "When Lou had first bought the car, Vincent was heartbroken: 'No more four-wheeling, Dad.'" So Lou ended up buying each of them dirt bikes: "We used to ride and come home looking like pig-pens. Victoria would just stand there at the porch with the garden hose and hose us down. We had fun." Lou taught Vincent how to clean the bike and how to check the oil. This was when Vincent was sixteen and they had moved back to Toronto. Lou then enrolled Vincent in a motorcycle driving course so that he could get his licence, which he did. Father and son went on a few rides together, even going as far south as the United States for motorcycle rallies.

While still living in Alberta, Victoria would bring Vincent to Toronto with her each summer while she took a summer course. During that time, Vincent was given every opportunity to try many different activities, such as St Mike's Hockey College and a summer art program at the Ontario College of Art. Victoria stayed with her family, but they had mixed reactions to their daughter's adopted native son. Victoria's mother was thrilled and thought of Vincent as her special grandchild. But, according to Victoria's uncle, her father did not treat Vincent well. And Victoria's brother cautioned her, "[Vincent] is very, very different when you're not around, you can't believe how different he is, and he's gonna give you lots of trouble." Apparently, her father ignored Vincent a lot and showed preference to the other two grandsons.

Vincent attended grade school in the same school in which Victoria taught. His performance was poor, because, as Victoria said, he was an underachiever and tended to have a short attention span for everything. He was the youngest in his class. He failed grade seven. His report cards reflected his underachievement and his lack of self-control. He did, however, display great artistic creativity, which his parents found mind-boggling. Although Vincent could summon up nice manners, which Lou and Victoria say impressed everybody, in class he was the clown, for which he got the strap a couple of times. Vincent's teachers reported that he was lazy, lacked initiative and motivation, and was immature. His teachers gave him a homework book, but it never came home. The Pelligrinis were anxious to be of whatever help they could and said to the teachers, "Call us, and we can help you get the work done." This, however, did not always work. Lou remembers one frustrating occasion when the art teacher told them the day before school was going to end that Vincent had only two or three days to get all his art work handed in. Vincent did manage to finish grade nine, because, as Lou says, "I had to spend three days standing over him to get art projects done. I was so pissed at him." Vincent acquired the desire to graduate from high school only when he saw his biological sister (whom he had contacted by this time) graduate. He said, "I'm going to be the first boy to graduate from high school." Finally, Lou and Victoria told the teachers that they were to speak about Vincent to Lou only, not to Victoria. Eventually, Vincent was expelled from high school. Victoria was very upset and says, "I took it as a personal affront against me." Discipline was also a problem at home, no matter what tactic was used: it made no difference whether he was grounded, sent to his room, made to go to bed early, or prevented from watching television: Vincent could circumvent the punishment.

By the time Vincent was twelve, his behaviour had grown increasingly worrisome. He started on his nighttime walk-abouts. "Sometimes, he'd take off for three or four days at a time. He'd pack his clothes, and he'd pack a baseball bat." He also made himself a set of *namchuk*, a martial-arts restricted weapon that consists of two sticks, one foot long, attached by a chain. Lou and Victoria used to drive to downtown Toronto with his photograph and look for him. When he was still quite young, Vincent began stealing things: a couple of ID bracelets and, then, loonies, which Lou and Victoria had been saving. As Victoria recalls, "One day, there weren't any left. He also took some screwdrivers, that kind of stuff. He'd always go into Lou's tool box. He took a small hatchet." Lou remembers another time: "I had a bottle of peach schnapps in the house, and, all of a sudden, it was gone. [I] had a phone call from the school. Vincent, they think, is drunk. Later, in his room, a bottle – jeeze! – it smelled like peach schnapps."

By the time Vincent was fifteen, more things started disappearing from around the house. His parents charged him. Lou explains, "We had just basically gotten it across to the judge, you know, that we were losing control of the situation. We wanted help. Time and probation is what he got. We even revoked his bail once." Shoplifting, too, became a problem. Victoria says, "When he saw something he liked, [he] took it." There was one event in particular when Vincent was in grade ten. Lou says, "[H]e went into our safe. They [Vincent and a couple of friends] pulled the safe out of the closet, [went] downstairs, got my drill, drilled seventy-two holes in the back of [the safe] and punched their way through."

After Vincent was expelled from high school, he lived at home on and off. The tension was great because his parents never knew what he was going to do next. Once, he robbed ten dollars from another boy, and when he appeared before the judge, he was not shown leniency, because this particular judge had already seen Vincent many times in his courtroom: "It was major, because the judge knew him. 'Cause [Vincent's] only been there like a bizillion [sic] times before that." It appeared to Lou and Victoria that Vincent's problematic behaviour operated in two-week cycles. The same pattern occurred when he was on probation. He also became verbally abusive and belligerent. For example, when he was told that he was late returning to one of the correctional houses he had been placed in, Vincent's reply was to tell the counsellor to f— off.

Lou and Victoria did not want Vincent to come back to live at home; they wanted him to earn the privilege, because, as Victoria admits, "the innocence was gone then, the minute he went into the system, the innocence was gone, and it would never come back." Still, Vincent called home often and cried to his parents that he would not get into trouble again. But when his parents told him that they wanted him to stay in the correctional facility or in a home for troubled youth, Vincent's response was to call his parents "fucking assholes." Victoria remembers that Vincent was terrible and would run the whole gamut of emotions, from good to bad in the span of four and a half minutes on the telephone.

Once, Vincent ran away from a placement facility. He and others stole a car, for which he was charged with possession of stolen goods. He did not have an easy time in jail either. Lou notes, "West Detention put them in ranges, and he was in the black range. He couldn't have been in the white range, because he wasn't white. [Still], they shouldn't have put him in the black range, because he definitely wasn't black." The Pelligrinis became increasingly fearful for their physical safety. Lou remembers one angry confrontation when Vincent "tried standing Victoria up one day. He would tower over her and try to make her back down, like, physically impose himself, and I saw him doing that, and I just grabbed him by the shirt collar and put him up against the wall and lifted his toes till he was barely having his toes on the ground, told him not to fuck around. That's the first time I ever talked to him like that. Sat him down and … said, If you wanna talk, you talk." Vincent became increasingly violent. His parents remember that, at some points, he would be away from home for weeks at a time. Since he did not have a house key, when he wanted to get back into the house, he would kick in the windows. But every time he did this, his parents charged him with public mischief. They say, "We charged him every time."

IDEAL-FAMILY MEMORY

Lou recalled his ideal-family memory, a time when he and Victoria had planned to surprise Vincent with a motorcycle. The gift was waiting for him outside, where they escorted him blindfolded: "A surprise for him. Sunny day, nice temperature. She took the blindfold off. The look on his face: total astonishment, surprise, disbelief, excitement! All those feelings that you expect a kid to have when you give him something like that. It started a whole trend of things that we used to do together. He wanted to drive it, really get on it."

The significance of this moment for Lou lay in his wishing that his own father might have done something like that for him. According to Lou, "I was giving [Vincent] something that I hadn't received."

DISRUPTION MEMORY

For Victoria, the episode during which she realized that their relationship with Vincent had irrevocably broken down took place on their front porch one morning when Vincent tried to come in the house after being on the streets or with friends. Lou was away on business, and Victoria was home alone, unwilling to let Vincent into the house:

Lou was away. Vincent had been out for a couple of days already. I wasn't sleeping very well. There was a knock on the door. It's 9:30 in the morning. Vincent was there, and my heart just stopped beating, because I knew just the way he looked he was in trouble. So, I opened the door, but I didn't open the screen at all. He said, "I want my clothes. I wanna leave." And I said, "You can't come in the house at all. Let's talk outside." We were in the carport and we were sitting at the table where there were some chairs. He kept saying, "I want my clothes. I don't have anything." I said, "You can come in when your Dad comes home, but right now I don't want you in the house."

He was very, very angry. He walked towards the lake. "I'm gonna, I'm gonna go stand in front of the train track; there's no reason to live any more." And I kept yelling. I remember running down the street, and I yelled at him to come back, and he didn't. Then I went in the house and I locked the door again, and I was calling the police to tell them where he was headed to and …

I heard a knock on the door again, and it was him again and … and I walked back out and this time he had a … lighter in his hand and he was flicking it, and finally he just put it up by his hand. And I didn't say anything, I didn't tell him to stop it or anything, he didn't even seem to be there – his eyes were very glazed – and, finally he put the lighter on the table. And he … he burned up his … he had burned up his motorcycle licence, and then he started burning his hand.

And I walked back inside, and I think I took the lighter, walked back inside the house and I called the hospital and I said, "What am I going to do?" They told me to go to the hospital immediately with him. So I asked him if he wanted

to do that, and he said, "Yes." So we went there, and they
called this psychiatrist in, and it took a very long time for the
psychiatrist to come in and [Vincent] fell asleep. And when
the psychiatrist came in, he said that [Vincent] didn't appear
depressed; he just appeared very tired and very bored and
that there were no beds on the ward for him because of his
age. And besides that, he wasn't depressed enough to be put
on the ward, and he didn't wanna give him anything for the
way he was feeling. So I said, "So, what are you going to
do?" And he said, "Well, nothing." And I said, "Well, what
do you expect?" He said, "Well, he can just walk out now,
and that's it."

So Vincent and I walked out together, and he said – the
last thing I can remember Vincent saying – "Well, I'll be seeing
you then." And he walked away from me, he was walking,
he walked towards the downtown sector. And I thought, at
that time, I felt very, very lonely, and I thought we've lost
him, that's it, you know ... I felt very frustrated because
nobody would believe that here was this kid who was just
so ... he was so suicidal at the time, and he didn't present
that. He presented as being very, very tired. So I ended up
walking home. I'm waiting for Lou to come home, and I told
him what had happened, and that's it.

The fact that I knew ... that I couldn't do anything about
it, absolutely nothing and the fact that I also knew that professionals couldn't either ... And the choice he made was to
go back out on the street, you know, when he had a perfectly
safe home, and everything else was there for him. And all
he needed to do was to keep the few rules we had and
he couldn't.

And I knew that when he went out on the street, that other
people wouldn't know how depressed he actually was. Like,
I didn't know whether he would live or die. I just had no
idea, because, I mean, his eyes were glazed; he was a mess.
I'd never seen him so badly off. I knew he hadn't slept for
days, and I wouldn't let him in – a stranger? Yeah.

For Lou, the disruption in his relationship with Vincent came
when Vincent was put in West Detention Centre by the court.
After Vincent had been taken away, Lou remembers going back

to his car, but when he got in the car he cried like a fool: "I really did. It was probably the toughest thing, and I think I knew then that our lives had changed already."

The Pelligrinis' feelings of helplessness and fear for their son's future were exacerbated by the fact that no one appeared to be able or want to help Vincent. Both parents felt that they were somehow blamed by society for not succeeding in raising a well-adjusted child. And they felt betrayed by the social-services system. The lack of sympathy and support they encountered in social institutions was also evident closer to home. Family and friends were equally capable of insensitivity. Lou reports, "One of the people I worked with said that the parents should be held accountable for the kid's crimes. I said, 'You know, I charged my son. What do you think of me, am I a bad person? So, why would you have me charged for something my son's done?'" The community's reaction to Vincent affected Lou and Victoria's sense of worth. Because they did not dare leave Vincent home alone, they spent at least three or four years as social recluses, with little contact with friends outside the workplace. But even in Victoria's workplace – the school in which Vincent was also enrolled – Victoria could not help but take as a personal affront her colleagues' expulsion of her son. When people did enquire after Vincent, a grateful Victoria always said, "Thank you for asking." And Lou appreciated the constancy of some friends of theirs: "We have this one couple that are very good friends of ours and they were always very good ... He was my sounding board."

The Pelligrinis' struggle with Vincent took its toll on their emotional and physical health. Victoria says, "I'd gone down to ninety pounds, and I'm five feet, six inches tall. I was emotionally unstable. I almost lost my job. I was obsessed, I have to admit. I got obsessed with him, to the point that I also lost a fair bit of weight. As well, I wouldn't sleep. It was terrible. Emotionally, I was in a tailspin." Lou went through lots of abdominal tests. He also did not sleep well and admits that he was extremely edgy and testy: "I mean, your mind was never really there exactly. You're never one hundred per cent into what you're supposed to be doing ... Geez! [Vincent] was killing me."

In their weakened physical and emotional states, Lou and Victoria suffered guilt and the erosion of self-confidence. Lou admits, "I ... feel guilty ... because of what we're doing ... More than anything else, it was my idea to come back here. I was part of the whole parameter – trying to figure out where we'd gone wrong. Then for the first six months, I wasn't home as much as I should've been and then I had a job that took weekends out of the summer. So I guess I was thinking, maybe if I hadn't done this, and maybe if I hadn't done that ... [But] we've done nothing wrong. In fact, we've tried to do everything as right as society supposedly says, but the way you feel is that you haven't done that well. And there isn't anybody that tells you you've done it well. No one – the social workers, probation officers, court judges ..."

For two years, the Pelligrinis did not know where Vincent was. Eventually, he hitchhiked to the prairies and reconnected with his biological family. Today, he has met a girl and is living with her in her own hometown. They have five cats. Vincent calls Victoria and Lou every weekend, using the calling card they send him every Christmas. He works and tells his parents that he cannot get into trouble out there because it is such a small town that everybody knows what everybody else is doing. He also works on his art work, something his father is very proud of: "He is an artist, his stuff is really good."

The Pelligrinis were devoted to Vincent and his upbringing; they took their parenting responsibilities seriously. Victoria took him to the library, and Lou went on picnics and bike rides with them. But because the Pelligrinis had no other children, they feel that they were perhaps too close to Vincent and that he simply was not comfortable with the closeness of their relationship. They now refer to their feelings as unhealthy co-dependency. During those difficult years, the parents felt that Vincent had rejected them. They also felt that their problems with Vincent had put a strain on their marital relationship. Nevertheless, when Victoria recounted her disruption memory, Lou sat close to her. Although the strain created a wedge between Lou and Victoria, the couple supported each other as best they could. Lou admits, "She used to get mad at me, at the peak of frustration and the tension and the bad times. At one time, I blamed Victoria." But he also says that, when Victoria changed, he realized she was not to blame: "We'd hug each other in the morning." The couple often differed on strategies for coping with Vincent. Lou says that, whereas he is black and white, Victoria is grey, and he often got angry at her for listening to what he called stupid social workers. Victoria appreciated Lou's approaches to Vincent: "I was ready to go for [Vincent's] throat, and Lou took over, which was great."

Both Victoria and Lou seem relieved that Vincent is now living several hundred miles away and managing on his own. While they do not think that he will ever come home again to live, they encourage him to phone. They had no other children to restore their confidence in their parenting ability, and Victoria wishes that they had adopted a baby instead of a youngster. She also wonders what might have happened if they had opted to raise more than one child. Lou notes that as parents they missed the regular benchmarks of their child's life: his first date, graduation from high school, first job, and so on. He says, "All the dreams were shattered." And Victoria says, "It was my chance at being a mom." She remembers one of her opportunities to be a mom to Vincent: "We knew he was going to West Detention, and here's this kid of seventeen, much bigger than I, much stronger than I, sitting on my lap, crying, crying. I felt like his mom. He still needed me, needed me as much as I needed him."

A variety of things helped the parents cope with their feelings. Victoria found that parents' support groups were helpful: "I really began to laugh when I got into the Armstrong group. I was reading a book on co-dependency, the funniest book. The group was good for that. It was good because we could laugh about it." Lou was encouraged by the occasional supportive professional: "[There was one] bailiff, a grandfatherly type and Vincent really, really liked him." For both of them, further studies and new information enlightened them as to what might have happened in Vincent's early life to have caused such a tragedy. Victoria says that she now understands that Vincent was not going to be rejected again, *he* was going to do the rejecting. "After speaking to Dr Armstrong, we got the idea that [Vincent] was in a dissociated state." When Lou acquired information on the effects of foster care on a child's inability to bond, he realized that Vincent's difficulties "had less to do with the fact he's an Indian kid and we gotta treat him no differently than we would treat a white kid or a negro kid." Vincent's problems, Lou came to understand, stemmed from the fact he was the product of too many foster homes. Something along the way snapped.

In order to alleviate their stress, they took up other pastimes: Victoria pursued further studies, and Lou focused on his love of motorbike riding: "Motorcycling kept me sane. I think because you had to be in control. I'd take back roads and there's some really good curves you can dive into. You don't want to make a mistake, obviously. So, it kind of gets you focused singularly." In the end, however, it was hearing Vincent's opinions about his parents that reassured Victoria and Lou. Vincent has told them that he thinks they did a pretty good job raising him. Furthermore, he says that he would like to adopt children as his parents did, so that he, too, can give a kid a chance.

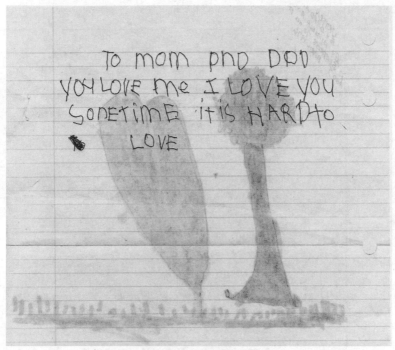

A note from one adoptee to his adoptive
parents when he was five years old

A cartoon drawing by one adoptee in elementary school

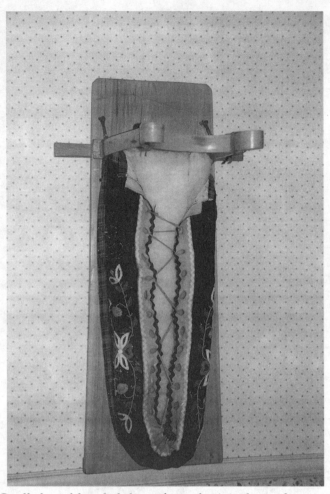

Cradle board handed down from aboriginal grandparents'
generation to adoptive parents

A drawing by one adoptee in his twenties

"Creation: a dream during a lifetime of reflection"
(courtesy of native adoptee Nathan Krebs)

"Eagle Spirit" (courtesy of Nathan Krebs)

Family photos of Tim's life displayed at his memorial service.
In the centre is the first picture we saw of Tim, and at the bottom
is one of the last photos taken of him.

We placed Tim's ashes under this young maple tree in 1993.

PART TWO

Conclusions

7 Why Do Some People Adopt?

I am not in this world to live up to your expectations
And you are not in this world to live up to mine.
You are you and I am I
And if by chance we find each other, it's beautiful.

– F. Perls (1969)

There are similarities as well as dissimilarities in the adoption experiences described in the previous section. The Brooks and Graves families each requested an infant for adoption, but when none was immediately available, both couples agreed to adopt older children. The Verdan and Adams families specifically asked for an older child so that the child would be close in age to their biological son. In every case, the parents were anxious to adopt and took the first children the agencies offered them. The Verdan, Pelligrini, Brooks, and Adams families specifically requested a boy when they began the adoption proceedings; all but the Pelligrinis planned to go on and adopt a girl later. The Brooks and Adams families did adopt a girl later, while the Verdans decided not to adopt again. The reason given for wanting a boy first was based on the order and number of their biological children. The Roethler and Graves families did not specify a preference and adopted a sister and brother(s) at the same time. All the couples except the Pelligrinis planned to adopt more than one child. The Verdans stopped with one, because they could see from the beginning that their son would need more attention.

As far as adopting native children is concerned, only Victoria and Lou Pelligrini began the adoption process with plans to adopt a native child. None of the other parents began by asking for native children. But Edward Verdan explained that he was aware that native children were being sent to the United States, because there was some difficulty in finding homes for native children in Canada, and, as a result, he and his wife specifically requested a native child. The parents were aware that minority groups, especially natives, were negatively stereotyped. Four of the fathers recalled stories of alcohol abuse and violence on reserves and in neighbouring small communities and the common perception that Indians were not reliable workers.

When asked by the agencies if they would take a child with special needs, each of the couples said no. Edward had worked in a home for disturbed children, and he was not looking for children with insurmountable problems. Rod and I said that, if the child's problem was physical and could be corrected, we were prepared to consider such a child. Neither the agencies nor the parents, at the time, considered adopted native children as having special needs. Edward said that the handicap of being native did not bother him. Later, the parents would reflect on the naivete of some of their requests, such as trying to match skin and hair colour to that of their own children and requesting problem-free children. With hindsight, these requests appeared quite ironic.

It was difficult for some of the parents to describe many positive characteristics or happy experiences with the adopted child. These memories had been obscured by the challenges surrounding the adoption breakdown. In order to understand what the parents lost, it is necessary to understand what they expected. Each couple was able to recount one ideal-family memory. Specifically, this would have been a time or event that captured what they had envisioned as the ideal family. The experiences the parents recalled closely resembled special times they had experienced in their own childhoods, or the experiences were ones that had been desired by them as children but that, for one reason or another, had not occurred. The memory of childhood experiences would help make certain experiences with their own children meaningful. Each parent developed the concept for his or her family by selecting the qualities that he or she enjoyed in life and by adding the qualities that were lacking. These recaptured, pleasant moments are important, because they represent what the parents found intrinsically rewarding as parents. Without these moments, the adoptions would not have been considered successful by the parents. When the adoptions broke down, the features that made up the happy memory were no longer present and would never again be present. In fact, for most of these adoptive parents, satisfying occasions seemed exceedingly rare.

What carefree family occasions there were had nothing to do with the everyday mundane chores of housework or school work. They involved nature, outdoor physical activities, and sports. They contained elements of peace and harmony, freedom, sharing, and the sense that all the family members were equal, natural, and separated from the rest of the world, with no competition or hassles. The children, especially the adopted sons, were happy in these scenes, at ease with themselves and with their environment; they did not seem guarded or aloof. They were open, honest, and accepting of themselves, their surroundings, and their parents. Three of the children enjoyed books, and three enjoyed their pets.

For the few happy occasions recalled by these parents, there were many more episodes and problems that were far from pleasant. All the families had grave concerns with discipline, bonding, relationships, school behaviour, and anti-social and illegal activities. Other problems were considered serious by at least four of the six families. These included unusual eating habits, sleeping disorders, speech patterns, toilet training, nosebleeds, and unusual staring. Four of the six adopted sons displayed similar behaviour that was of concern to the parents and to other adults. The parents were particularly disturbed by the appearance of their children's eyes. They described them as glazed over, vapid and lifeless, dark and empty, surly and obstinate, and trance-like. After the children began going to school, the parents worried about their sneaking out at night, running away, lying, lack of motivation, and anger. Later, there were problems with alcohol and drugs. The parents spent considerable time discussing concerns unique to their son: the Verdan family, echoing the experience of Rod and me, spoke of unusual treatment of household pets; the Brooks family spoke of Jon's controlling personality; and the Roethlers, again like Rod and me, were disturbed by their son's obsession with weapons.

While the ideal-family memory focused on the child, the disruption memory focused on how helpless and frightened the parents had felt. In these moments of disruption, there were common elements between the stories recounted by the parents. The moment of disruption was not the time when the child physically left the adoptive parents' home. It was a time when the parent *realized* that the child would never be the child they had wished for. This was the emotional disruption, the *real* disruption. It was an event that would change the parents' relationship with their child forever. It would be a turning point, and, from then on, the parents' attitude towards the child was altered. Expectations for the child, for themselves as parents, and for their idealized image of their family were irrevocably changed. What makes these moments so significant is that the parents realized that they were operating with a new frame of reference and had adopted a new way of viewing their child.

In the ideal-family memory, the adoptee is open, confident, free, happy, and interacting with family members, but in the disruption memory the adoptee is distant, strange, and empty of emotions. When the parents saw their son as a stranger, they felt the loss of the child as acutely as if the child had died. The scenes described were empty of the usual sources of tension that would usually cause conflict and irritation between parent and child; they were scenes of ineffectiveness and helplessness for the parents.

What can we learn from the experiences of these adoptive parents? And, to start at the beginning, what do these experiences tell us about why people adopt?

The desire for a certain kind of family and the impetus for fulfilling that image through adoption can be partially explained by the political and sociological contexts in which these parents grew up. Although six couples are a small sample, these parents provide a brief glimpse of what it was like to grow up in Canada in the 1940s and 1950s. This context explains, for example, the parents' assumption that a careful plan and many resources – stable marriage, love, health, money, and possibly older and younger siblings – would be sufficient for any child, natural or otherwise, to develop into a healthy, happy, and productive adult. It also explains why the parents can comfortably conclude that these are the factors that are essential for a happy and successful family. The attitudes and values on which these parents set goals and acted were based on their life histories and experiences. Their backgrounds helped them create personal meanings for what constituted their basic or root image (or construct) of family. None of the parents could readily explain why their original family image had not been fulfilled, nor why an adopted child who is loved would wilfully leave a safe and comfortable home, refuse all available opportunities, and take up a self-destructive lifestyle. The parents had been acting on their personal and socially constructed meanings of structure and purpose of the family, their roles in it, the family's role in society, and the nature of adoption.

All these parents had had similar experiences in their past that shaped their attitudes and values. Generally, they were confident in their motives for adopting children, in their belief that, if given love and the right kind of guidance and support, *any* child could be raised to be a responsible and sensitive citizen, and that good parents produced good children in a healthy family environment, convictions that some of the parents appeared to prove correct in the raising of their own biological children. The parents were confident and optimistic that they could provide a nurturing home environment for adopted children. Ten of the twelve parents were confident that their childrearing abilities would enable any child to grow up well adjusted and happy. They believed in nurture over nature and that being home while the children were young was important. In all of this, they were supported by the theories on childrearing in vogue at that time which stressed the importance of the child's early environment; psychological behaviourist theory even went so far as to state that one could mould a child to become a doctor, a lawyer, a beggar, or a thief simply by appropriately reinforcing the desired behaviour. There was evidence to the contrary even then, in particular a growing body of research that pointed to the critical role of parent-child bonding during the first three years of life in shaping character development (Karen 1990). Yet these ideas had not yet infiltrated the child-welfare sector; none of the couples in this study was told by any of the professionals they encountered, during the adoption process or afterwards, that the child they were considering adopting had not bonded with their birth parents and that this absence of early parental attachment might hold trouble for the future.

The belief that the determinative influence in a child's life was the environment and that parents could direct a child's development was evident when Rod and I initiated the adoption procedure. At that time, we were visiting with friends, the Brooks family, on Vancouver Island. One evening, our discussion of the issue of nurture over nature continued into the early hours of the morning.

Mary and I argued that, if a neglected native child was given a caring environment, he or she had a good chance of developing into a responsible, caring adult. Arnold and Rod were less optimistic and believed that the child's background and early years were strong determinants and could overshadow parenting factors. But, within two years, both Rod and I and Mary and Arnold had adopted older native children. Both of the adopted boys had suffered physical, emotional, and possibly sexual abuse in their early years. About ten years later, each of these two sons left their adoptive homes prematurely.

Although not all the parents were born in Canada, they shared a common cultural background with European roots. All but one of the parents were raised in traditional, intact homes, and only three of the twelve parents came from divorced families. Honesty and hard work were two characteristics that were displayed by most of their parents. The traditional family structure included a working father, who was usually the seat of authority, decision making, and counsel. Their fathers were perceived to be distant by their children, and fun times with them were scarce but much desired. With one exception, their mothers were described as supportive and did not work outside the home, and, even in the case where the mother did work outside the home, she was also responsible for the care of the home and the children. Four of the fathers felt that their mothers were more than just supportive; they were the ones who really took charge of family affairs. While her children were growing up, she usually stayed home to raise and nurture them instead of continuing to work outside the home. The movies and television shows of the day, such as *Father Knows Best* and *Leave It to Beaver*, reflected and helped perpetuate these structures and characteristics.

Most of the couples felt that they had to obey their parents, and they did so. For many, this behaviour was reinforced by the religious teaching that each parent had been exposed to. None of them had come from a particularly religious family, but as children most had attended church, if only sporadically. When they became parents, they took their children to church; today, few of the participants go to church regularly, but most spoke of some kind of inner faith.

Most of the couples were from small families, and if there were many years between siblings, it was felt that they had been actually raised as single children. Seven of the parents were the eldest child in their families. One had more than three siblings; six had two siblings; one had an adopted sister; another a half-sister; and another a stepsister. Three of the parents had relatives who had been adopted: one of the mothers had an adopted sister, and the other two each had a relative who had been adopted. While these adoptions were challenging, they seemed to be working. This helped to explain the optimism they felt when they themselves decided to adopt. The parents came from traditional nuclear families that had had little history of trauma such as ill health, death, separation, or divorce. They were all well educated and held steady jobs from the time they completed school and/or raised their children.

The parents had been capable in other areas of their life; their determination and commitment had brought them the results they wanted. Not only were the fathers successful at school, all of the them played, and most of them excelled in, sports. Even the two fathers who had fooled around and who had not taken high school seriously still earned their high school diplomas. These academic achievements were crowned with the ease of getting a job that paid well and offered a secure future. This increased their self-confidence, and they went on to be successful in their careers. Two of them worked for over twenty years with a large utility company. One had a successful career in sports. Another was successful in the business world. The remaining two were in education; one was in administration, and one was an instructor. The mothers were successful too. Half of the women were expected to get a good education, which they did. Although it was generally accepted that women would and should finish school, marriage and children should follow soon after. All the mothers had jobs after they graduated from school. Those who did bear children did so within three years of marriage, and then these mothers stayed home, as was expected, to raise the children, look after the home, and support their husbands, as the men continued their education and/or careers. In every family, the husband's job required him to spend some time away from home. The amount of time away from home varied from a few days, once in a while, to a week or more, quite often. During those absences, the responsibility for the home and children rested on the mothers. Two stay-at-home mothers completed university degrees through part-time studies, and, after their children were in school, they began to work outside the home. The four women who had paying jobs fell into the category of superwomen, as they managed job, home, and children. Four of the mothers had received a university education and were teachers. (It is interesting to note that, at the time of this study, two fathers and four mothers were teachers. In other words, four of the six families had at least one parent teaching.) The two remaining mothers were successful in their career choices but chose to stay home and raise three or four biological children.

The parents were also determined to make the adoption work, to live up to their image of the family and to their own self-image as parents, and to have their adopted child be a happy part of that family. The parents often defined happiness or success by how well the child fitted their image and expectations, hopes, dreams, and needs; they expected their child to be contented and law-abiding and to respect and accept both himself and those around him. In order to achieve such goals, people choose certain paths and perform certain actions. They come to know themselves – at least in part – through the eyes of others, whose feedback and reactions act as a mirror reflecting aspects of themselves. For the parents, a rejection of them or of their and society's values by a child can be viewed as a personal failure, a flaw, a fault, something lacking in *them* rather than as a problem that may be inherent in the child, in his or her pre-adoption experience or in some other unknown factor. Each couple was determined to do everything possible. This determination forced them to push the system to help their adopted child(ren). When help was not forthcoming, all of them experienced frustration. Their frustration was made worse when they realized that their child was not going to get the help needed, it seemed, until he broke the law. The parents chose to enter the public arena in many ways: charging their children, confronting judges they felt were too lenient, and writing desperate letters to public officials, agencies, and government representatives. One father even ran for public office in order to try to change the way foster children were treated by the system.

The rules that shaped the way these parents took on the task of childrearing were learned during their own formative years. As these individuals grew up, they were taught the general principles by which life is ordered. Their parents and grandparents had followed these principles and had repeated them to their

children, who accepted their veracity unquestioningly: love con-
quers all; obey the rules; when you start something, you have to
finish it; where there's a will, there's a way; and if you work hard
enough, you will succeed (with the corollary, of course, that if you
do not succeed, you didn't work hard enough). At that time, there
was no reason to doubt these maxims.

While each parent had personal reasons for adopting, there
were also reasons that were common to all six couples: the issue
of world overpopulation, general optimism about the future, confidence in the power of a good childrearing environment, and the
influence of the media in promoting native adoptions. We and the
families we interviewed adopted during the late 1960s and 1970s,
a period when many people felt that they could make a difference. At this time, as well, native Canadians were making their
voices heard through national political bodies, such as the National
Indian Advisory Council and the National Indian Brotherhood.
These groups and others raised the profile of native Canadians in
the country, and at the same time the Canadian government, concerned with problems on the reserves, actively promoted the
adoption of native children by white families. The negative con-
notations of the Sixties Scoop, as it was called, were a product of
a later day; at the time, the parents profiled here were convinced
that they were engaged in a rescue mission, not a campaign of
cultural genocide (Johnson 1983; Wharf 1993).

In all cases, the adoptions were initiated by the women, a fact
that confirms the finding that women are generally more comfortable with the prospect of adoption than men (Kirk 1981: 140–5).
At least four mothers saw large families as being happier than
small ones. Each of these four women came from families in which
they were the first-born in a two-children family. All the parents
met their spouses either while they were at school or shortly
thereafter. They married in their late teens or early twenties, and
nine of the twelve moved directly from their parents' homes to
their own marital homes. The four couples who did have biological children had their first baby within three years of their weddings. All the children were healthy, bright, good-looking, and
easy to raise; they were absolutely perfect. Of the eleven biological
children, only one child had a learning disability.

Never having had a live birth is cited as the stated reason
for adopting in 70 per cent of cases (Bachrach 1986: 248). The

contributing factor for failed adoption in this instance is not the infertility itself but rather the parents' reasons for not having a child of their own or their attitude towards their infertility or impotence (Seglow et al. 1972: 31). Infertility may lessen self-esteem (DiGiulio 1988: 428), and parents may feel that they must undo previous failures by being perfect parents (Fishman 1992). However, in my research, none of the parents gave infertility as a reason for adopting. One mother found out *after* adopting that she could not have children; another, after experiencing trouble with her pregnancies, reached the conclusion that, although she would not have any more children of her own, she was willing to adopt. One mother had had difficulty carrying her pregnancies to full term and had suffered greatly when one child was stillborn. But she and her husband did try again, and, in spite of the doctor's warnings, went on to have two healthy children. Another found out that she had cancer and needed a hysterectomy, but even before the diagnosis of cancer and after delivering four healthy babies, she wanted to adopt children, as well as have more of her own. In another case, the mother had had a stressful second pregnancy and thought that, if a couple had two natural children and wanted more, they should consider adoption because there were already so many children needing good homes. For the two couples who chose to adopt *instead* of having their own, the decision to adopt was based on the desire to provide a better home environment for native children and on the idea that *adopting* children would be a good way of fulfilling the desire for a family.

The amount of persuasion that the women used on their husbands varied from making a simple proposal of adoption to bull-dozing the husband into thinking that adoption would be a good idea. Four of the husbands were as enthusiastic about adoption as their wives were. One father stated that, although he fully supported the adoption, he was always more sceptical about their ability to make it work. Nevertheless, he was encouraged by the fact that he knew a couple of native youngsters who were excelling in university and in sports; he felt that native children would be more successful if they were given good homes. One father had not wanted to adopt.

The parents all felt that adoption produced a situation wherein everyone benefited. None of the parents saw adoption as a self-sacrificing act, and all resisted the suggestions made by friends and relatives that they were do-gooders. They insisted that they were adopting for themselves as much as for the children. The parents wanted to share the experience of family so that all family members, including the adopted child, could benefit from it. They believed, too, that they could make a difference in the lives of these children; both parent and child would have a rewarding experience. The adoptions also fulfilled dreams. In one case, adoption itself had always been a dream; in another, adopting spoke to a desire to have a big house and lots of children.

During the interviews, the parents spent time trying to determine what their motivation had been when they decided to adopt. They were clear that they adopted for themselves as well as for the good of the child. In psychology, incentive draws a person towards a goal and is associated with certain behaviour and objectives (Landy 1987: 415). This means that we, the adoptive parents, had learned that there are certain inherent rewards in having and raising children. We learned this from our observations of our background experiences *as* children and from our own experiences *with* our children and those of others. The goal that we desired is an *intrinsic reward* and it comes from inside a person, without any involvement on the part of others. As Frank Landy explains, "After completing a difficult task successfully, you feel proud of yourself. You feel pleased (rewarded) in spite of the fact that no one praised you" (ibid.: 416). The parents' intrinsic reward was the sense of pride, contentment, and satisfaction derived from establishing a good relationship with the children and seeing them happy and relaxed in the home environment.

Those parents who had biological children also had many *extrinsic rewards* from their happy and fulfilling experiences with them. These came in the way of praise for their children (for the good job they had done) from friends, relatives, and teachers, as well as positive feedback from their own children. They wanted the rewards of childrearing and felt that they could obtain them by adopting. Certainly, the media promoted the idea that there were children needing homes and that the only thing missing in the lives of these children was love. The parents felt that they could not only love the child but also provide him or her with a good home with many opportunities.

For many parents, this preliminary stage in the adoption process is filled with unfailing optimism that the adopted child will happily integrate into the family and that he or she will feel a sense of belonging to the family and grow up to be a successful and well-adjusted adult. This confidence *must* be sustained, if the adoption is to be completed. At the same time, however, parents may be unwittingly impervious to warnings that adoption may not be the simple matter they believe it to be. All the parents profiled here, by their own admissions, had underestimated the potential warning signals before the adoption and during the early years. Each couple could remember someone who had warned them. I remember seeing my father shaking his head when I told him we were going to adopt a native toddler: "You can't make a whiteman out of an Indian." I deliberately chose to downplay his warning, not because I believed he was necessarily wrong, but because I had faith in the current belief that the environment was more important in the upbringing of *all* children. His comments still haunt me today. When one family we interviewed approached their priest for a reference they needed for the adoption, he refused because he was of the opinion that the white-couples-adopting-native-children scenario never worked out. A native psychiatrist who worked with the adopted children of another couple told them the same thing. Yet another family was told by their social worker that they should wait as long as possible before legally finalizing the adoption, because in so doing they would still be able to obtain assistance from the social agencies.

As the adoptees began behaving in a troublesome fashion, the parents sought professional help, only to be told that there was no cause for concern. Teachers' comments – such as "there's nothing the matter" or "what do you want from this kid?" – caused the parents to doubt themselves. Many arranged to have special testing done to evaluate the child's behaviour patterns. Then, when they found that they could not control their sons, some of the parents avoided, albeit not deliberately, the problem. This avoidance took two quite distinct forms. First, the parents engaged in acts of circumstantial distancing that enabled a kind of avoidance or escape. This behaviour expressed itself in a strong focus on fulfilling the demands of the workplace: all of the fathers and two of the mothers had full-time jobs. Two mothers worked part-time. In addition, many of the fathers travelled and were away from home for a few days at a time. The second type of avoidance was less overt. Four of the women spoke about their husbands' ability to dissociate themselves from, block out, or not talk about the problem. Naturally, this disengagement made coping with the child more difficult for the spouse who lived with a tense situation on a daily basis.

This stage in adoption is similar to the first stage identified by Elisabeth Kubler-Ross (1981) in her study of the feelings that affect those facing death or who have experienced the death of a loved one. The first natural reaction or coping mechanism when someone is faced with a potentially insurmountable problem is denial, that is, to deny its insurmountability or even its existence. When faced with a terminal condition, the patient may cling to the belief that there is still a chance for recovery. When the couples in this book contemplated the possibility of adopting an older native child, a potentially troublesome adoption, they unconsciously denied the concerns voiced by professionals, friends, or other adoptive parents. Steadfast and single-minded about the many benefits that can accrue to a disadvantaged child when he or she is adopted into a loving and caring family, the parents pointed to their many resources, their own happy children, and other success stories. The chance to help a child would be worth the risk.

8 The Effects of Adoption Breakdown on Parents

Once we see differently, we act differently.
– Glenda Blissex, in Andrea Fishman,
Amish Literacy: What and How It Means (1988)

It has been argued that, for adoptive parents, the process of adoption breakdown consists of six distinct stages: there is at first diminishing pleasure in their relationship with the adopted child; as the relationship worsens, the child is seen as the exclusive cause of the problem; eventually, the parents cannot tolerate their isolation any longer and they tell someone – a relative, a friend, a colleague – that all is not well; a turning point is reached when the parents begin to give voice to the thought that the adoption might not work after all; increasingly desperate, the parents give the adopted child an ultimatum – change or else; and finally, all attempts at saving the adoption having failed, the parents and the adopted child go their separate ways (Partridge 1986, in Reitz and Watson 1998: 213).

Though there is much truth in this model, I would suggest another approach – and arguably a more helpful one – which treats adoption breakdown as an emotional journey. On this journey, parents progress through a series of emotions, beginning with denial and then proceeding through frustration and anger, shame, guilt, and grief before finally concluding with acceptance. All these emotions are experienced in connection with concrete events, but it is the emotions and not the events that demarcate the stages of adoption disruption.

Adoption breakdown, it has rightly been said, has a devastating impact on all the parties involved; the almost unbearable grief and sense of loss that accompanies it leaves no one untouched (Avery 1997). For the parents studied in this book, adoption breakdown was an unremitting process that took place in the midst of daily routines. Family members went about the normal day-to-day activities of family life – cooking, cleaning, shopping, balancing the household budget – and the routine responsibilities of school and work, while the adoptee's escalating problems gradually eroded the stability of the family and affected the ability of its members to function in it. The resolve of the parents to seek any and all possible sources of help for their adopted sons was matched only by their sons' unwillingness and inability to accept help. And as the parents discovered that there was little they could do to help their sons, their sons left home, prematurely and, in some cases, permanently.

The departure from home by the adopted sons was a complex and emotional experience. The parents were devastated and they grieved over that rejection and loss as they would have grieved over a death. The details surrounding this separation and what preceded it reveal three kinds of losses around which different kinds of emotions clustered: the loss of the son, the loss of the parents' self-image, and the loss of hope. The effect of losing their son expanded outwards to incorporate, in ever-widening spheres, the parents and their self-image, the family, social agencies and civil servants, the community and the wider society, and the family's place in the community. The adoption breakdown had a ripple effect that eventually forced the parents' constructs of family to change. It also resulted in a sense of personal failure.

The expectations the parents had concerning the adoption influenced and were influenced by their concepts of the roles they occupied vis-à-vis themselves, each other, family, and society. They experienced frustration, anger, fear, helplessness, guilt, shame, and tremendous sadness. It was through this emotional journey that the parents were forced to recognize and to accept new constructs. The emotions the parents faced were rooted in who these people were, the values and ideals they had grown up with, their reasons for adopting, and the aspirations they held for themselves, their children, and their families. These emotions bear examining more closely, since they reveal the substance and poignancy of the losses the parents experienced. The most pervasive emotions throughout the adoption breakdown were frustration and anger, which were directed towards every player in the drama. The most self-destructive emotion was guilt, while the most insidious and incapacitating was grief.

For these parents, frustration and anger, shame and guilt, and grief were part of a process that led to acceptance of circumstances for which they were not prepared. These feelings were accompanied by fear, confusion, and despair, and they were all experienced in stages of varying length and complexity. They did not surface and then simply disappear; they reoccurred periodically during the struggle and even after the journey seemed to be over. However, generally, the emotions tended to cluster. Denial, mostly unconscious, was the first, present even before the trouble was obvious. As the difficulties manifested themselves, frustration and anger were experienced, often accompanied by fear and confusion.

In an attempt to understand and deal with the devastation, the parents looked for explanations and reasons for the unexpected turn of events. Part of their attempt at understanding was self-examination. The parents asked themselves about the role they may have played in causing all of this. They wondered if they could have prevented it. They felt blame and embarrassment. Some parents projected the blame onto themselves and experienced tremendous guilt. As the troubles continued and the reality of the situation became apparent, the parents felt intense helplessness and overwhelming hopelessness. They recognized what they had lost – the child, their self-esteem, their confidence as parents, and their role in society. They grieved for what might have been. This painful process eventually led to acceptance of a new, albeit less appealing, construct of their family. But it happened slowly. The emotions mentioned above – frustration and anger, shame and guilt, and grief – were felt in a continuous cycle, so that on any given day, all three might be present. The duration depended on many factors: the individual's previous experience and personality, the severity of the adopted son's problems, and the availability and quality of help and support.

DENIAL

Denial is a normal human response to a situation that is too painful, too incomprehensible, too overwhelming. Each family arrived at its decision to adopt based on deep-rooted values enmeshed in a system central to the parents' existence. Their decision to adopt arose from a strong belief that they could influence the development of events within their family.

When doubts were raised about their sons' ability to bond with the family and to interact positively in his school or community, the impact was not limited to the adopted son. It resonated throughout the parents' value system. These inconceivable situations were too difficult to accept, so parents entered into denial of their sons' adjustment difficulties. Inextricably woven into their sons' limitations, however, was the parents' own ineffectiveness in influencing and shaping the course of events for their family and for themselves.

Denial first emerged with the early predictions and warnings that were ignored but that later appeared as glaring precursors to the devastation that followed. In the beginning, the parents also unconsciously denied, or overlooked, the severity and duration of the difficulties in school and in the community that their sons both caused and would experience. However, in cases where the parents did push and challenge the system for extra help or testing, the school and/or professionals denied that there was any cause for concern.

Denial is an important tool of self-preservation. We use it to protect ourselves from things that are too painful to face. Denial buys time and allows the mind to prepare for the challenges and changes that inevitably lie ahead. A person diagnosed with terminal cancer, for example, will not believe it. My own father refused to believe that his smoking had any effect on his lung cancer. It was something that he adamantly refused to accept and acknowledge throughout his life. To accept the cause-and-effect relationship would have meant a permanent change in his behaviour and in his belief system. At first, the parents studied here did the same thing: accepting the severity and the hopelessness of the situation would have meant a drastic change in their expectations and in the quality of family life. They fought against that.

Denial is useful when it is temporary. I think that the parents and social agencies moved, with difficulty, from denial of the problem to acceptance. Eventually, the son's behaviour escalated to the point that the feedback from the community and social agencies made it impossible for everyone *not* to move to acceptance. However, the parents' denial of *their* inability to shape the course of events was more difficult. They continued to receive messages of how it was their responsibility to manage their son, to change his behaviour. His difficulties were somehow within their power to change. They heeded maxims like "bad kids mean bad parenting" and "change the family, change the child." These ideas were so ingrained, so prevalent, that parents continued to believe that they as parents could be effective in shaping their families. The acceptance of their obvious powerlessness was central to the parents' ability to move through the stages that followed. Without a firm acceptance of powerlessness and recognition of their own limitations, parents – mostly fathers – felt less guilt and more anger. The mothers, on the other hand, felt far more guilt.

FRUSTRATION AND ANGER

When denial of their situation was no longer possible, the adoptive parents felt a great deal of anger. Frustration and anger are emotions that well up when one's efforts are thwarted, when one's worth is denied, when one's presence is resented, when one's opinions and values are ridiculed, when one's energies are exasperated, and when one's movements are confined and constrained at every turn. Anger is the emotion of rage, hostility, and retaliation towards the object, person, or idea that prevents forward and positive movement or that hurts, opposes, offends, or annoys. Anger is the emotion that Kubler-Ross (1981) identifies as the second stage in a person's response when faced with a terminal illness or with the finality of the death of a loved one. How these feelings are experienced and described, what they are called, how long they last, and what damage they cause is a subjective process.

Among the adoptive parents, the women found anger a difficult emotion to acknowledge. It was an emotion that was not easily dealt with or overcome and that reappeared many times before the parents came to accept the new circumstances. Anger was not a singular emotion but was embodied in feelings of rejection, helplessness, fear, and confusion, and it was a reaction to the loneliness and isolation they experienced. The parents expressed anger about the wasted potential and self-destructive activities of their sons. Ella Graves's attitude towards Ken hardened when, in the face of other people's misfortunes, he wilfully threw away what she believed could have been a productive life. Much of what the parents said revolved around their sons' rejection of the family's values of honesty, respect for self and for others, truth, and hard work. The parents were affected by their adolescents' apparent lack of respect for them personally or for their way of life. This youth was someone who had little if any friendly feelings for them. Some reports described these sons as filled with an all-consuming primitive rage, perhaps originating in early childhood experiences. However, each parent gave their adopted children the benefit of the doubt, tried to see through their anger, and made repeated efforts to communicate with them in meaningful ways. They loved their sons and empathized with them and recognized their pain and agony.

The parents expressed anger about the effects the son's behaviour had on the rest of the family. Homes were filled with tension, fear, and confusion. The parents were angry about the insensitivity their sons displayed towards the health and happiness of their siblings. Elaine Verdan admitted that she did not exactly feel relief when Gerald left home, but she conceded that the others probably felt better. The angry confrontations in the home – over everyday matters such as curfews, lying, theft – were often accompanied by fear of the sons' possible suicide, of fire-setting, of open and physical attacks, and of the loss of the parents' own self-control. A lot of energy was spent avoiding conflict, physical and emotional; it was everywhere. Mary Brooks remembered how Jon would sit in a chair opposite her and stare at her for hours on end. But, although she was often unnerved by this behaviour, she held out against Jon's "head game" and would not capitulate to his attempts to wear her down. In four of the families, the tension became so great that one of the other siblings left home for a time. The parents felt that, because so much time had been devoted to the adopted sons, the other children had suffered. Parents questioned whether they as parents had responded in the best way. So much of their energy was focused on the problem child that the basic pleasures of family life – when they took place at all – were fraught with conflict and tears.

The parents saw the effects on the other children in the family when they were threatened, explicitly or implicitly. In all cases except one, the other siblings did not want to see their brother again. Some were angry and/or bitter, but most seemed to mellow over the years. It is interesting that, during the interviews and the discussions the parents had with their children, at least two parents learned, for the first time, that their children had worried about their parents' safety during these troubled years.

Not being able to do anything for their sons was one of the biggest sources of frustration for the parents. Sometimes, it was like watching helplessly as a person drowns while he or she refuses – or is unable to catch – a lifeline. Edward Verdan said that he tried to figure out why Gerald was doing what he was doing, but he never could. The parents also feared their own loss of self-control. This was a concern in the area of discipline. John Graves explained that constant exposure to ongoing threats of defiance and emotional and physical outbursts and the strain that this created resulted in him becoming more of a disciplinarian than he really wanted to be. The parent's self-image as a tolerant father or mother slowly eroded, and their inability to control reactions heightened the fear and uncertainty that lurked just below the surface of most interactions with their sons.

Some of the anger was self-directed when the parents felt frustrated and inadequate in dealing with the stress of the disruption and the unpredictability of their sons' behaviour. Certainly, the parents felt they had lost control of their sons and, in some cases, of themselves. The behaviour they encountered was both frightening and erratic, and when things quieted down, they found themselves bracing for the next round of crises. Experiments have shown that when danger is unpredictable, it is more damaging psychologically (Badia et al. 1973; Martindale cited in Worchel and Shebilski 1983; Seligman 1975). One of the best pieces of advice I received to combat the anxiety of unpredictability came from Dr Armstrong, who, as I mentioned earlier, told me to imagine the worst possible scenario, because it would ultimately happen. Frightening though this was, it did relieve a lot of tension, since there could be no surprises.

The parents also experienced anger about the changes that took place between themselves and their spouse. In addition to targeting each other with displaced anger, the parents often experienced conflict over what decisions to take regarding their son and disagreement about how best to implement a plan of action. Having to make decisions between two unappealing choices was most stressful, but often it was necessary in the interests of all concerned.

There was frustration and anger, too, about the insensitivity and judgmental attitudes encountered in the social-service agencies and about the system's general betrayal of them as adoptive parents, the same system that had earlier seemed so available and supportive and that had encouraged and facilitated the adoption. Now it was closed to them, difficult, even impossible, to access. It was one thing for the parents to exhaust their own ideas and strategies for helping their sons, but when the people in social-service agencies could not or would not help, the parents' frustration often grew to desperation. When I went to the Children's Aid Society, I found that the people there did not seem particularly interested in helping us work through the problem. This child we had adopted was *our* problem, not theirs. In fact, it seemed that we were the faulty ones, so we had better fix the rest of the family to accommodate Tim. The plan seemed to be to destroy and rebuild rather than to renovate and repair. Ultimately, we had to wait until Tim broke the law before anyone could or would offer us any help. I was also frustrated when I came to realize that adoption of native children, who, we once had been told, were in desperate need of good homes, was now no longer viewed as desirable.

GUILT

The parents were committed and determined to make the adoption work, but when their childrearing methods did not produce the intended results, many felt shame and guilt. In order to work through their feeling of inadequacy for this lack of success in the adoptive relationship, they looked for answers to the "Why *didn't* it work?" questions. This theme permeated our interviews, as each person tried to integrate his or her conclusion with those of the other parent.

Each couple over the years had partly decided what the reasons might be for their adolescent's disturbing behaviour. They discussed fetal alcohol syndrome, alcoholism, abuse, and lack of bonding. On the surface, these reasons seemed quite diverse. Then, it became clear that they were indeed related and all contained elements of neglect, abuse, separation, and inadequate bonding. An interesting discovery was not the particular reasons themselves, but the fact that it was essential for the parents to have *some* explanation that made sense to them and that helped them to share responsibility. Finding the cause of the problem was the key element in enabling the parent to try one more approach or finally to begin to accept the changed circumstances. It was akin to the bargaining stage that Kubler-Ross says people go through when they try to determine the cause of a terminal illness or come to terms with the death of a loved one. Identifying the reasons enabled the parents to move from this guilt stage to the final stages of grief and acceptance.

Guilt is a subjective and complex feeling, and it can exist on many levels. As a result, some parents took longer than others to work through it. The language the participants used in the interviews illustrated that the blame could be placed in one of three areas: the child's background, their own conduct as parents, or society. If the parent felt responsible, then he or she would experience guilt, and the journey through this stage would take longer. In *Composing a Life* (1990), Mary Catherine Bateson says that women in our society tend to be disproportionately damaged by family trauma, because they too readily accuse themselves of failure and internalize their loss. This seems to have been true of the parents profiled here. There were distinct gender differences in the way fathers and mothers responded to the insurmountable difficulties they faced. The mothers spoke more often than the fathers did about the change in the way they evaluated their parenting abilities. They took as a personal embarrassment the child's anti-social behaviour at school and in the court system. The childrearing practices they had learned and had successfully used on their other children were not effective, and they lost confidence in themselves and became emotionally distraught. The mothers also accused themselves of spending too little time with the child who was less troublesome and of being overinvolved with the adopted sons. Two of the daughters who were adopted with their brothers also moved out of the family home earlier than expected, before they had completed high school. Both the Roethler and Graves families described their daughters as quiet and withdrawn. Each of these girls became pregnant in her teens. Carol Gilligan describes a typical female adolescent's quiet reaction as the silencing of her own voice, a silencing enforced by the wish not to hurt others, but also by the fear that, in speaking, her voice will not be heard (1982: 51). Freud stated that puberty, which brings about so great an accession of libido in boys, is marked in girls by a fresh wave of *repression* (cited in ibid.: 11). There is evidence that boys act out against society more often than girls do. In Dr Armstrong's Parents for Youth group, boys made up 64.5 per cent of the children with conduct disorders (Armstrong et al. 1994).

The mothers spoke with surprise at the fathers' ability to distance themselves from the situation and their unwillingness to talk about their sons as much as the mothers wanted to. What the fathers spoke of was their frustration with two elements of the situation: one, they were not able to control their son, even though they had tried everything; and, two, they had difficulty with their wives' reactions and obsessiveness, their excessive crying and talking. Rod regularly pointed out in the interviews that I seemed to have lost my usual zest for life and that I had a heaviness of spirit. Like most of the other mothers, I felt more guilt for what I was not able to do: like them, I was not able to help my son adjust to his family and his community.

Most of the men admitted that they felt some guilt and that they had somehow failed their children. Lou Pelligrini laughed when Rod asked him why he felt guilty. Moving the family and his frequent business trips, he noted, probably had something to do with their son's troubles. Rod said that he felt sorrow that things did not work out, but he insisted that he did not feel any guilt. He was confident that the problems Tim had would not have been eased or solved if he had come home early from work three times a week: Tim's difficulties were larger than any of us could comprehend. Rod later admitted that, if he felt guilt, it was due to the effect of the tension on our other children.

It became evident as Rod and I talked about the interviews that we had noticed different things. We each chose to notice and interpret different parts of the interviews that resonated with each of us on a personal level. Carol Gilligan summarizes this by saying that male and female voices typically speak of the importance of different truths (1982: 98). Likewise, in this study, when the fathers and the mothers talked about their feelings and how they reacted to the situation, there were obvious differences about how responsible each of them felt. The women spoke a good deal about their sense of responsibility to make the adoption work. Generally, they felt more guilt than the men and thus took longer to reach the stage of acceptance of the failed adoptions. The mothers were more closely connected with the adopted children than the fathers, and they spent more time with the children. The extent of the mothers' guilt and their ability to absolve themselves depended on their background, their assessment of the situation, and their ability to come to some other, more satisfactory explanation for the problem. Mary Catherine Bateson explains: "[There are] two kinds of vulnerability that women raised in our society tend to have. The first is the quality of self-sacrifice, a learned willingness to set their own interest aside and be used and even used up by the community ... The second kind of vulnerability trained into women is a readiness to believe messages of disdain and deroga-tion. Women [in her study] became vulnerable to distorted visions of themselves, no longer secure that their sense of who they are was matched by the perception of others" (1990: 54).

At the time of the adoption, the mothers who had biological children felt that their parenting skills were good. Each mother had done her best, and this effort seemed to have succeeded. And so each had chosen to adopt. Why did these good parents later feel so lacking, flawed, ignorant, and guilty? Why did the women appear to feel the guilt more than the men, and why were they more susceptible to the (real or imagined) unsympathetic reactions of others? Recent research (Mandell and Duffy 1988; Armstrong et al. 1994; Eichler 1988) examines the different expectations we have for men and women in our society, in our culture, and in our families. Women are held responsible for the private domain of the home: "there was a time, not too long ago, when what went on in the family was considered private; nobody's business but one's own, and perhaps God's or the parish priest's" (McDaniel 1988: 436). "For women, the public world belongs to and is owned by men. [The wife] is dependent upon what the man earns but is responsible for the private sphere, the family" (Rowbotham, cited in ibid.: 436). Even today, what goes on in one's home is relatively private. This division was clearly articulated by the parents, both in the worlds they had grown up in and in their present world. So, when the son had to appear in court or when Jon Brooks chose to beg on the corner with a rat on his shoulder or when Tim was interviewed as the most popular boy prostitute in Boy's Town, this was a public disgrace and embarrassment for the mothers. The women felt that they had failed to look after their domains.

Women are also assigned the caregiver role in the family and in society, and with that assignment they assume the responsibility for the success of how well the family functions. For those women studied here who were determined to succeed in the career of full-time mother, the adoption breakdown and the early leaving of their children was taken as a personal failure. Studies by H.F. and M.K. Harlow in 1962 emphasized the importance of the primary-caregiver role in the development of an infant and his or her ability to relate to others. The literature and theories that were widely accepted in the 1970s and 1980s were also mother-blaming. A large proportion of these studies focused on the controlling mother, the ambitious mother, the perfectionist mother, and the narcissistic mother. Thus, when a child had a problem and when almost all the literature available described flaws in the mothers as the possible root cause of this problem, women looked at themselves and asked, "Which one of these mothers am I?"

In addition to the caregiver role, mothers must undertake the role of peacemaker in the family. The families that these parents encountered on television, when they were young, were perfect. Everyone played his or her role very well. But, in addition to acting as household manager, it was also the mother's role to keep the peace and, in many cases, to ensure that the children did not bother Dad. When the control she was supposed to exercise over these areas slipped from her, the woman felt that she had failed in her responsibility. Seeing it as her responsibility to keep peace in the house and to guide her children towards independence and the acceptance of the couple's values, she could only conclude that it was her fault when this did not happen: "A concern for individual survival comes to be branded as selfish and to be counterposed to the responsibility of a life lived in relationships. And in turn, responsibility becomes, in its conventional interpretation, confused with a responsiveness to others that impedes a recognition of self. The truths of relationship, however, return in the rediscovery of connection, in the realization that the self and the other are interdependent and that life, however valuable in itself, can only be sustained by care in relationships" (Gilligan 1982: 127).

And so the mothers in my research often felt more guilt than the fathers did. Gilligan states that "instead of attachment, individual achievement rivets the male imagination, and great ideas or distinctive activity defines the standard of self-assessment and success"(ibid.: 162). Mothers, on the other hand, "stay with, build on and develop in a context of attachment and affiliation with others ... Women's sense of self becomes very much organized around being able to make and then to maintain affiliations and relationship ... [and that] eventually ... the threat of disruption of an affiliation is perceived not just as a loss of a relationship but as something closer to a total loss of self" (ibid.: 169).

A closely knit family seemed particularly important to the women. Is this because society promotes the idea that women are not worthwhile or complete unless they are mothers, or is this because women see their worth being assessed and judged by how good they are at mothering? When women do not mother or do not foster good children, their value is diminished by society. Men, on the other hand, find recognition and approval in their jobs. For the most part, fathers tend to leave the nurturing, supporting functions of the family to their wives. When the husbands in these profiles were absent from the home for long periods of time, the disciplinary role as well as the supporting roles were left to the women. This was a difficult, full-time challenge for which the women had not been trained and with which they were uncomfortable, and, at times, even frightened. The child's emotional difficulties were so complex that even trained professionals could not overcome them.

One other difference between fathers and mothers is that a mother who believes in equality and feels that she has a right to a career can choose as her career the role of caregiver in her family. Mary Brooks tried to equate the important traditional role of childrearing and mothering with a career in a capitalist economy. She may have been ahead of her time, but she believed that, for her, the job of mother was the one to which she aspired. Consequently, if a woman in this particular job raises children who are less than perfect, she is likely to feel the same disgrace as someone who gets fired because of inadequate performance of duty. She also loses the rewards of the job and the personal fulfilment that is at the top of everyone's list of needs for self-actualization. Women who choose motherhood as a career find fulfilment in being the best mother they can be. In the workforce, a person can climb the ladder of success by taking on more responsibility and doing equally well; for a career mother, taking on more responsibility and excelling at parenting may mean increasing the size of the family, through natural means or through adoption.

Because of their different views of the world and of their place in it, men and women require different strategies or action plans to help them cope when difficulties arise. Gilligan says that men are task-oriented and women are process-oriented. For men, it is important to see the problem, find the solution and fix it, and then to move on to the next problem. Women are more concerned with feelings and emotions, with working through things, with developing understanding and reaching out. And so, in my research, Arnold Brooks could say: "In terms of looking after your children, you [women] get involved in all the small things. The [man] says, 'Well I'm not going to get into this. I'm not going to get into it this deeply.' We'll just accept this and go on and do things. Men seemed to face it and say, 'This is the way it is and if there's no answer then it's not worth dwelling on it, so let's go on.' Whereas women tend to look for the answer, and they need to discuss and discuss." Some of the fathers seemed to treat adoption as a challenge, which they had tried to meet but unsuccessfully. Having failed, they wanted, as Rod said, to move forward. Gilligan states that when women lose a tennis game or a point in a match, they tend to blame themselves, while men tend to blame something else, the weather, the racket, and so on. Rod's attitude supports this view; he explained, "I tend not to point to myself, so, I finally did see the event or the adoption process as a failure, but I'm not sure that I really felt that I was a failure."

For the parents, there were at least three paths leading through the guilt stage to the final stage of acceptance. Parents who believed that their children's problems originated in genetics, abuse, and/or other sociological factors spent the least amount of time in the guilt stage, because they did not believe that they were to blame. This was also the path travelled by parents like Rod and Arnold who did not need to explore the reason why their child was having difficulty; they acknowledged the problem but just wanted to get on with their own lives. Parents like Lou who believed that bad kids were always the result of bad parenting and that they or their inadequate or ineffective parenting was partly responsible for their child's poor adjustment spent more time in this stage. For the women, there was yet another path. Mothers who believe that bad kids are the result of poor and inadequate *mothering* in particular will need even more time and/or some therapy or other intervention to help them reduce their guilt and enable them to accept the situation and to go on with their lives. In order to pass through this feeling, the mothers profiled here had to shift the blame away from themselves.

In addition to guilt, the parents also felt shame. There was a reluctance to speak to other friends or family members about their son's behaviour; they were embarrassed by it. Often friends and relatives had quick solutions or seemed not to welcome the exposure to the angst and pain of others and to their own feelings of helplessness – much in the way people who do not want to visit nursing homes or palliative-care units or even attend funeral services. Lenore Terr in *Too Scared to Cry* explains the difference between guilt and shame: "Shame comes from public exposure of one's own vulnerability. Guilt, on the other hand, is private. If follows from a sense of failing to measure up to private, internal standards. When others know that you once were helpless, you tend to feel ashamed. *They* know. If on the other hand, you feel you caused your own problems, you cease feeling so vulnerable and blame yourself, instead, for the shape of events. *You* know. But you are the only one" (1990: 113).

GRIEF

The parents were often unable to articulate the tremendous sense of loss they felt for the child they had known and loved. They did not know until much later that they were, as Elaine said, grieving. The parents grieved for the child who might have been, who was *supposed* to have been, and who died or who ceased to exist at a particular time. He was not going to be there in the way that the parents expected, needed, and wanted. The stranger who replaced him was threatening and uncaring, an unknown quantity they grew to fear. The persona each of these sons assumed was in complete opposition to that expected by the parents. Even before the boys left home, the parents described their son as a stranger, both in appearance and in behaviour. In each family, the parents spoke about him as being gone, and, in some cases, as if he had been replaced by an impostor, who had pierced body parts, missing teeth, glazed and vapid eyes, marks of self-mutilation and drug abuse. The past no longer mattered. In fact, the adoptee seemed to have taken deliberate action to destroy or hide the identification he might have had with the parents and their values. Vincent Pelligrini burned his ID card. Jon Brooks cut himself out of family photos. The parents were truly forced to behold the figure who had lurked just beneath the surface of the individual they had perceived as their son. This moment marked a turning point; any last chance at meaningful communication seemed lost forever. Now the parents had to adjust to the fact that their son was gone, and they would have to build a new relationship with a stranger.

The parents described with flat voices some of the stressful times when they observed their son being out of control. Edward Verdan recalled trying to intervene when his son was handcuffed and led away. Lou Pelligrini remembered the obscenities that came out of Vincent's mouth. I remembered how Rod and I felt when we went down to the Dalewood Crisis Unit and saw Tim being brought into the unit in a straitjacket. We were frightened of our sons. There was always an impending threat that they could and would do anything, including hurting family members. One of the siblings admitted years later that he had slept with a knife in his bedroom door frame in order to protect himself against his brother. Others were just angry, disgusted, or embarrassed. Still other siblings worried about their parents' safety. The adopted children seemed to oppose all of their parents' values, and worse. They were involved in prostitution, drug abuse, and criminal activities. These were no longer the children the parents thought they had raised. Those boys were effectively dead. Ella Graves described the turbulent time, before Ken moved out, as one during which her son seemed to have had a kind of cancer that had lasted three years, before it finally consumed him. Mary Brooks coped with the change by saying, "Jon was dead."

The second loss incurred by the parents in the adoption breakdown was that of their self-image. This stemmed from a profound sense of helplessness, inadequacy, and limitation: they had been unable to parent, unable to achieve what they had hoped for, unable to help their adolescent in any meaningful way. In some situations, the parent felt compelled to assume the position of turning against the child. This situation stripped the parent bare and forced him or her to come face to face with the realization that any opportunity to change the course of events was lost. Victoria Pelligrini recalled how she was forced to realize that there was nothing further that could be done when Vincent, her son, opted to return to the streets. John Graves recounted how he had hoped that, by showing control over the situation, he could get Ken to talk to him. When Ken chose not to talk, there was nothing left to do but to tell Ken that he could not stay around the family home anymore; he had done enough damage to the rest of the family. Even when Edward Verdan thought that he had secured one moment to be close to his son, Gerald, things did not work out. Edward concluded that if Gerald was going to live his life in this particular way, he would have to realize that he would be alone to face the consequences, because his parents would not continue to bale him out. Rod said that he had felt sad and almost beaten somehow, filled with hopelessness and disbelief when he realized there was absolutely nothing he could do that was going to make an impression on Tim. The hole in the family that Tim's departure created left us both feeling empty and useless. There was no longer any bit of hope that we could make him adapt to our family.

There was no disguising the rejection that the parents experienced when the child deliberately rebelled against them. The parents felt that they were crippled. Not only were they compelled to change their expectations of their child, they were also forced to change the image they held of themselves as parents. When they were faced with an altered son who did not act as they had expected, they had to re-evaluate everything. Although they had perceived themselves to be determined and committed parents, circumstances pushed them to struggle simply to *salvage* the relationship. This took its toll on other aspects of their lives, and, in some cases, it affected their performance at work. They lost confidence in their ability to secure help for their sons and themselves and to maintain their self-control. These types of concerns were most often expressed by the mothers: Victoria had not succeeded at her one chance to be a mother; Ella began to doubt the sanity of thinking that she could ever have been a good mother and wondered if perhaps Ken would not have been better off if he had been raised by someone else; and Mary concluded that she must have been deluded about her mothering abilities, because, in her words, "I just screwed up royally. I was disappointed with myself, because I discovered I wasn't the wonderful person I thought I was."

The parents described their behaviour as obsessive, emotionally heavy-laden, and empty of spirit. Ella described how she had built walls around her heart, because the pain was too abominable. This protective device hardened her all over. Elaine said that when she thought about their situation, when the lid came off the box in which she stored their difficulties, things looked horrendous indeed. Edward summed up the potential risk he was at by saying, "It was him or me." In each case, when the parents felt they had lost a part of themselves, their spouses also felt that loss. This had a domino effect: the parent lost the child, a part of him or herself, and a part of his or her spouse. In each family, the parents walked parallel paths as they tried to deal with the stress, but they could not lean on each other too much, or they would have knocked each other over. Because they responded differently to the stress, they could not always be there for each other. If a father's reaction was one of anger and the mother's was one of hurt and guilt, sometimes it became impossible for them to find support and solace in each other.

Distancing and avoidance strategies were also unconsciously used, but mainly by the fathers. Though these strategies, on the one hand, served to reduce stress, at least temporarily, they also had the effect of separating the couple even further. While the men could dissociate themselves and the women grieved, a wedge, to quote Lou, was driven between them. In trying to cope with the trauma in their own ways, the parents drove themselves apart. I would cry and want to talk about Tim, but Rod would say, "Oh, forget it for a while." It was very important for me to have Rod listen to me as I tried to clarify and make sense of things.

Statements made by the parents displayed a disappointment in the way that his or her spouse was reacting. This often made the other spouse a target for further displaced aggression. The fathers expressed frustration with their wives' responses to difficult situations. Lou recalled that, at one time, he blamed Victoria for reacting as she had and for taking advice from a social worker whose suggestions Lou thought were less than helpful. Victoria would get angry with Lou at the peak of frustration and tension, and, as a result, Lou admitted, their relationship was strained. Rod and I experienced tension between us, too, because he found my feelings of guilt irritating and my desire to take the car out late at night to drive around the city in search of Tim pointless. He also remarked that through the experience I had lost my lighthearted side; I had become a much more serious person. Elaine regretted not having talked more with her husband and their three children as a way of dealing with the conflict; instead, she did what she usually does when she experiences frustration: she became even more withdrawn and quiet. The women referred to the support they expected but did not receive from their husbands. Mary recalled being hurt when her husband did not recognize or respond to her needs, and Alison said that even though she wanted to cry at times, she refrained from doing so because she knew it upset Georg.

There were disagreements and conflicts over what action plan should be implemented. The parents usually held different opinions as to what to do with their adopted sons, because each saw the problem in a slightly different light. The women perceived the men as being able to repress and dissociate themselves from the situation, and the men perceived the women as being too eager and too hasty to take any and all advice, good or bad, from social workers and to want to give in to their sons. This seemed to be the case with the Roethlers and the Verdans and also with Rod and me.

The hopelessness of the situation was tragic. Even though many of the sons did return home for short periods of time, the moment when a son first left home was the one most often chosen by the parents during the interviews as the time when they realized that the child was unreachable and was forever lost to them. This I have labelled the disruption memory. By contrast, the ideal-family memories of the parents illustrated what kind of family situations and interactions they had anticipated. They wanted experiences that were open and comfortable, with the family members being mutually supportive and the adoptee as happy and natural as all the others. The parents described moments that were similar to what they had experienced or had wanted to experience as children and what they were hoping to replicate in or add to their own families. These hopes were dashed when the adoption broke down.

The parents talked about the loss in descriptive phrases and metaphors: Alison spoke of her family image being chipped away slowly and painfully, with repeated disappointments; Lou said that all his dreams had been shattered. Some of the metaphors used to illustrate their altered family revealed the parents' assumptions about the dynamics involved in the parent-child bond. Mary Brooks envisioned the parental bond as a filled well from which the child could draw support and sustenance. She said that the adoptees had drawn the well dry, because they had not done anything to replenish its supply of goodwill. When the parents had no more to give these children, when they had depleted and exhausted their resources, the well dried up. Arnold Brooks used a grittier metaphor to illustrate his perception of his son's behaviour: he resembled a hunting dog who, having been sprayed by a skunk, rolls in feces to rid itself of the smell. Jon, having been contaminated by the stench of his family ties and values, also attempted to shed himself of the smell of his identity by getting involved in anti-social activities.

The situation seemed all the more hopeless when the parents did not receive support from family and friends. Overall, and surprising to me, the extended families were not seen as supportive. In families where there were other adoptions, the support and understanding was forthcoming. But in most cases, the relatives and friends did not know how to act or what to say, or they judged and blamed the adoptive parents for not being good-enough parents. Challenged by a work colleague's opinion that all parents should be held accountable for their children's crimes, Lou retorted that he had charged his son for the offence the son had committed. In Lou's opinion, this was the most responsible thing to do, and in no way did he feel that he should be the one charged with the crime for which his son had sole responsibility. Ella remembered that a close relative felt that she and John had really screwed up with Ken and Grace. Her relative said that Ella and John had done it all wrong and that they had been the worst parents. Edward said that only one person ever asks how Gerald is doing; it is as if Gerald had never existed. Edward concluded that the problem with most people is that they do not want to believe that the sorts of family problems that one sees portrayed in television programs and in movies can actually be taking place in the midst of their own families. Mary found that people were judgmental and hurtful in their comments. She sensed that people flattered themselves with the belief that, if *they* had raised her boy, the problems the Brooks family was having would not have taken place. These people chose to see Jon as a good boy and could not understand why he would find it necessary to misbehave in the way that he did. When family and friends did not offer the minimum of help or empathy that was expected of them, the parents found themselves in this strange world where familiar faces did not respond in the way that they thought they would. When someone asked how her son was doing, Victoria felt deep gratitude, because it meant that this person was acknowledging the struggle and the loss. The recognition helped to normalize the experience.

The parents in every case were embarrassed by the actions of their adopted children. When the community did not acknowledge the parents' efforts, the shame the parents suffered increased. As well, the parents were afraid for the community, for their other children, and for themselves. The mothers spoke of this more often than did the fathers. Rod and I, for example, worried that Tim's arsonist behaviour would sooner or later cause serious injury or end in someone's death. All the families had been respected members of their community, but the anti-social/criminal behaviour of their sons changed that. The mothers felt ashamed in front of other parents when their sons were suspended from school, and the parents did not dare leave their children alone or with local sitters for an evening. Thus, over time, many couples became reclusive and found it hard to interact with neighbours or to make new friends. Going to court was an especially painful ordeal, and the mothers especially commented on it, indicating that they felt singled out as bad mothers, exposed and vulnerable. Victoria even suggested that the stigma they felt could be made up into a T-shirt with "I'm the criminal's mother" written across the front. Hearing herself admit to someone doing a survey for the Young Offender's Act that she was the mother of a young offender made Ella feel that she herself was the offender.

The failure of the child-welfare system in meeting the needs of families who have adopted special-needs children is finally beginning to attract serious study, with particular attention being devoted not only to the attitudes of social-work professionals but also to the biases and assumptions built into the system itself (Avery 1997). Certainly, none of the parents in this book found family-therapy sessions helpful. In fact, in suggesting that the family adapt to accommodate the behaviour and needs of the out-of-control adopted sons, the sessions increased the parents' feelings of inadequacy and guilt. The family therapists at that time seemed convinced that the families were dysfunctional and that their own role was to fix the family. This was done in several ways. Each family was asked to come to a family meeting, usually once a week. They sat in a room with a therapist. Outside the room, watching through one-way mirrors and listening with the help of a microphone, were other therapists. The latter, not necessarily parents themselves, observed the family members as they interacted. The observers could phone into the room and talk to the therapist in the room with the family to request more information or to suggest interventions. The focus of this kind of therapy was to analyse how the family interacted, who talked and who did not, their body language, and so on, and then to set up homework. The homework would include outings or a change in the way the family members related to each other, sometimes trying to shift the power relationships within the family. If the family seemed to be interacting in a fairly normal way, the therapist would try to stimulate lively interaction or conflict to assist the assessment process. It appeared that the assumption was that the family – not the child – had created the problem. During the stressful times when the families were in crisis, the parents were feeling insecure, anxious, blamed, angry, sad, and guilty. They did not respond favourably to having others poke at them, looking for failings and then creating a crisis so that it could be fixed.

Until their child broke the law and appeared in court, there was no person or agency that was able to offer the solid support or assistance the parents needed so desperately during the time before and after the adoption breakdown. The parents rightly assumed that in Canada, with its variety of social programs, there was bound to be agency that would be willing and able to help people in their situation. Yet, as it turned out, there was little help available. And even when they did receive help, it did not amount to much, particularly for the parents, since the child was cast as the victim and the family or the parents as the perpetrator. Moreover, in the pre-adoption interviews, if there was *any* mention of the adoptee's early experiences with abuse and neglect, these reports were felt by the adoptive parents to be too sketchy to be useful. Either the child's troubled background was glossed over or it was ignored as much as possible. Later, when early experiences of abuse and neglect manifested themselves in troublesome behaviour by the adolescent, the severity of the problem was belittled or discounted. The result was that the parents felt as though they were looking for excuses and avoiding responsibility. This is not to say that everyone in the system was to blame. On the contrary, each couple had met someone in the legal and social-services system who was caring and helpful. Yet the fact remains that the parents tried everything, asked all the questions they could, pursued every possible avenue, attended all the sessions they could stand, and nothing worked. They said that the treatment they received at the hands of some social workers, the constant turnover in staff at the agencies, the useless advice, the lack of fit between their sons' needs and the agency criteria, the waiting lists, and the tendency of "experts" not to listen or to dismiss their opinions made the family-therapy sessions a colossal waste of precious time.

The parents often felt as if they and their sons had fallen between the cracks of the system. It particularly irked Arnold that Jon was never referred to by name. To the system, Jon was just a ward of the court. When Arnold once phoned to ask after Jon, he was told that if he felt that he could not deal with this ward of the court, they would be glad to take him off his parents' hands. The implication was that being unable to deal with their son made the Brooks unfit parents, and, if the Brooks wanted to rid themselves of their problem, they could. John Graves remembered how a psychiatrist worked with Ken from the time the boy was seven. After two years, the psychiatrist ended the sessions with the report that the family and Ken would be "A-okay." Clearly, this doctor had no clue as to the depths of the boy's difficulties. Edward Verdan felt a bitterness towards an adoption and social-services system that did not consider older adopted native children to be special-needs children. Had these children been understood to be in need of particular attention, and had this information been related to the parents at the time of adoption, the parents might not have felt betrayed. Four of the couples spent hours writing letters to various officials about the inadequacies of the system. They had been given defective goods, to use one parent's term, from the beginning, and there was no recourse available. The parents had been deceived by an advertising campaign that painted a rosy future with adopted native children that was full of love and possibilities. To this day, I struggle with my naive participation in what was a covert campaign on the government's part to assimilate native peoples through adoption into non-native homes.

The parents grieved that they would not be able to witness the usual milestones in a young man's life: first date, graduation from high school, driver's licence, first car, marriage, and so on. Their sons were also not present for special holidays, Christmas, and birthdays, and they missed celebrations such as family weddings. The extended family, for its part, did not know what to do about Christmas and birthday gifts; sometimes these family members took it upon themselves to stop giving. And, when they asked about the adoptive parents and their children, the parents found it awkward to respond truthfully or they simply did not know how to respond. It was not easy for these parents (and their other children) to say, "My son (or brother) is in jail ... or living on the streets." One parent was bitter that their adopted son did not take the trouble to acknowledge family events or celebrations, even though he often treated his friends to gifts. Neither the Graves nor the Verdan family was invited to the weddings of their adopted children, and they did not feel that they would be able to experience the joy of being a grandparent to their adopted children's offspring.

The parents felt their loss in all areas of their life and so their grief was all-encompassing. Yet no one diagnosed their feelings as those of grief until we began the interviews. The parents grieved over the changes in themselves and the lost hopes for the family. The sentiments that were repeated from one interview to another reflected sadness, loneliness, disappointment, and defeat. Labelling the overall sensation as grief clarified the feelings and made sense of them. In Elaine's words, "I didn't even know it was grieving. I didn't have a word to apply to it. You just knew that that person died at a particular time in your experience with the individual. It's grieving for this child that might have been." It was apparent to me that some of the parents were stuck in the guilt and grieving stages, and I believe that the interviews helped to shift their perception of the adoption breakdown so that they could continue on the way to coming to terms with their experience.

This stage, the last one before acceptance of reality, has recently gained more prominence in psychological literature (Petruccelli 1993; Bridges 1980). As we change our perceptions about our role, our responsibilities, and our abilities, we begin to grieve all the aspects of our loss. Kubler-Ross identifies this stage as the point at which the individual is stripped of all feeling, emptied of all strength, and becomes resigned to fate. Grief is the necessary precursor to acceptance. William Bridges explains that it is important to reflect on these things, for with realities, as with identities and connections, the old must be cleared away before the new can grow. The mind is a vessel that must be emptied if new wine is to be put in. Bridges believes that "the first task of transition [is] unlearning, and in order to change … you must realize that some significant part of your old reality was in your head" (1980: 100–1).

Physical problems, be it an abnormality or a disease, can be easily observed and understood. A physical injury means that a diagnosis can be made, a treatment prescribed, and a recovery expected. Get-well wishes will be sent, and support will come from all sides. These are all accepted guidelines that we can act upon to deal with a disruption to the order of things. With an emotional struggle, however, the disruption may not be readily visible, but it is there nonetheless. The parents I interviewed spoke of the struggle they all had experienced as if it was a physical illness, but none of them could convey that reality at the time it was happening. Because she was seldom asked about her son, Victoria was always touched when Vincent's lawyer, whom they sometimes met by chance, would ask how the boy was getting along: "That's the kind of question people would ask if somebody was physically ill, but not when a child is acting out." When the question was asked, it had the effect of validating and acknowledging that there was indeed a problem with the child and that there were emotional consequences for the parents. As Victoria so aptly put it, "Carlton cards hasn't discovered us yet." Avoidance on the part of others, intentional or otherwise, is hurtful and isolating. Furthermore, an emotional problem, like mental illness, especially if it involves acting out against society, is stigmatized. Emotional problems are sometimes attributed to a person's weak character. If the parents' child has the problem, then the parents must have done something wrong. If the parents are seen to be experiencing emotional difficulties, it may be assumed that there is weakness of character in them as well. Worse, it could even be perceived that the defects in the parents' characters may have given rise to those in the children. Finally, because of the invisible nature of the source of the difficulty, no one says, "I'm sorry," or "You're doing the right thing, just hang in there." These are statements that someone would make if somebody was physically injured or sick.

The emotional strain took a toll on the parents' health. Victoria, who is a slim woman, admitted that her weight dropped from

116 lbs. to 92 lbs. at the time of the adoption breakdown. Her emotional distress and the sleeplessness almost cost her her job. For her husband, the stress caused sleeplessness, irritability, and distraction and led to counselling. Edward Verdan experienced chest pains, coughed up blood, and was put on intravenous fluids for a week. Mary Brooks admitted that she was so consumed with her grief that she talked about Jon twenty-four hours a day, to anyone who would listen, for two or three years. She says that she focused on her dislike of Jon and told others that she no longer wanted him in her life, that he was dead.

9 The Search for Answers

Lord grant me the serenity to accept the things
I cannot change,
the courage to change the things I can
and the wisdom to know the difference.

– Reinhold Niebuhr

Through the years, I searched for an explanation for our adoption difficulties. My husband and I were isolated and shocked at the lack of support for our struggle. We were unable to find information, research material, or an agency that addressed the experiences of adoptive families. In trying to find answers, the blame for Tim's behaviour shifted from one target to another: his Indian heritage, his bad blood, his weak and "loose" birth parents, his narcissistic mother, his absent father, his working mother, his ambitious family with its high expectations of achievement, the discrimination, the pre- and post-natal abuse he suffered, the adoption stigma, the fact that he was the third child, the second boy, that he never had his special time (we adopted Melanie only six months after him), and so on.

Since Tim's adoption in 1973, there have been advances in the understanding of the unique nature of adoptive relationships as well as of the effects of heredity, pre- and post-natal neglect and abuse, and separation trauma on the degree of success an adopted child will have in bonding with his adoptive parents and in growing up as a stable and productive adult. For parents whose adopted children are out-of-control, this information is helpful, because it enables them to see the adoption breakdown from a different perspective. When adoptive parents realize that the causes for the breakdown of the adoption could be factors external to them or the family, a substantial amount of guilt is alleviated. The parents can appreciate that their child's inability to bond with them and his or her struggle with identity in adolescence has less to do with them as parents and their home environment than they might have first feared. Thus, the love, persistence, support, and encouragement (with or without professional help) that the parents provided were almost predestined to make little difference to the child's development.

I never asked the parents outright what they thought caused their child's problems, but we certainly discussed possibilities many times through the series of interviews. We arrived not at one answer but many. Not one was complete by itself; there was no simple explanation. It would be easier if there *were* one answer, but the realization that there is not enabled me to support and help other struggling parents. As well, we were aware before we started the interviews that our personal explanations for the disruption would not be the same as those proposed by the other couples. For example, Mary Brooks said to us, before Jon left home, that she felt that my return to work was a factor in Tim's troubles. She focused on the difficulty that older abused children have with bonding and their need for a full-time mother.

Each couple had some ideas about the source of the difficulties: Rod felt that being native was a factor, while I focused on the neglect and abuse that Tim had suffered previously. (I was outraged at my inability to make up the difference!) Edward considered fetal alcohol syndrome a possible cause. Georg spoke about the genetic element when he said, "[These children] are not homemade." Alison firmly believed that it was not the children's fault. Lou cited his and his wife's inexperience as parents, while Victoria focused on Vincent's sad story. John discussed the cultural differences, while Ella wished that she could have had more influence.

Every suggested cause did not guarantee that a particular problem would appear. Although there is a great deal of evidence to support the detrimental effects of abuse and neglect, these factors do not necessarily guarantee problems. Yet, in varying degrees, the parents profiled here were able to attribute at least part of their adopted son's behavioural problems to external factors. What also helped the parents to sort out, objectify, and apply these factors to their circumstances was the realization that they, as parents, were not alone – other families were having similar problems with adopted children – and that they, like other couples, had been unwittingly misled by social-service agencies. The parents were also able to relieve guilt by realizing that the government's policy of allowing older native children to be placed outside their communities was a risky policy fraught with ulterior motives.

In the following section, I will expand on some of the external factors that may have contributed to the adopted sons' difficulties, their inability to bond with their adoptive parents, and their anti-social behaviour. Then I will discuss what sources of support the parents made use of in trying to come to terms with their emotions, their self-image as individuals and as parents, and the new realities facing them.

NEW INFORMATION

Information is power, and it has a sort of liberating quality about it; it allows us to exercise more control over ourselves, our emotions, and our lives, as well as to make rational choices among many possible alternatives. Learning more about the factors that played a role in the lives of these adopted children initiated the process of deliverance from the emotions – anger, sorrow, guilt, grief – that overwhelmed the parents. Focusing on the possibility that pre-existing factors *may* have contributed to their sons' anti-social behaviour offered the parents a way towards healing and acceptance.

Heredity

Genetic predispositions can offer a partial explanation for criminal/anti-social behaviour in some populations, and the environmental effects of having a criminal adoptive parent also increases the risk of adoptee criminality (DiLalla and Gottesman 1989). In this regard, the problems that result from the adoptive parents not knowing their children's hereditary history would be minimized if adoptions were more open and if contact between adopted children and birth parents were allowed to continue after the adoption.

With such rapid advances in genetic research, the knowledge about how genes affect personality and behaviour will continue to expand. Recent research on identical twins who have been raised separately seems to establish that much of what we think of as personality is inherited. Predispositions towards shyness or sociability, thrill-seeking or placidity, affability or irritability are inherited traits (Karen 1990: 66). There have been a number of studies done on identical twins. Robert Feldman (1994) describes twins who were separated at birth and then reunited thirty-four years later. They had similar personalities: neither was married; they both worked in firefighting; they shared hobbies such as forestry; they liked the same foods and drank the same beer. The data on twins also suggest that there may be a genetic predisposition for the psychiatric disorders associated with suicide. (We learned that Tim's mother had committed suicide in the 1980s.) Research into this area has not demonstrated whether there may be an independent genetic component for suicide.

Pre-Natal Abuse

There is a growing body of research that provides compelling evidence that exposure to drugs and alcohol in the womb can result in brain damage as well as learning difficulties and serious behavioural difficulties later in life (Cole, cited in Avery 1997; Wente 2000). In addition, one study, by Richard Barth, draws a direct connection between drug exposure in the womb and adoption breakdown. Barth compared pre-placement experiences and child–adoptive–parent outcomes for children who had been exposed to drugs and children who had not been exposed to drugs. Of the 1,269 families who responded, one difference emerged: "Couples adopting independently had somewhat lower satisfaction if they adopted a drug-exposed child (Barth 1991: 323–42).

On the subject of fetal alcohol syndrome or its milder version, fetal alcohol effect, one newspaper report states that children suffering from this condition "are out of control. They can't tie their shoes and can't learn to read. They lie, cheat and steal. Kids with full-blown FAS are mentally retarded. Kids with ... fetal alcohol effect ... often look normal and have normal intelligence but are cursed with learning and behavioural problems. They have no sense of conscience, no sense of consequence, and no impulse control. They're walking time bombs who explode again and again." One FAS victim mentioned in this report was a "violent, sexually promiscuous crack addict" by the age of fourteen, and her adoptive mother describes how the family "went through a string of experts. They told us to improve our parenting skills" (Wente 2000). Fournier and Crey (1997) write that "bathing a fragile fetus in alcohol is like spilling a drink on a computer: the circuitry is scrambled in ways that are hard to predict and impossible to repair"(175).

FAS is not a problem unique to Canada's native peoples but it is particularly prevalent among them. The National Native Association of Treatment Directors estimates that 80 per cent of aboriginal people in Canada are affected by alcoholism, either through being addicted themselves or through dealing with the addiction of a close family member (Fournier and Crey 1997: 174). A leading researcher in the field, Albert Chudley, asserts that every native child adopted in the last two decades has suffered alcohol damage in utero, and that this fact – rather than alienation from white society – is at the root of their difficulties in later life (ibid.). Chudley may or may not be overstating his case, but there can be no doubt that the consequences of FAS for Canada's native population have been severe. Records from medical institutions in Saskatchewan showed that in the past decade, out of 450 children born with FAS/FAE, 75 per cent were aboriginal (Fournier and Crey 1997: 178). A 1990 survey at native treatment centers across Canada found that 80 to 90 per cent of their clients had experienced sexual abuse (116).

Post-Natal Abuse

Abuse – physical, sexual, or emotional – is common in the history of children whose adoptions fail. In a 1986 study, 80 per cent of children in broken placements had been physically abused, and 58 per cent of those children who remained with their adoptive families had also suffered physical abuse (Hornby 1986: 8). Children who were abused manifest problematic behaviour as they grow older: refusal to eat or serious binge-eating; hoarding food and excessive vomiting; suicidal behaviour, including threats and attempts; and sexual behaviour characterized as promiscuous by the social worker (Cole, cited in Avery 1997). Sexually abused children have a seven-times greater chance of alcohol or drug addiction than the average child, a ten-times greater chance of suicide attempts, a much higher chance of living on the streets and in juvenile prostitution, a higher rate of mental disorders, including multiple-personality disorders, and a higher rate of eating disorders and various psychiatric problems (Kellington 1993). First Nations suffered generations of sexual abuse at residential schools and in foster care and many brought this learned behaviour back home. It remains a major problem today and aboriginal communities have begun initiatives to take control of their justice system and deal with the offenders in more traditional ways (Fournier and Crey 1997).

Many abused children see themselves as bad, a problem, or unlovable. Children usually blame themselves, not their abuser, for what happened. This deep-rooted negative sense of themselves haunts them all their life. It affects their ability to choose good friends. Their sense of being a failure reduces their opportunity for achieving success at school, in the community, and in the workplace (ibid.). The behaviour is difficult for adoptive families to understand and accept, especially without forewarning or support. Some of the most problematic children are those who have lost their ability to trust, show affection, and form lasting relationships. In addition, children in their early adolescence may confuse the normal desire for independence with their rejection of parents in the new adoptive home (Hornby 1986: 8).

Abused children do not feel safe. Their ability to trust is undermined and, in some cases, destroyed. It is difficult for them to ask for or accept the help they need to develop into healthy, productive adults. For many abused children, the journey into adulthood is a lonely and difficult experience (Kellington 1993), often marked by what Michael Hehir (1991) refers to as "avoidant attachment" behaviour. Another writer observes that "although most adopted children have suffered abuse, the cause-effect connection between child abuse and crime [is uncertain]. By no means do all children who are abused become antisocial. They have a variety of reactions, including becoming withdrawn, depressed, insecure and anxious. Many abused children grow up to be responsible adults who are good parents" (Samenow 1989: 184). However, there is strong agreement that early abuse contributes to difficult behaviour patterns.

Sex of the Adoptee

Another factor that accounts for how a child will respond in an adoptive situation is the sex of the adoptee. "Maladjusted behavior was higher among adopted boys than adopted girls. Moreover, adopted boys showed a higher prevalence of maladjusted behavior than all the boys in the cohort whereas there was no such difference between the adopted girls and all the girls in the cohort" (Seglow et al. 1972: 144, 145, 153).

Age at Adoption

Usually when a child is abused and subsequently removed from the home, he or she is older when placed for adoption. Not all older children have been abused, but certainly every older child has had to deal with the trauma of separation and loss. When adopted older than age three, aggressive and hyperactive children displaying anti-social behaviour were at greatest risk of adoption instability (Berry and Barth 1989):

Children placed at two or three years of age who experienced a disruption will have more problems than counterparts who do not experience disruption. Being moved from one home to another is inherently disrupting. We're seeing a lot of that in foreign adoption. Psychological problems associated with adoption is restricted to children in the middle childhood years and adolescence ... On average, adopted children are more likely to manifest psychological problems than non-adopted children ... [but] only a minority of adopted children manifest clinically significant symptomatology ... [They have] a unique set of psychosocial tasks that interact with and complicate the more universal developmental tasks of family life (Brodzinski, cited in Fishman 1992: 46)

Research published between 1948 and 1956, although not proved, commands general agreement on the desirability of early placement (Seglow et al. 1972: 30). This is often paired with the previous determining factor of abuse or the prolonged early deprivation and separation trauma. According to Bowlby and other attachment theorists, "maternal deprivation and separation are damaging in the early years largely because the child's precious central figure has been removed, causing his attachment life and all its emotional and developmental derivatives to become disrupted" (Karen 1990: 99). The period of greatest vulnerablity with respect to later development is under three years of age (Bowlby cited in Karen, ibid.; Spitz 1965); even at the young age of three or four, the young child cannot easily attach himself despite being provided with the most favourable conditions for the formation of a human bond (Magid and McKelvey 1987: 66). Humphrey and Ounstead (1963) found "a greater tendency to lying, stealing and destructive behaviour in the ... group, which included a number of children known to have been adopted after two or more years of very unsatisfactory upbringing" (cited in Seglow et al. 1972: 34).

Previous Disruptions

Sometimes the child is removed from the home and placed in a foster home or has several foster placements before being adopted. Previous adoption disruptions increase the likelihood of more disruptions, because the child who has not had a satisfactory relationship or has had it disrupted will have great difficulty forming a subsequent one. At the end of 1988, there were 4,400 crown wards in the care of 52 Ontario Children's Aid Society agencies. Only 636 children were placed for adoption that year. When the adoptive plans for 152 were examined, 102, or two-thirds, experienced one or as many as ten moves to different foster homes. This is interesting because the expression "long-term foster care" surely, but incorrectly, conveys a suggestion of permanence (Adams 1990).

Ken Magid and Carole McKelvey interviewed many violent offenders. One of them, Charles Manson, stated, "Rejection, more than love and acceptance, has been a part of life since birth" (Magid and McKelvey 1987: 23). Rejection seems to breed disruption, according to Magid and McKelvey. "It [abandonment] is as if a voice inside their heads is saying, 'I trusted you to be there and to take care of me and you weren't. It hurts so much that I will not trust anyone, ever. I must control everything – and everybody – to ward off being abandoned again'" (ibid.: 26). Reading such books as *High Risk* gave Mary Brooks the insight she was looking for with respect to Jon's rejection of certain situations. Having been rejected, children like Jon become experts on rejection and, in order to ensure that they will never again be victims of rejection, they take the initiative by rejecting others first. Mary speculated that what Jon was probably unconsciously saying to himself was, "You've touched me, but I can't deal with that so I'll reject you by taking your money." This also made sense to Victoria with respect to Vincent. In the interviews, Lou and Victoria spoke of Vincent rejecting them before he could be rejected again; he would not allow them to get close to him.

The key factor that is now gaining increasing attention – owing to the work of John Bowlby and his disciples – is the attachment process itself. In their experiments on rhesus monkeys, the Harlows signalled to the world how important a warm, soft, primary caregiver was to the normal emotional and social development of baby monkeys. Similarly, a primary person to whom the child can become attached, who responds to the child's needs and who initiates positive activities with the child, seems to be indispensable (Fahlberg 1979: 7; Karen 1990). Today, instead of regarding parent-child bonding as a one-way street, experts such as Gunther (1963) state that there is now little doubt that "attachment is a two-way thing which is of the utmost value in survival ... and that how and when the attachment between mother and baby is interrupted have a lot to do with deciding the infant's behavior later" (Gunther, cited in Seglow et al. 1972: 146). Disruption of the parent-child bond before the age of three can have damaging results for the child's subsequent development (Karen 1990).

Foster Cline defines a person's soul as those unique, special human qualities of thoughtful caring for others and the internal belief of something beyond us and far greater than ourselves (cited in Magid and McKelvey 1987). The development of these human qualities is accomplished through the cycle of infant feeding. When the infant suffers hunger pangs, and his mother is there to feed him, that relief leads to satisfaction and a sense of trust. This trust can be damaged by separation or abuse but also in natural ways such as in situations where the parents cannot take away the pain of chronic illness or congenital problems. This sense of trust comprises three distinct parts: trust of self, trust of others, and trust of humanity. By the age of six months, the cycle has been completed hundreds of times; it basically locks in the first associational patterns. New studies now indicate that changes occur in early neural development in the brain when infants experience early stress. Certainly, the parents profiled here recognized the importance of bonding for the child and for themselves. But often the closeness that the parents desired was difficult for their son, perhaps because his ability for attachment had been damaged beyond repair in his early years by disruption of the bond with his birth parents. The Brooks and Pelligrini families spoke of being too close to the child, and that their son responded negatively. When Lou and Victoria tried to get too close to Vincent, he would put his guard up, and in order to create more space between him and his parents, he would have to leave. This confirms the view of attachment theorists that children who have been separated from birth parents in their first years of life – whether or not the separation was the result of rejection on the parents' part – have a particularly deep-seated feeling of abandonment that constrains their ability for social relationships. Such children "cannot believe that a caring gesture is any more than a passive fancy. So [they are] likely to keep testing and testing, keep mixing clinging with hostility and unreasonable demands, perhaps driving away the parent who wants to initiate something new (Karen 1990: 227).

Magid and McKelvey (1987) are convinced that society, particularly North American society, is placing many children in high-risk situations, where the children do not attach and do not learn to trust. In adoptive situations, the risk is even higher because of the separation trauma and, in many cases, neglect and abuse. They describe techniques – rage-reduction therapy, wilderness therapy, spiritual therapy – that have been used to try to attach unattached children. There appears to be limited success with abused children.

Adoptee's Search for Identity

Insecurely attached children need to be reached by adolescence, because it is in childhood that change is most easily accomplished without therapeutic intervention (Karen 1990: 66). All adolescents seem to search for their unique identity, but for adopted children this is even more difficult: "Adoptees are missing an important part of their identity ... Adopted adolescents are often at a disadvantage in their struggle to develop a secure identity. Lacking knowledge about their origins, including who their birth parents are, and why they were relinquished, adopted adolescents often find it more difficult to form a complete and stable sense of self" (Fishman 1992: 48). Recognition of this reality has led to demands, on the part of adopted children and adoptive parents alike, for a more open adoption process with easy access to birth records (Avery 1997; Wegar 1997).

The search for origins was judged to be a healthy response by those adoptees who feel a need to complete their own sense of individuated identity (Haag 1989). Many researchers have been able to demonstrate that the severity of emotional problems correlates directly with the age of the child at the time of the adoption placement and the extent of maternal deprivation (Karen 1990). The effects of these early childhood traumas may not become manifest, however, until adolescence or early adulthood when the adoptee has a tendency to develop identity conflicts or difficulties in forming intimate relationships (Sorosky et al. 1984: 98). Children adopted after the age of three, as noted earlier, are more vulnerable to feelings of rejection and to the development of an "abandonment depression." The identity conflicts they experience in adolescence and adulthood are even more intense than those of other adoptees (ibid.: 200). Erik Erikson described the essential task of adolescence as the development of a sense of identity and showed how the failure of the process results in a state of identity confusion. This results in a sense of shame, embarrassment, and lowered self-esteem; the adolescent feels vulnerable to any additional experiences of loss, rejection, or abandonment (ibid.: 110, 112). Genealogical connection is one important aspect of adult identity, relating each individual to past and future generations (ibid.: 14). There are many concerns and feelings that revolve around the formation of identity. This is "not only the identity modelled after the adoptive parents," Erikson notes, "but also the identity that has been surrendered," an identity that in most instances "is based on minimal information and maximal fantasy about the birth parents" (Pavao 1989). "Statistical data and case histories of the adoptees who have successfully searched for their birth parents validates the impression that adoptees are more vulnerable than non-adoptees to the development of identity conflicts in late adolescence and young adulthood" (Sorosky et al. 1984: 40; Reitz and Watson: 1992). A few well-known adoptees who experienced such difficulties are Margaret Laurence, Rod McKuen, and Betty Jean Lifton.

Lifton's book *Journey of the Adopted Self: A Quest for Wholeness* (1994) is filled with moving life stories of adopted men and women. The book examines how separation from the birth mother and secrecy in the adoption system have affected adoptees' sense of identity, as well as their attachment to their adoptive parents. She introduces the concept of cumulative-adoption trauma. According to Rollo May (1975), anxiety comes from not being able to know the world you are in, not being able to orient yourself in your own existence (Sorosky et al. 1984: 195). These children may have problems in integrating the past with future, in Oedipal resolution, in identification with the new family, and in attitudes to adoption. "It is clear that there are some stresses for the adoptive family that are not present in the biological family, thus leading to crisis and difficulty for the adopted adolescent in completing this stage of development and emerging with a strong ego identity" (Stein and Hooper 1985, cited in Brodzinsky and Schechter 1990: 166). Lack of knowledge and sense of one's true identity cannot be overcome, no matter how warm and nurturing the adoptive parents are (Sorosky et al. 1984: 14).

The children in this study had yet another element of their identity with which they had to come to terms: their native ancestry. Native adolescents are faced with the triple crisis of being adolescent, aboriginal, and adopted. From an early age, these adopted boys recognized that they did not resemble their parents and siblings in terms of colouring and that this set them visibly apart from their adoptive family. The difference was plain for everyone – relatives, friends, neighbours, classmates – to see. While there may have been other local instances of transracial adoptions in their midst, where the child was clearly not the biological offspring of the parents, the stigma borne by the boys profiled here was that of being an Indian. As young children, they grew up in an environment where being Indian also meant laziness, shiftlessness, no work ethic, being drunk, a down-and-out, and the bad guys in cowboy movies. The pervasive negative stereotyping that First Nations people have had to endure throughout this country's history was not lost on these adopted sons. They knew that they were descended from a people who have been treated with injustice and cruelty: dispossessed of their ancestral lands and confined to unproductive reserves or in urban ghettoes; administered as dependent wards of the state by a department of the federal government; long denied the right to vote and still denied the right to self-determination and self-government; victimized by political oppression and systemic racism; and forced to live in horrific social conditions, both on and off reserves, from which there is little escape (Wharf 1993; "An Indian and a Québécoise search for roots" 2000).

The government legislation and treaties over the past three centuries have isolated 550 bands on more than 200 reserves. In the early part of the twentieth century, the government changed its strategy for dealing with the Indian problem from one of isolation to assimilation. Officials seized hundreds of native children from their homes on the reserves and forced them to attend residential schools that punished them for speaking their native languages and for practising their cultural traditions. The children were required to worship the god of the white people, to speak their language, and to adopt their culture. The price Indians have had to pay for the government's policy of isolation and its covert policy of assimilation has been high. The standard of living for Indians on reserves has dropped to levels comparable to the lowest in the world. In comparison with the average Canadian, native peoples have a life expectancy that is ten years less, a 2.5-times higher rate of infant mortality, a six-times higher incidence of children in care, a thirteen-times higher incidence of alcoholism, a fifteen-to-twenty-times higher rate of fetal alcohol syndrome, a five-times higher rate of incarceration, and (on reserves, where 80 per cent of the population lives below the poverty line and in appalling housing) a 70 per cent higher rate of unemployment. For those under the age of thirty-five, the death rate is three times the Canadian rate, and these individuals are most likely to die from accidents or violence, including suicide. The rate of suicide among Indians is the highest in the world. Indians are the most economically disadvantaged people in our country, both on and off reserves, compared to Canadians overall, and they have much lower levels of educational attainment, especially off reserves (Boldt 1993: 7–18). These are the facts of life for Indians today, and it was out of this setting that Indian children have been removed, first, to be put into white residential schools and, later, to be put up for adoption into the homes of white families.

The history of Canada has been an institutionalized dehumanization of Indians and a denial of all the wrongs committed against them in the interests of this country and its newcomers, then and today. In *Surviving as Indians: The Challenge of Self-Government*, Menno

Boldt makes the poignant observation that most Canadians are unable to recognize Indians as people with whom they share a common humanity. "[Canadians] seem not to place the same worth on an Indian life that they place on the life of a Canadian. Such a conclusion is indicated by the sheer indifference Canadians display towards the ongoing tragedies in Indian communities that they regularly see, hear, and read about" (idid.: 15). When an Indian is seen seated on the sidewalk of a busy city, it is easier for the average person to see the Indian as a victim of his own self-imposed vices and laziness (that is, his bad blood) than to see him as a victim of systematic disenfranchisement by a racist and paternalistic government. While national surveys show that the average Canadian is supportive of native rights, few Canadians have any real idea of what is involved in redressing the wrongs committed against Indians. Canadians want to see themselves as enlightened, but few would be prepared to face the economic and political costs – certainly politicians would not be – in righting historical wrongs (ibid.). The Canadian government, for its part, continues to talk less about the tragedy – the "ethno-spiritual holocaust" (ibid.: 60) – of our native peoples than about the high cost of welfare support for them.

Social Environment

Most of the research done before the 1980s focused on the impact of environment on adoption breakdown. Agencies concerned themselves with the study of the dynamic interplay in the post-adoptive relationship between the adopted child and other family members – nature of relationship with family members, degree of fit, community reaction, child's identity formations and dealing with rejection, abandonment, self-blame, sense of worthlessness, and so on – and hence with the "family-systems" approach to therapy. Only recently has reference been made to what the child and his early environment contributes to the disruption, intentionally or otherwise: "John Bowlby's monograph in the early 1950s demonstrated the deleterious effects on the child of early maternal deprivation and was instrumental in bringing into adoption policy the current mental health theories with an emphasis on early placement. It catalyzed a shift from the interests in heredity and genetic determinism to environmental and psychodynamic concerns" (Sorosky et al. 1984: 34). All of this underlines the essential truth of the view that the "acknowledgment of differences" in adoptive kinships – that is, the recognition of the uniqueness of the adopted family – is vital to the success of any adoption (Kirk 1990).

In addition, the model of symbolic interactionism, as set out initially by H. Blumer and later elaborated by Stanton Samenow (1989), Ken Magid and Carole McKelvey (1987), and particularly John P. Hewitt (1997), indicates that the child's *choice and response* to the environment is more crucial than the environment itself in determining behaviour (Samenow 1989: 18). Proponents of this approach do not believe that the environment plays the conclusive role that was once thought: "Deterministic explanations of human behaviour have furthered the tendency to blame what is external to self: poverty, racism, broken home, child abuse, the glorification of violence, deficient schools, unemployment, peers, role models, but *individuals differ in how they cope*. Deprivation does not force them into crime, some [children] look for ways to improve themselves" (ibid.: 102 [emphasis added]). Of course, this is not to deny that in some cases a person's background will result in low self-esteem which in turn will shape that individual's perception of the world and limit his or her ability to transcend difficulties in later life; nor is there any doubt that a condition such as fetal alcohol syndrome may cause behavioural problems or undercut an individual's capacity to cope. What is clear, however, is that there is no easy and clear connection between environment, personality, and behaviour. So many ingredients go into the mix that it is facile to blame a person's conduct simply on, for example, poverty or, as in the cases studied in this book, the alleged failure of adoptive parents.

Temperament and Personality: Choice and Response

Tim's poor self-image, which began with his early abuse and neglect, his repressed anger, and his confusion about his identity, were incompatible with our desires for a close-knit family of achievers and contributors. The choices he made in his life were the result of his personal interpretation and assessment of his background and his opportunities. Whether that process was a

voluntary one or conditioned by factors in his early life – exposure to alcohol in the womb, neglect, the trauma of separation
from his birth mother – does not change the end result. Tim's
interaction with his own feelings and perception of his situation,
as well as his interactions with us and his family and *our* perception of family and expectations of him, shaped his social actions
and ours. We also came to understand that, along with the environment in which we raised Tim and his early childhood experiences, the other determinants in his behaviour were his particular
temperament or personality. These shaped the choices he made
vis-à-vis his interpretation of his environment, and the choices he
made and the behaviour that ensued forced all of us to reconfigure
our image of family. A. Bandura (1981) refers to this as reciprocal
determinism, that is, how the interaction of the environment, behaviour, and the individual give rise to certain reactions and actions.

Knowing the effects of temperament and personality on behaviour offered us a much broader perspective than had previous
explanations that focused *exclusively* on Tim's heredity and his
early childhood. This perspective was also more encompassing than
any explanation that revolved entirely around the ultimate power
of the family or the environment in defining Tim's responses.
Most children, after all, are resilient; some, even after suffering
extreme loss, survive and do well. "Studies of teenagers who
experience deprivation when very young [show that they] have
rebounded handsomely in adolescence" (Kagan, cited in Karen
1990: 66). In a five-year study of 112 older neglected children
who were adopted, A. Kadushin (1970) found that 74 per cent of
the adoptions were successful, 15 per cent were unsuccessful, and
11 per cent were equivocal. The conclusion is that this remarkable
success rate argues for a recognition that children have varying
capacities to deal with potentially traumatic conditions and that
these strengths enable them, when provided with a healthier environment, to surmount the damaging influences of earlier developmental insults (Seglow et al. 1972: 37). However, this remarkable
success rate – in a five-year period – still meant that one in four
adoptions did not succeed. And, again, such statistics do not illu-
minate *why* some children can overcome adverse circumstances
and others do not. The roots of personality are complex and,
despite all our research, deeply mysterious.

SOURCES OF SUPPORT FOR PARENTS

While information did much to satisfy the parents' need to understand and to ease their sense of responsibility and guilt as to why their children had experienced so much difficulty, the support the parents received through support groups and from individuals, usually in the last stages of or after the adoption breakdown, allayed their sense of isolation and helped them work through much of their anger, sorrow, and grief.

Parent-Support Groups

The most useful single source of help came from parent-support groups. The main purpose of parent-support groups is to *support* the parents in a way that society, agencies, and family-therapy sessions cannot. Whereas family-therapy sessions are child-focused, parent-support groups are parent-focused. There are different types of parent-support groups. Some are run by parents, others by social-service agencies. Some meet once monthly, others meet weekly. Some operate on a drop-in basis, and parents come when they wish. Some are educational and others have a series of steps and homework that the parents are expected to follow each week.

With the exception of Dr Armstrong's Parents for Youth group, Rod and I did not find support for our particular needs. Dr Armstrong acknowledges this lack of support: "Today ... society lacks this kind of cohesive structure. We have a number of children growing up in an environment where the behavioral expectations are incredibly diverse, the values within the home are not supported by the community at large, and the feedback systems to parents are not very clear" (Petruccelli 1993: 24). He argues that society's refusal to set and enforce limits and boundaries has devalued parenting and disempowered parents, and it is this disempowerment that lies at the heart of the matter. Thus, parents need to turn to each other for the help they need.

Parents for Youth has groups of ten to twelve members, and they meet regularly. New members are admitted only when parents already in the group feel they are ready to leave. In these groups, it is recognized that the parents of children with conduct disorders suffer greatly. Most of the parents seeking this kind of help have been made to feel abused, blamed, patronized, and humiliated in their contact with child-oriented professionals and family therapists. Parents for Youth believes that the parents know their children better than anyone else and that, consequently, they are the best people to help their children.

Parent-support groups are designed to support the parents as they learn to change what they can and to accept what cannot be changed. The groups are composed of parents who have or who have had similar problems. It is facilitated by a group-leader who has been trained to work with groups. The parents discuss their children's behaviour but also their own feelings about that behaviour. The discussions may include their experiences and expectations from their own families of origin. In the safety of this group environment, the parents can discuss the conflicts and differences of opinion that they may have with their spouse over the way they should react to their child's behaviour. The parents encourage each other to make changes and to set realistic limits and to follow through with natural and appropriate conse-quences. They exchange information and strategies for utilizing available resources, such as police, probation officers, the courts, the hospitals, and social workers.

In the support groups, the parents are not blamed or judged; they are comforted by the fact that they are not alone and that other good parents have troubled children. Sometimes they feel blessed by comparison to other parents. They also feel good about themselves for having helped others and they feel safe to talk about their worst fears and disappointments. While there are many tears, there is a great deal of laughter, too. Parents who are paral-ysed with fear and shock and isolation are slowly able to feel again, to mourn, and to move towards making improvements in their relationships with spouses and children.

Every parent we interviewed who had attended a support group commented on how much it had helped him or her as individuals and as a couple. The groups helped them in the pro-cess towards acceptance (Bridges 1980: 100). First, Rod and I real-ized that we were not alone; other caring people were having trouble with their children, both biological and adopted. Second, it helped us to be able to talk about our problems with other parents who had similar difficulties. The other parents did not judge; they understood exactly how we felt. Professionals, on the other hand, did not seem to acknowledge the problem. It was not until Tim deliberately broke the law, when he was eleven, that we finally got the help we had been seeking, and then in a small pilot project located at the Family Court Clinic.

Four of the six couples attended a parent-support group, although none of these was a group designed specifically to deal with the issues surrounding adoptions. Two of the parents, the Pelligrinis and ourselves, attended Parents for Youth support groups. Another couple, John and Ella Graves, attended Tough Love, and Alison and Georg Roethler attended some parents' groups at the Dalewood camp for troubled children. Each of the three couples attended these groups for a one-year period. The remaining two couples had not had the opportunity to participate in any support groups.

The Interviews as a Form of Group Therapy

The interviews were more therapeutic than any of us expected they would be. They helped the parents accept their situation, offered an opportunity for them to let go of the old and open up to the new, and, by allowing them to talk to others about their children, broke their isolation. They also stimulated meaningful dialogue between the parents and their other children about the disruption. The parents commented on several factors that contributed to the formation of what turned out to be a therapy group that helped all of us.

Irvin Yalom has studied the benefits of support-group therapy. With the benefit of hindsight, it was easy to match the benefits he identifies with those offered by our interview sessions (1985: 92):

1 Hope: In the interviews, this sometimes took the form of negative benchmarking. The participant knew that their sons were managing on their own and could still turn it around. There was also the hope expressed by the parents we interviewed that this book might help other parents in similar circumstances.

2 Universality: All of the participants had difficulty with their native adopted children. The interviews made them aware that they were not alone, that others were engaged in the same struggle. In Lou's words, "Scary how our lives parallel each other."

3 Information: I was able to tell the participants about the experiences of the other participants, and they were able to tell me about people, books, and televisions shows that might be useful for this project.

4 Altruism: The interviews sessions were helping all of us and we were hopeful that this book would help others.

5 Recreating the family: We all had to adjust to the new family format.

6 Socialization and feedback: I knew how difficult the adoption experience was and so was able to empathize with and console the parents.

7 Imitative role models: The other parents knew that Rod and I had survived the breakdown, and our response to Tim's death gave the parents confidence that they, too, would be able to cope.

8 Interpersonal input: Talking itself is therapy. We had many laughs and enjoyable meals together.

9 Catharsis: The participants had not had any cathartic experiences or many opportunities to tell others, sometimes even each other, exactly how they felt.

10 Support: We supported and encouraged each other.

11 Self-understanding: By telling and discussing their stories, the participants were able to learn more about themselves.

12 Existential factors: We were able to articulate the universal truths that consoled us: life is at times unjust and unfair; there is no escape from some of life's pain; all we can do is face the basic issues of life and death and thus live life more honestly and be less caught up in trivialities. Personally, I learned that I must take ultimate responsibility for the way I live my life, no matter how much guidance and support I get from others.

13 Closure: The Pelligrinis felt that the interviews were a good way to signal the end of an adjustment period and that now they might be able to begin to enjoy the next stage of their lives.

14 Try out things: The interviews provided the parents the opportunity to give voice to their own theories. It was here that each participant tried to fit the new information into his or her previous framework. This was particularly evident when it came to finding the reason for the adoption breakdown. For example, I realized that a native adoptee had special needs.

The participants combined the following factors: the adoptee's age, any history of drug abuse with the possibility of fetal alcohol syndrome, identity confusion and native cultural discrimination, and so on.

Particularly important to the participants were three of the benefits cited above: universality, information, and altruism. I will elaborate on a few situations where this was apparent.

The first telephone contact proved to be more crucial to the process than I had anticipated. In Victoria's words, "You know what I found interesting, too, was I think the first telephone conversation we had put me at ease. I felt like you really wanted to talk and open up to what it is we were actually going to be in for." It was evident from the beginning that the parents felt vulnerable. Even the source of the referral was important. Lou said, "Had you phoned through that whole organization ... if you'd gotten our names because you knew somebody in Alberta, and you knew we'd adopted or something, then I would've said no, regardless of what you went through."

The fact that Rod and I were able to conduct the interviews together was valuable. The men felt that having Rod there meant their point of view was taken into account, and his presence allowed the two of us to present our experiences and listen to those of others *as a couple*. The location of the interviews, in our homes, enabled us to get to know each other more quickly. We felt more comfortable in each other's homes, and the personal surroundings disclosed more than we would be able to glean from an office setting. Lou's comments summarized the way the couples felt: "We had very open conversations and you're sitting in our house, and we're talking about some very intimate times, emotionally intimate in a painful sense in a lot of ways. This is the second visit in your house and it's very comfortable and very warm, and in that respect, I don't think anything needs to be changed." His wife added, "I found this very comfortable, and I don't get comfortable with people quickly at all." To this Lou added, "Yeah, you're lucky you got anything out of Victoria, to be honest."

A trusting, warm, relaxed atmosphere was necessary for the parents to recall their significant memory experiences. The ideal-family memory captured the essence of the parents' hopes and dreams, while the disruption memory was powerful and emotional. These really were the most difficult moments that the parents had experienced. To re-experience them was frightening for both parents. The spouses were supportive and protective, sitting close to each other, leaning forward and sometimes touching each other. There was occasionally a silence as we waited for the person to go back in time. Finally, the person tried to find the words to describe his or her feelings in that setting. The reader cannot fully appreciate by simply reading the text how powerful the experience was. What is missing is the tremor in the voice, the tightness in the throat, the tenseness of the muscles, and the sobs that shook the parents. Although each situation was unique and quite different from the others, what stands out are the similarities. All the parents referred to their son as gone, going, hidden, a stranger. Their helplessness and sense of hopelessness and despair were overwhelming.

In the interviews, there were a few times when one parent would make a comment that had little to do with the emotional issue and seemed to be simply an unconscious attempt to break the tension. It was usually the father who did this by asking a question about some detail or feelings; he focused on relaying the series of events that took place. Rod admitted that he had the most trouble with the first significant memory experience. He described it this way: "I think it's like hypnosis almost. You get a real kind of no-bullshit approach. It gets really underneath some of the superficiality, which is natural. People can kind of protect themselves. When we get into that process some of that protection goes away."

At first, Rod and I found it as difficult to listen to the parents as they did to talk about such painful memories. With time, we grew more comfortable, but it was not uncommon for one of us to say on the way home, "I feel almost physically ill," or "I've got a headache," or "It's really draining." After one interview, I said to Rod, "I find that I'm kind of living each of those steps with them. I'm sensitive to their feelings. When their feelings become more open, I have a greater degree of sensitivity." I think that we uncovered in us and in them some emotions that had been obscured. I felt a great pressure, since I did not want the parents to be hurt all over again, in the way they had been by professionals. I wanted the interviews to have a positive impact on the parents.

We feel fortunate to have met these couples. New friendships have been formed in the process, and each couple expressed a desire to meet the other couples as well. We keep in touch once or twice a year with all the couples, except one, through Christmas cards and letters; with two of them, we even have the occasional lunch or dinner. As well, we have a continuing friendship with the Brooks family out west. Three of the couples attended a celebration we had when I received my doctoral degree; two couples were unable to come.

Professional Support from Individuals

While the parents' experiences with social-service agencies and the legal system were often negative, there were some individual workers who gave the parents support. These people came from many different walks of life: lawyers, probation officers, police officers, teachers, and friends. They were unique and special individuals. While the parents could not identify one helpful agency, they could each name one or two people who had been helpful to them. Victoria recalled how Vincent really liked a grandfatherly bailiff; Alison remarked how their social worker had gone beyond her duties to help her out in the early years, and later, the doctor at the Family Court Clinic demonstrated his support by not making Alison feel small or stupid or giving her the sense that she had done something wrong.

Other Sources of Support

Although there was disappointment among the parents at how particular friends and relatives responded to the parents' difficulties with their adopted sons, some relatives provided a good deal of support. Some babysat so the parents could get away, even though the task was a difficult one. Rod's parents and my mother did this for us, and some of the other couples had friends with whom they shared family holidays. Most of the couples had at least someone, friend or relative, with whom they could share their anxieties.

Certainly not least was the support and companionship the parents gave each other. One mother, feeling rejected and helpless and depressed, went away with her husband for a few days.

Sex helped to reaffirm her sense of self-worth and strengthened the bond between them. Sometimes it was not so much what the parents did for each other as what they did not do: blame the other spouse for shortcomings or direct excess frustration towards the other spouse. Often when one parent felt defeated, the other was able to rally and handle the immediate crisis; at other times, when one parent lost his or her temper, the other parent could take over and bring a calm to a particular situation.

Important, too, for many parents was the presence of other children in the family. The interviews did not focus on the other children in the family, but certainly they were discussed. One of the main reasons for adopting was the enjoyment that the parents experienced with their older, natural children. They spoke about how easy these children had been to raise and what wonderful times they had together. Even when the parents were struggling with the anti-social acts of their adopted son, they found solace in the knowledge that their other children were well adjusted and doing well. One couple, however, Victoria and Lou, had just the one adopted child, and so they were unable to find the support the other parents found in their other children. Alison and Georg were in a similar situation, because their only children were adopted children.

In retrospect, the parents agreed that their adoption difficulties placed a lot of pressure on their other children, as they tried to be extra good and to help Mom and Dad. In one family, the concern the children felt surfaced only during the course of the interviews, when they stopped by to check us out. In our family, we believe that much of the responsibility rested on our eldest daughter, who, perhaps in her efforts to help keep things under control, fell into a struggle with an eating disorder. In the interviews, the parents often spoke with joy and pride about their children and also at their sorrow and guilt at what these children had had to endure and for the happy times that were sacrificed in their struggle with their adopted sons.

For Ella and John, their grandchildren played an important role in helping them accept what happened to their adopted children. The fact that their biological children were successfully raising their children with the same childrearing attitudes and practices that John and Ella had demonstrated comforted them. It helped restore their confidence in themselves as parents: "You say to yourself, what did you do wrong? But once you start dealing with your grandkids, I convinced myself I didn't do anything wrong. Because you kind of go through this again with your grandkids and you see what they're doing and their response. You look back to those times when things weren't so great around here but really in my mind, I don't think we did anything wrong. We tried very hard. I didn't do anything different then than I do now, so … We have these kids that have done very well for themselves."

While in the process of writing my doctoral thesis, our daughter became pregnant. Our family was very excited, and I, in particular, enjoyed the opportunity to spend time with her, visiting and helping her through some difficult months in which she experienced nausea. Those months were filled with a wonderful anticipation of a new life. We were ecstatic when we held our grandson for the first time, soon after his birth. Lorie is determined to be a full-time mother and strives to provide an environment in which her son Joseph can develop trust and confidence in himself and in those around him and in which he can enjoy being a child. He is just a little older now than Tim was when we adopted him. We are constantly reminded that two and a half years is a long, long time for a baby. He is so vulnerable, helpless, and impressionable. It is difficult to ascertain where Lorie's strong determination to stay home comes from. Does it come from experiencing the devastating effects of Tim's early deprivation? Does it come from our family history of stay-at-home mothers, from my example of staying at home until she was fifteen? What other factors are there in this equation?

My husband and I find that we enjoy the times we have with our grandson. We look forward to his visits and to our growing relationship with him. He seems to be a catalyst in helping us turn a corner, helping us move our focus from the events of the past ten years to the present and the future, which we now view with increasing eagerness and optimism. In the midst of my grief over the adoption breakdown, the wall of pictures in my study helped me reconnect with the wonderful memories of happy family occasions and carefree holidays. Photos of Joseph are slowing taking over more space on my wall. What started out as one picture of a newborn is now eight pictures of a little boy experiencing his happy world, caressed and loved.

All of the parents found sources of comfort and strength deep within themselves. For some of the fathers, their own earlier experiences seemed to reduce the personal blame. For example, they may have had black sheep in their own family. Arnold's early childhood experiences in particular helped him understand some of the more outlandish things their son did. Arnold was the youngest in a family of nine children. Although he remembers the different personalities of his siblings and how they each had their good and bad sides, one sibling in particular experienced a lot of difficulty, was often in trouble, and once had returned to live with his parents, who were, by this time, retired. While some of Arnold's siblings reacted with bitterness and anger at this black sheep and his transgressions, his parents saw their difficult child as one who needed their love. Everyone was still able to meet and enjoy the family at get-togethers. His parents did not equate love with their children's ability to earn it. This is a lesson that Arnold carried with him when he considered Jon and his difficulties.

The adopted son, himself, sometimes made it easier for the parents to accept the situation. The parents wanted positive feedback from the adopted children themselves. Although most of the parents did not verbalize this need as much as Arnold did when he said specifically that what mattered to him was what Jon thought, it was evident that the feedback of the adopted sons was important to them. For example, the parents spoke with a smile on their faces when they told of phone calls from Vincent, Jon, Jimmy, or Ken and when the Graves's children acknowledged to their parents what a challenge they had been to raise. When Vincent told Lou and Victoria that he thought they had done a pretty good job with him and that he would like to adopt to give a disadvantaged child a chance in the same he way he had been given a chance, the parents felt gratified. I valued my last lunch with Tim when he told me that he was not that badly off, that he was okay, and that there were many people worse off than he living on the streets.

Why did these parents value the opinion of someone who had rejected their values and, in doing so, caused such heartache? The feedback from the adopted child affected the parents' sense of self-worth. We rely on others to provide us with the different parts or aspects of our self-concept. Our self-concept is built with the parts that are provided by the reaction of others. As parents, we need positive feedback to establish our hope and dream of being good parents. The parents had something to offer the child. When the child rejected it, their concept of themselves was shaken. Research recognizes the importance of children's reactions to parents in the formation of their self-image (Peters 1985; Ambert 1992). When Vincent sat on Victoria's lap and cried because he did not want to return to the detention centre, Victoria felt that she was needed as a mother and that Vincent was still such a little boy. On another occasion, when the police came to the house to arrest Vincent in connection with a robbery, Victoria said that they, as parents, were personally affected and felt wretched.

When the parents saw that their son was making positive steps, they felt better. Parents spoke of their sons' good social manners and their ability to communicate. They enjoyed the adopted child's sense of humour and found comfort in his concern for and loyalty to others. For example, Alison was impressed by how much volunteer work Jimmy did, as well as little odd jobs for others, and that he seemed to care about his little community of street kids. Three of the six adopted boys had a special talent in art, which was a source of pride for their parents. Elaine and Edward gave Gerald some money for buying art supplies.

Now, as young adults, the adoptees communicate with their parents, and the parents feel good about this. Understandably, the best medicine was when the adopted adult commented positively about his relationship with his adoptive parents. Jon Brooks told his parents that he was sure that if they had not taken him in, he would be dead today. Ken Graves told his parents that they must now take things more slowly, because they are getting older and deserve the rest. A few of the parents felt good about the way they had been able to communicate their positive feelings to their sons. Arnold took Jon's hand and told him quite directly that he, as his father, was proud of him for Jon was a self-made man in the way he was now in charge of his own life. Arnold also stated that, if his son felt that there was goodness in life and that it was worth living, then he and his wife had done their jobs as parents. Arnold felt especially that, in the end, it was not the material things he had accumulated or the things he had accomplished that would be a testament to the kind of life he had lived. The things on which his life would be evaluated had more to do with the kind of family he had raised, the kinds of individuals his children had become, and how his adopted children felt about the job he and his wife had done as parents.

In their study of a select group of non-native parents who adopted native children, Fournier and Crey (1997) acknowledge that these parents had good intentions and did everything they could to make the adoptions work: "There were many non-native foster and adoptive parents who did their very best to nurture, heal and raise the First Nations children entrusted to their care. Tragically, the outcome of adoptions even by conscientious non-native parents was often disastrous, as the adoptee reached adolescence only to suffer the triply painful identity crisis of being adolescent, aboriginal and adopted. Canadian and American social service agencies now estimate that adolescence is the period when up to eighty-five per cent of transcultural adoptive relationships fail" (89).

OTHER WAYS OF COPING

Physical Separation from the Problem: Time Out

For the parents who worked outside their homes, their jobs provided a welcome get-away from the constant pressure and tension in the home. The fathers who travelled were also more removed from the situation. This is not to say that being away did not create problems of its own, like frustration and, in some cases, guilt for leaving the spouse behind to deal with the situation single-handed. In every case, the fathers were away from home for short periods of time, which meant that total responsibility often fell on their wives.

I found my job a wonderful refuge, a place where I did not think about Tim and his escalating bad behaviour. Having the job to go to probably saved me from a nervous breakdown, and the same was true for some of the other parents; jobs and careers definitely helped them maintain a degree of self-confidence and retain their self-image. This was especially the case with the men, because less of their respectability rested on their degree of success with their children. Unlike some of the women, the men all had another area that helped them feel good about themselves. Victoria, however, did not derive these benefits from her job, because she worked at the school her son attended. She was the one who got phone calls at school from his probation officer, from his lawyer, and from people in his group home to say he had run away. This was somewhat alleviated when the school was told that, where Vincent was concerned, Lou was the one to call.

There were also some activities that worked to reduce the pressure or tension and the stress caused by the adolescent's behaviour. Alison took up playing the clarinet, and Rod found tremendous relief in playing tennis. It was an outlet for his frustrations, and while he was on the court he was not thinking about Tim. Lou realized that motorcycling probably saved his sanity. While on the road, he not only felt the exhilaration of the drive, he knew he had to exercise control over his machine. His singular focus on this activity took his mind off the problems at home and helped him regain control in his life. Arnold felt that, because he and his wife were busy with kids and work at a new business, they were able to move on with their lives.

What helped one parent did not help all. For example, tennis did not serve as an escape for me, because it was yet another thing I could not control. Where Rod found the control he exercised over the game to be a great antidote for the lack of control he had over Tim's behaviour, I found that my lack of control in tennis merely exacerbated the lack of control I experienced with our son's behaviour.

The time our sons spent in jail and in closely supervised or locked facilities also provided a circumstantial distancing. Every parent saw the time the adopted adolescent spent in jail as a time when they could sleep without worry about their son's whereabouts or his safety on the streets. These interludes were like mini-vacations during which the parents could catch up on lost sleep. This distancing was blocked in one case when the court made the Verdans their son's probation officers.

Factors Affirming the Adopted Children's Native Identity

Another important source of help stemmed from factors that gave positive reinforcement to the adopted child's native status. There were two contributors. One was the white community's recognition and provision for native culture. This was relatively new at the time, though now there are courses and classes about native culture in all levels of school and university as well as special college/university programs for aboriginal students. The second contributor was the help and recognition received from the native community itself. Three of the adopted boys have reconnected with their native families. In the case of the Roethlers, this was a very positive experience for the adopted young adults and the adoptive parents.

Letting go

As the parents moved along the road to acceptance, they had to let go of their expectations of their child and of themselves as parents. The unexpected difficulties encountered during the adoption and the subsequent breakdown forced the parents first to question and then finally to change their perceptions or root images. By drawing on Blumer's theory of symbolic interactionism, we can better understand how the adopted child's unexpected and often anti-social acts forced the adoptive parents to reassess their son's actions and intentions. They had to let go of old expectations and patterns of behaviour; they had to respond differently. To quote Blumer:

Such things as requests, orders, commands, cues, and declarations are gestures that convey to the person who recognizes them an idea of the intention and plan of forthcoming action of the individual who presents them. The person who responds organizes his response on the basis of what the gestures mean to him; the person who presents the gestures advances them as indications or signs of what he is planning to do as well as of what he wants the respondent to do or understand. Thus, the gesture has meaning for both the person who makes it and for the person to whom it is directed. When the gesture has the same meaning for both, the two parties understand each other ... If there is confusion or misunderstanding along any one of these three lines of meaning, communication is ineffective, interaction is impeded, and the formation of joint action is blocked (Blumer 1969: 19).

When you are no longer dealing with the person you knew, you must judge which course of action is most appropriate. If the person does not respond in the usual manner, you need to re-evaluate your plans. When this happens repeatedly, you begin to doubt yourself. The adoptive parents doubted themselves as parents. Bridges quotes one woman who describes how the loss of her husband affected her: "My self-esteem as a woman and as a person were all tied up in his reactions to me. I lost my way of evaluating myself." He also explains that divorces, deaths, job changes, moves, illnesses, and much lesser events "disengage us from the contexts in which we have known ourselves. They break up the old cue-system" (Bridges 1980: 94–5). The disappearance of the old system forces us to devise a new one. Moreover, the difficulty comes not from these changes but from the larger process of letting go of the person you used to be and then finding the new person you have become in the new situation (ibid.: 75). As the parents' perception changes, so do their expectations of the child and of themselves, but the basic piece of thread of your own expectation of yourself is changed (ibid.: 71). The parents were firm in their convictions that they wanted to give a disadvantaged child a good home, but they were also using the adoption as an opportunity to fulfil their lives and their dreams and their idea of what they could do, could accomplish, of what they wanted in order to fulfil their hopes and *their potential*; Mary, Victoria, Ella, and I were all clear about our personal desires to be good moms. Along the same lines, with respect to the ending of old relationships, William Bridges notes that "usually people find endings frightening because they break our connection with the setting in which we have come to know ourselves, and they awaken old memories of hurt and shame" (ibid.: 118). Mary Brooks connected Jon's feelings of rejection and his behaviour with her own feelings of rejection when she was a child.

The early departure of our sons left us feeling helpless and wounded, with low self-confidence. We were not the people we thought we were: As one of Bridges's subjects says: "We [came] to identify ourselves with the circumstances of our lives. Who we [thought] we [were was] partly defined by the roles and relationships that we [had], both those we [liked] and those we [did] not … the personality style that [made] us recognizably [us] and [them] is developed within and adjusted to fit a given life pattern" (ibid.: 13). The reaction of others is a vital part in the formation of self-concept. The interactions with others, the feedback received from others, shapes a self-concept. Some of the feedback can be ignored, and some may be camouflaged so the self-image is more acceptable to the individual and more like the person the individual wants to be. Therefore, when the parents in my research moved to accept the new circumstances, they developed new ways of viewing their son, new ways of interacting, and new expectations of those interactions. As Blumer states, "the new form of joint action always emerges out of and is connected with a context of previous joint action ... growing out of what went before. In the fact of radically different and stressful situations people may be led to develop new forms of joint action that are markedly different from those in which they have previously engaged, yet even in such cases there is always some connection and new form without incorporating knowledge of this continuity into one's analysis of the new form" (Blumer 1969: 20).

Opening Up

It is interesting that what each parent wanted in a family was created, or re-created, in his or her mind. Each parent created his or her own reality. Each parent had an image or construct of their desired family, their ideal family, the family that they would consider to be a successful family. When the son leaves the family home prematurely, the broken family is seen as a failure; intact families are successful. There seems to be little place in our society for broken families, for families who fail to fit the accepted structure of the family. There is little tolerance for the family that cannot control its kids and little understanding for emotional difficulties. A broken family is neither respected nor respectable.

In psychology, perception is sometimes seen as a three-part process. First, the person, bombarded by stimuli, guesses about the meaning, based on the information available. Second, the person actively searches for important-to-me features that begin to stand out. The patterns that appear depend on what you are interested in and what you have available. Next, the person organizes the stimuli into some recognizable shape. Gestalt theory (1935) includes the ground-figure principles to identify what is important (figure) from that which is less important (ground). It is here that we try to reduce ambiguity and fill in any gaps that may exist. The final step is to interpret or make sense of all of this. The human mind strives for coherence and consistency. We are determined to make sense of things (Landy 1987: 130). When one pattern does not work, we try another.

Accepting the failed situation was difficult for the parents. They asked, "Why did this happen?" To remove the guilt, they needed to change the perception of their expectations and responsibility and power. With the mothers especially, this led to an examination of their roles in the relationship. In the process, they often experienced guilt for not making it work. Because of the information they had available to them and the experiences they had weathered in their lives, the mothers felt the responsibility for family relationships. The blame was placed on their shoulders. The more weighed down the parent was, the harder it was to move towards relinquishing the ownership of the problem and eventually placing it, or at least sharing it, with other factors such as the adopted child's genetic background, his early years, discrimination, and so on.

The opposite of to accept is to reject. When a child rejects his parents' values, the parents read this as a personal failure, a flaw, a fault in *them* rather than a problem that is inherent in the child because of his or her background or whatever. Parents define happiness or success in terms of how well the child fits into their image and expectations, hopes and dreams and needs. They see themselves and come to know themselves through the eyes of others, through their feedback and reactions. This feedback is meant to verify their images, expectations, and evaluations of who they are as human beings. Each of them wants to feel a little special or a little better. As Ella said, she used to ask herself, "Why me?" And then she thought, "Well, why *not* me? Why should I be exempt from all this? Why should I be so special?"

For many who struggle to accept new circumstances, the core of letting go is opening up. C. Glesne and A. Peshkin write: "Do not mourn who you are now: learn who you are and how you operate, and make the best of it" (1992: 76). Similarly, R.E. Palmer observes that "experience is painful ... Experience often suggests the pain of growth and new understandings. It has constantly to be acquired and nobody can save us from it. We would like to spare our children from unpleasant experiences we have had, but they cannot be spared from experience itself. Every experience runs counter to expectation if it really deserves the name experience" (1969: 196). Accepting reality and moving on is what Rod did when he said, "It just wasn't going to work with Tim."

Acceptance

The transition in thinking that moved the parents from the stage of guilt to the stage of acceptance was achieved through the articulation of a number of facts and a gradual resignation to them: the son would never come back to the family home to live, as they had expected he would; the son was safely established on his own far away from his parents' home; the parents' expectations for the child's success and future had been far beyond what the adopted child could accomplish; and the parents had tried to raise an adopted son, but things did not turn out as they had wished. John describes the parents' journey of acceptance and realization and of letting go as a series of cycles through which adjustments are made. He described his gradual acceptance through an ever-increasing diminution in the level of his expectation for his son. When finally their son left, his level of expectation of anything else happening *other than the son's departure* coincided with the son's actual departure from their home. He says that he had been emotionally prepared for the event through his decreasing level of expectation and his inability to accept the damage the son had done to the family. The result was that he saw the son's departure as the only solution to a long-standing problem: the son had done enough damage, and he should now continue on his own.

I believe that, for all of us, our objectives were flawed from the outset, and things could not really have happened otherwise. If our objective had been to do the very best we could with these children, to bring them into our homes to love and provide for them, then we could have called the adoption a success. The fact that we wanted these children to be successful and to fit into white society and adopt the rules and values of that society was a misguided notion spawned by a variety of personal factors and a duplicitous government policy in which we were naive participants. If we could have readjusted our expectations and just seen Tim as a member of our family for a while, then we could have confidently concluded that the adoption was a success. After all, we had been able to enjoy some good times together as a family.

Because the parents had discussed the many aspects of loss, many new constructs were formed and accepted. The parents had to adjust their construct of their son, of themselves as parents and spouses, of their families, and of what they could expect from friends, relatives, and society. Ella and Victoria tried on these new persona when they referred to themselves as the criminal's mother and the mother of the young offender. For Rod and me, the healing process was slow and painful as we tried to find out who this new Tim was. It involved shaping and designing our family in one of two ways: including Tim, or creating a different kind of relationship with him in his new status, which still had to be structured. Each person's role was affected. My role of nurturing, caring, supporting, and providing fun and comfort had changed to one of appearing in court, visiting the hospitals, meeting with workers, participating in family-therapy sessions and parent-support groups, and trying to cope with a society that was attempting to impose a shape on our problem family that it thought was appropriate but that to us seemed inappropriate and even dangerous to our other children. We wondered whether we should allow Tim's space to be filled in, leaving him out, or whether we should try to maintain the old shape with its rough, naked edges. What kind of role would he play in the family now? The process accompanying Tim's relocation was a difficult undertaking for each member of the family; we resisted for a long time, clinging desperately to what was familiar. Ultimately, through our many encounters with representatives of social agencies, support groups, and friends, we were able to create a new, more fluid shape that facilitated further changes as we adjusted to further interactions. Encountering new and challenging experiences that were not part of our original root image caused still further introspection, reflection, interpretation, and shaping, and we modified our image as we encountered Tim's feelings and actions.

The pilot parents-support group set up by Dr Armstrong was the most important agent that helped Rod and me identify what Tim's struggles meant to us and then to see how we needed to revise and change our expectations before we could alter our old actions and disciplinary practices. Further modifications resulted from our interaction not only with Tim and with agencies but also with each other in the family. Our acceptance lay both in redefining the role of the child who did not live up to or fit our earlier expectations and in reshaping new identities and roles as parents. With Tim, the same interpretive process was part of his struggle on the streets. He was struggling and I think beginning to see the meaning of his indigenous heritage and of his being what he called a red apple. We had hoped that his encounters with the native agencies, his long-time worker, Lydia, and the new Street Outreach Service Programs would help him reinterpret his circumstances and determine a new action that would lead him away from the streets. His untimely death robbed him of that opportunity.

A COMMENT ON THE NOTION OF FAILURE

We and all the parents we spoke to struggled with the notion of failure. We recoiled from the word; it confused and angered us. Were we *failures*? It is a word that haunted me throughout the years with Tim and does so even now as I write this book. I cannot dispute the fact that in many ways all these adoptions failed, but my research was not about failure. Rather, it was about the struggle to accept what we were powerless to change.

There were certainly times when we did feel, and were made to feel, like failures. The onus for success of the adoption was put on us as the parents. We were often treated as "duds": we were said to have had unrealistic expectations; we had undertaken something that was clearly doomed from the beginning; we seemed to have inflated opinions of our abilities; we had botched our duties and obligations as parents; we were an embarrassment to ourselves, our families, and society; we were somehow weak and incapable; we were at fault and guilty. Yet were we truly failures? I do not think so, if failure implies a personal responsibility through neglect and wrongdoing. We may have *failed* in our attempts, but, although the adoptions were not successful, we were not, personally, *failures*!

Each parent had struggled to overcome this label and the feelings of discrimination that accompany it. We had raised other children who were good and productive citizens. How many law-abiding children does one need to raise to counteract the blight of a child who was overcome by a combination of circumstances that were not within anyone's control? Good parents stand by and help all their children as they try to overcome the challenges of life, be they physical, emotional, or psychological. We could even say that all the families profiled here were successful, if by that we mean that the families have survived. Today, most of the adopted boys are in contact with their parents. Although the relationship may not be what had been hoped for, it is now a connection that is not filled with as much angst and anger. The families have survived not only the challenge of a troubled child but also the condemnation and shame inflicted by society.

10 Applying What We Learned

The problem of adoption breakdown involves a large number of children, and, for that reason, it would certainly appear to be serious enough to merit increased awareness from all sides and more careful handling of all players. Although only about 2 per cent of ever-married women adopt, the total number of children involved in this process is large. In 1980, in the United States, there were 300,000 children in foster care, and in 1982, 594,000 children were placed for adoption (Bachrach 1986: 250, 254). The National Association of Homes for Children in the United States reported that failed adoptions range from 10 to 33 per cent (up to 178,200 children) (Magid and McKelvey 1987: 149). In 1997 the Adoption Council of Canada announced in a public-awareness campaign that there were 40,000 children in foster care (16,000 in Quebec and 24,000 in the rest of the provinces) and 14,000 were legally available for adoption (Hilborn 1997). In any given year, the total number of children for whom homes are found is 1,250. This figure is less than 10 per cent of the total. None of the provinces or the agencies involved conducts any follow-up inquiries as to how an adoption is working out.

The impact of these large numbers is felt everywhere: disruptions cause an enormous emotional and financial strain on the adoptees, adoptive families, schools, social and judicial agencies, and society in general. Therefore, the minimum response from policy-making bodies and social agencies must include further education for adoptive parents and social workers, further research to help recognize, prevent, and minimize the difficulties adoptees experience, and government commitments to fund a variety of family-support initiatives, including funding for daycare facilities and paid maternity leaves for adoptive parents. Furthermore, governments must ensure that the standard of living for native peoples on reserves improves and that family-support structures are put in place so that native peoples can properly care for their own children. Finally, there must also be a change in society's attitudes towards troubled youths and towards their families: schools, social services, and the courts must show some leadership and responsibility in targeting the circumstances that give rise to delinquency in our children. As well, research into the effects that children with conduct and other psychological disorders have on their parents will increase public awareness to legitimize the struggles of these parents and increase the likelihood of adequate support services. Although these areas of concern may appear unrelated, they are related insofar as the well-being of *all* children and their ability to grow up to be productive and well-adjusted adults are affected.

EDUCATION

Under this category, we can include the education of agency workers, social services, parents, and adoptees. Finding a fit between the needs of the child and the needs of the parents is the responsibility and duty of the adoption agency. This is a task of vital importance, and there is currently increasing awareness that it requires fundamental changes in the adoption system, particularly in terms of the training of professional staff (Avery 1997). Such people must be well trained and have reasonable caseloads. They must recognize the unique problems facing adoptive families and be ready to listen, show empathy, and offer assistance in a spirit of collegiality, recognizing that their job is to work with adoptive families rather than dictate solutions to them. As well, the individual agency worker assigned to a particular case must prepare the child and the parents by disclosing the child's social and medical past and by providing for intensive services, a long-term follow-up program that will anticipate, address, and support the parents in any potential behavioural problems that may arise in the child.

A recent study of the adoptions of children from Romanian orphanages in the late 1980s and early 1990s has revealed stories that are remarkably like our own. Of the estimated 10,000 foreign adoptions of Romanian children, Canadian families claimed 633 of them. Elinor Ames of Simon Fraser University in Burnaby, British Columbia, studied the development of forty-six such children within their adoptive families (Hilborn 1997). She recommends that these Romanian adoptions be regarded as special-needs adoptions because of the extra commitment required of the parents' time and energy. Ames states that each month a child spends in an orphanage contributes to lower intellectual ability and increased potential for behavioural problems. The people arranging these adoptions must be fully aware, and must make the parents fully aware, of the greater commitment that will be involved. She also recommends that there be pre-adoption preparation, specialized pre-school programs with parent participation, and extra stimulation and guidance for the child in the home, as well as post-adoption support to promote parent-child attachment and to teach good social behaviour and constructive ways of dealing with behaviour problems (for example, attention-demanding behaviour, short attention span, hyperactivity, and indiscriminate friendliness).

Proper training would also give the worker the necessary discernment as to whether a child, in particular circumstances, should or should not be taken from his or her birth parents. Thorough investigation, participation of all parties, and sound judgment will determine whether a child's life is in jeopardy if he or she is *left* with birth parents or whether that child's best interests are served if he or she is *removed* from birth parents and put up for adoption. If discretion is exercised in all the cases that come before the agency and if the agency is organized and efficient, its workers educated, available, and empathetic to the needs of the whole family, the kinds of bureaucratic bungling and delays that can injure a child permanently will be minimized.

DISCLOSURE

We knew little about Tim when we brought him home. The brief written assessment we had and the introductory videotape we viewed about this little boy did not tell us much. We did not receive (nor would we have received even if we had asked) an accurate picture of Tim's abilities, potential, or limitations. A striking and concrete example of this, already alluded to: we were told that Tim had good teeth, but our first visit to the dentist resulted in six teeth requiring caps because they were in such bad state. If it was known then what an important role heredity and pre- and post-natal care play in the later development of adoptees, we were not privy to the information when we adopted. Protecting the identity of the adoptee and the birth parents was thought to be more important:

Parents have an undeniable right to a full disclosure of the medical history of the child they want to adopt and of his or her birth mother during the pregancy, and they are now demanding recognition of this right from governments and child-welfare agencies (Avery 1997). If adoptive parents are prepared to invest time, energy, and love in raising a child, they need to have information about any potential problem so that they can adjust their expectations for the adopted child. The effects of the birth mother's drug or alcohol abuse and/or of any physical or sexual abuse of the child in the early years can induce patterns of behaviour in the child that are uncontrollable and dangerous.

Although care and love can mitigate some of the negative effects of the child's early history, love in itself is not enough. Parents need to know this. Beyond love and commitment, parents who adopt traumatized children with behavioural and emotional problems need ways to understand what these problems are, how they might manifest themselves over the next fifteen to twenty years, and what can be done about them. For example, children who have been removed from their biological homes because of parental abuse and neglect have difficulty bonding with the adoptive parents and in forming any other meaningful attachments. These children lack confidence that their adoptive parents will be available and responsive, helpful in meeting their needs, and a comfort to them in adverse or frightening situations. Children who suffer from an inability to bond with any adult may be diagnosed officially as having some other treatable handicap, but when the child becomes an adolescent, he or she will begin to manifest uncontrollable behaviour that causes turmoil and grief all around. The silence about these kinds of potential difficulties in the adopted child needs to be broken so that parents can be apprized of and prepared for potential crises. The adoption agency has a moral obligation to disclose the hidden baggage the child is bringing into the new family. One parent whom we interviewed reported receiving only one page of information from a thick file, and there was no mention of the fact that the birth mother was a heroin addict at the time she gave birth.

While agency workers need to be well trained, they must also ensure that adoptive parents undergo preparatory training. For instance, running away to another family is common among adoptees. What happens between birth and age three is repeated in adolescence, and in a way they are just changing families again. It upsets adoptive parents greatly if they are not prepared for this kind of behaviour (Pavao, cited in Fishman 1992: 49). With support services and education for the parents and professionals, these common adoption problems can be effectively handled. If agencies and parents work together from the beginning of the adoption process, they will establish a good consultative relationship that will enable parents to access and utilize the support services if and when the need arises. Workers will more confidently and quickly offer the most appropriate service if the agency had already developed a relationship with the parents when things were going well. This practice would not only serve as a *preventive* measure, it would also be an effective intervention strategy. Agencies would feel an ongoing sense of responsibility.

Society's attitude towards adoptions has changed dramatically over the years. After the Industrial Revolution, adoption was viewed as a solution for the needs of homeless children. After 1870, the prevailing principle was a child for every home, where the child who was chosen was the one who best suited the parents; he or she was expected to assume the identity of the adoptive family and to ignore his or her own. The child was usually selected by the parents, and there was little or no investigation or preparation of the adoptive parents. Much later, after the Second World War, when requests for adoptable children exceeded the number of infants available for adoption, the thrust was more towards a home for every child, where the child's needs would be considered but where the adoptive parents were to be held accountable for any ensuing problem. When parents are held accountable, then we can also say that a factor in the adoption breakdown was their unrealistic expectations. Yet this is the same as recognizing that they were ill-prepared to face the challenge, and the fact that they were ill-prepared implies that someone did not tell them what they needed to know. The Brooks family, for example, felt that if they spoke about their concerns, the agency would think that they were not good parents and would look for another placement for Jon. When the Roethlers were nearly at their wits' end with their children's bad behaviour, they were afraid that if they contacted the agency or even if they tried to return the children, the children would be split up and placed in separate homes. These parents felt that contacting the agency with questions might not be in their best interests or those of their children.

Today, there seems to be a more balanced outlook. The contributions and limitations of both the parents and the children are recognized in the challenging adoption process (Avery 1990). If we want to minimize the heartache and stress that all parties suffer through adoption breakdown, more investigation and disclosure is crucial and all interested parties must be heard. The trend is currently towards a more open adoption process. The latter includes complete and honest disclosure of all relevant history, as well as the adoptee's right to access information about the birth parents; in some cases, the birth parent(s) can maintain limited contact with the adoptee. Parents who adopt such children need to be armed with knowledge, experts say. They must know how to read a child's cry for commitment no matter what. The head of an adoption agency in Pennsylvania, Barbara Tremitiere, maintains that "openness with children and adoptive parents is crucial to success." Parents who go through parent-preparation courses learn about dealing with anger and jealousy and about their temptation to hit a child, because, as Tremitiere says, "we are *all* potential child abusers under enough stress (Adams 1990: C1). Some of Ontario's Children's Aid Society branches hold mandatory parent-training sessions that are about as intensive as the nine-week sessions run by Tremitiere at her agency.

FOLLOW-UP

Follow-up studies of adoptions were not done in the past. When new adoptive parents turned to officials for help and support, little was available. With a pall of privacy and non-disclosure hanging over the process, formal follow-up on the success or failure of the adoption was impossible. It was assumed that the adoptee would assimilate into the adoptive family and that he or she and the parents would all live happily ever after. Now there is increasing recognition that follow-up services may be needed long after the legal process of adoption has been completed (Avery 1997).

Adoptions require *dynamic* not *static* assessments. Assessments of the needs of the adoptee and of the adoptive family should continue long after the papers have been signed. Regular and continuous communication will provide for appropriate use of resources when they are required. Static measures in a single assessment cannot be final or comprehensive indicators of ability, personality, or probability of success. An assessment is a complex process, and more studies on the challenges of adoption are necessary before social agencies can help parents through the adoption experience. One or two follow-up home visits do not mean that everything is fine. After the adoption papers are signed and the adoption is legal, it cannot be assumed by the agency that the adoptive family will thrive. Ongoing and long-term support services need to be available in one form or another so early intervention can minimize the difficulties and maximize the assistance.

In past years, the success of adoptions and the ability of the child to fit happily into the family depended mainly on luck. Today, post-adoptive services are recognized throughout the adoption field in North America as crucial to the success of adoption. Yet, in Ontario, owing to lack of funding, only two or three of the fifty-four branches of the Children's Aid Society offer these services (Adams 1990: c1). In December 1996, the Society reported that reductions in funding and resulting cutbacks in employees made it highly unlikely that such services are or will be widely available any time soon. With a budget reduced to pre-1990 levels, over 545 full-time equivalent positions (3,675 full-time equivalent positions in 1996) have been lost since 1991, in spite of the fact that the number of children requiring care has increased. In 1992, 47,000 reports of maltreatment of children were investigated. Annually, 52,000 families contact the Children's Aid Society, but they receive less than one hour of brief service. In 1995, 87,000 families with 150,000 children and youth received counselling and support services from the Society. The agency provided substitute care for 20,000 children in 1995. It reports that more children and families are coming to the attention of child-welfare authorities as a result of unemployment, decreased social assistance, fewer community services, and family stress, yet "programs aimed at supporting youth during their transition to adulthood have been reduced by government cutbacks" (Ontario Association of Children's Aid Societies, December 1996). In 1997 the Ontario Association of Children's Aid Societies reported that support services for adoption cases were available but that each office would have to be contacted to see exactly what kinds of services were being offered.

Barbara Tremitiere's agency in Pennsylvania has few adoption disruptions. To adoptive families in crisis, she offers lifetime support through therapy, respite care, a support group, and residential treatment; all these services can come into play to keep an adoption placement together (Adams 1990: C2). These services are what Richard Barth and Marianne Berry refer to as "preservation help" (1988). This ongoing support while the child is growing up could take the form of family activities and resource workers. There should be parenting courses available and opportunities to meet and talk with other adoptive parents. If parents adopt children of native ancestry, they need to be educated in native history and culture.

The message of the importance of funding preparatory courses for families and follow-up programs is beginning to be heard, but whether or not Canadian governments are going to respond is still unclear. A few families who have adopted cross-culturally have formed groups to share information and stories and educate and support each other. The participants in my interviews hope that this book will also have a positive impact on society's attitude towards the families of troubled youth. They asked me to contact the Children's Aid Society and to send the agency a summary of my findings so that a repetition of the pain they have suffered can be prevented.

David Brodzinsky and Marshall Schechter (1990) strongly advocate post-placement services (290). These services would be offered between the placement of the child and the legalization of the adoption. The services would include remedial work, crisis intervention, and ongoing supportive services. This adjustment period was one that was especially critical for the Roethler family, since they adopted three children all at once. Their adoption worker suggested that the Roethlers extend this service as long as possible so that all the agency's services could be used to their fullest extent. For the other adoptive families, where the adjustment of the adopted child was perceived as going well, the post-placement visits were viewed as a formality. In our case, until Tim was eleven, his Dennis-the-Menace behaviour was thought to fall within the broad range of what was considered normal. I myself remember thinking how wonderful and well adjusted our family was. It was only when Tim entered puberty that his destructive behaviour propelled all of us into crisis.

Brodzinsky and Schechter also strongly advocate that support services be available for adoptive families well after the final adoption papers are signed. To my knowledge, these were not formally available to any of the parents in our study. Brodzinsky and Schechter suggest that, although some children will need only occasional counselling, some children and their families will require ongoing therapy (ibid.: 291). Of course, whether or not these services are utilized rests with the family and with the adoptee. If these services were offered as an *integral* part of the entire adoption process, then parents would know of their availability and would not hesitate or be embarrassed about using them. And these services should be available until the adoptee is an adult. With this sort of preparation, agency workers would be better able to understand parents' apprehension and doubts about their parenting abilities and would be more effective in helping the parents. As I look back now, if these services had been available unequivocally, without the agency trying to assess our *degree* of need, we would have benefited enormously throughout our years in Alberta, when Tim was not displaying any of the normal desires for affection. I am confident, too, that ongoing services would have enabled everyone in our family to connect in a positive way with Tim's native culture, to learn his native language, and participate in camps and outings. Gatherings with other adoptive families would have provided role models and connections for each member of our family. Of course, by the time Tim turned twelve, the problems had escalated so dramatically that the crisis our family was in would have almost been beyond the reach of these supportive programs. Still, if *any* support and therapy had been available for us and for Tim before he entered the court system and left home – even temporary respite care as he began the frightening period of adolescence and identity formation – I believe that the trauma would have been minimized, he might not have broken the law, and the adoption may not have ruptured.

The measures offered by social agencies must be understood as being preventive and cost-saving in the long run. If a family is supported in its efforts to avoid potential difficulties with their adopted child, substantial emotional effort, time, and money can be saved by health-care and legal services farther down the line. With early detection and treatment, the hospitalization, incarceration, and fatality rate among these adopted children would decrease in the same way regular medical check-ups and screenings help us detect and treat many potentially dangerous medical conditions.

RECOGNIZING NATIVE IDENTITY

In the cases described here, the additional complicating factor was the children's visible difference in appearance, compared to the rest of the members of their families, and their Indian ancestry. The growth and development of the child's self-esteem through the bonding process with the new family, or at least with one significant person, was affected. For the adopted native child, there needs to be a recognition by the parties involved in the adoption process of the difficulties of being a native child in a white family. Support services must be available to both the child and the family, and this help must be available *before* he or she breaks the law, not after, as was the case with Tim.

Since 1970, there has been an increase in media attention devoted to the devastating difficulties experienced by many native adoptees in North America. These adopted adults are currently recounting the frustrations, abuse, and pain that they suffered, and are continuing to suffer, because of the government's misguided plan to use native children as a means of facilitating the desired assimilation of native peoples. It should be noted that not all native-white adoptions rupture, but the majority do. In his eight-year study, Christopher Bagley found that among the 47 adoptions he followed in Calgary in 1993, 60 per cent of them had broken down. This figure is much higher than with other transracial adoptions, where he found only 20 per cent had had serious problems or had failed (Bagley 1993). More recent statistics indicate that 95 per cent of native adoptions fail (*To Return: The John Walkus Story* 2000, Fournier and Crey 1997).

When native children who have come from troubled backgrounds and who have been the victims or pre- and post-natal abuse are available for adoption, they should be considered special-needs children. There is certainly a great deal of evidence in this book to support this view. The term "special needs" captures all facets of what is involved in adopting an older native child with a troubled history: it implies proper investigation, recognition of potential problems, and preparation of the parents and the child. But, in addition to the child's early history, the other good reason to consider the status of native children as special-needs is that these children will have to grow up trying to reconcile their visible ethnic identity with the surrounding white society. Indeed, to say that native children who are available for adoption into white homes have *extra-special* needs would not be an exaggeration. For the parents I interviewed, adopting a native child was not seen by them as requiring any special considerations. Some parents had refused to adopt children with learning disabilities or severe physical handicaps and yet had welcomed (for the most part) native children. The parents thought that they knew better, despite the undercurrent of derogatory notions about Indians. The parents, after all, did not hold such notions nor did they believe that these notions should even be taken into account when making their decision to give a disadvantaged native child a home. Being of native ancestry per se was simply not an issue.

Yet today we know that native ancestry is certainly a key issue when such a child is adopted. To designate the native child in an adoption as a special-needs child is to appreciate *all* the facets of the child's background – not only his or her own social, medical, and psychological background but also the cultural, ideological, and historical background of the birth family. This designation implies, too, that the adoptive parents are undertaking a great responsibility towards that child.

SUPPORT GROUPS

Support groups as a source of help for the adopted child and for the parents were highly recommended by those parents who had been part of them. These groups helped the parents regain their confidence and a positive self-image. Especially important was the sharing of emotional experiences in a safe and non-judgmental setting and with other adoptive parents of troubled youth. What makes these groups so vital is the commonality of experience; the parents do not want someone who does not know their situation telling them what to do or not to do. As Glaser says, when speaking of researchers analysing their qualitative data, "what a man in the know does not want is to be told what he already knows. What he wants is to be told how to handle what he knows with some increasing control and understanding of his area of action" (cited in Merriam 1988: 146). The parents were able to discuss anything and to say exactly what they wanted to say. As with all support groups, the intimacy of being in the company of those who had suffered in the same way was felt to be paramount in moving the parents from one emotional stage to another; the group members could sensitively provide the encouragement each of them needed.

The adoptee must also have a venue in which he or she can find compassion, support, encouragement, and information. What the parents found was that specialists and other professionals were unable to reach the adopted children. So, when all avenues of help had been exhausted, the adoptee often turned to more familiar alternatives: new persona, his own friends, the street. Victoria felt that no one was able to help Vincent. There did not seem to be anyone available or capable of helping him: "The fact that I knew that I couldn't do anything about it, absolutely nothing, and the fact that I also knew that professionals couldn't either ... And the choice he made was to go back out on the street, you know, when he had a perfectly safe home." But, then as now, a child has the right to refuse treatment or a placement that might be of benefit. We had this difficulty with Tim, because he often refused help, and this was frustrating for us and for the social workers. Tim was always a great lover of the outdoors and a keen observer of nature. We believed that he would be safer, more stable, in a rural, structured setting. But because of his fire-setting history, and later when he was a year or two older and had become attracted to the risky life on the streets of downtown Toronto, the rural setting was not deemed appropriate by the agencies or by Tim. The Roethlers' son was inadvertently sent to the wrong jail, but he settled in and seemed to be benefiting from the setting. About half-way through his sentence, he was moved. The officials made no attempt to recognize this facility as beneficial to Jimmy, and, rather than make use of this rehabilitative opportunity, they moved him to another institution where he failed to thrive.

A few support groups specifically geared to native children and their non-native adoptive and foster parents have sprung up in several cities. Nineteen years ago, in Manitoba, Glenda and Jack Armstrong, Vi and Tom Holens, Geraldine Bjorson and Norm Velnes, with their adopted children of native ancestry, started Project Opikihiwawin to expose their families to the positive aspects of being native. According to literature about the project, the children involved have the opportunity to interact with traditional elders, teachers, and role models and to participate in cultural ceremonies and events. As a result, these children acquire far better self-esteem than adoptees who seek these contacts as adults. The project works with approximately one hundred families annually and provides numerous opportunities for families to participate in cultural events. The twelve young adults who have grown up with Project Opikihiwawin are reported to have a strong self-image and a deep respect for and acceptance of the aboriginal community of which they are a part. Some of the adopted young adults may have experienced a certain degree of difficulty or challenge because of other factors, such as attachment issues, fetal-alcohol syndrome or effect, or learning disabilities; however, their self-identity and self-esteem as natives remains strong and positive.

In Ontario alone in 1996, there were thirty-two support groups for adoptive parents, some of them independent and others working with local branches of the Children's Aid Society. But most of these services are for the short term, and they are made available only when the family is judged to be in crisis. Even then, help is not immediate; names are first put on a waiting list. Furthermore, any long-term support, where available, is almost always on a fee-for-service basis. Virtually no preventive services are available. When Tim was eleven and just beginning to exhibit disturbing behaviour, the numerous agencies I phoned were not forthcoming with help. I even walked into some agencies and literally begged for some kind of intervention on their part. Only in one agency was I asked to sit down and given a tissue for my tears. And even there, as I filled out yet another form requesting all sorts of irrelevant information, no one took the time to enquire as to the nature of our troubles. No one listened, no one questioned me. I was simply told that they were too busy and that I could expect to be phoned to set up an appointment in a few weeks.

In some parts of the country, the Canadian legal system has made some allowance for the use of traditional healing circles for offenders and there has been increased support for visits in correctional facilities by elders and the use of sweat lodges and other traditional methods for troubled youths of native ancestry to come to terms with themselves and their behaviour. Such appreciation by authorities of the importance of these traditional means of "healing" is an encouraging and positive sign that the value of aboriginal culture is being recognized generally and that some aspects of it could have application *beyond* the legal system into other areas of life – *before* the legal system has to come into play.

One encouraging sign is the advent of adoption-related magazines. In the United States, *Adoptive Families* is published by Adoptive Families of America, a national, non-profit adoptive-parent-support organization. Through first-hand stories describing – and offering suggestions for – the difficulties often encountered by adoptive families, this magazine provides another type of forum for the exchange of supportive ideas for adoptive families and their children. In Canada there are now two adoption-related magazines being published: *Adoption Helper* (Robin Hilburn, editor) and *Post-adoption Helper* (Jennifer Smart, editor). The Internet also offers many websites to adoptive parents.

RESEARCH

While there is a general consensus that heredity and early environment are important factors in the adopted child's ability to adjust to his or her new home, new studies suggest that the extent to which an individual adjusts successfully to changing circumstances is an enormously complicated issue that involves a host of factors, including parenting styles, inborn temperament, cultural mores, the critical role of the father, and the influence of same-sex and opposite-sex friends, siblings, and other non-parental figures (Karen 1990). Much more research is needed on this issue before firm conclusions can be reached. What is clear already, however, is that the old idea that parents and family are the key determinants of personality and behaviour no longer commands wide acceptance. For a long time, the mother as prime caregiver was often the target for whatever difficulties her children manifested, and the explanation for shortcomings or defects in parenting abilities was often seen as a result of traumas in the parents' childhoods. Few now subscribe to such ideas.

There is also growing recognition that it would be instructive to focus on the *effect of children on parents*, natural and adoptive. Understanding the parents' feelings of fear, anger, despair, and powerlessness tells us about the effects children have on their parents and the parents' image of themselves and of what constitutes a successful family. Researchers are just beginning to investigate the stress that children who are out of control bring to their families. In *The Effect of Children on Parents* (1992), Anne-Marie Ambert examines how parental health, employment, financial concerns, marital and familial relations, human interaction, community, personality, attitudes, values and beliefs, goals, and feelings of control over life are affected by difficult children. She is a strong advocate of the kind of research I have undertaken in this study:

Family reconstruction after a delinquent child has been removed or has left home is a topic which has not been adequately researched ... Researchers might want to explore what changes occur in a family after a delinquent is removed from the family. Admittedly, the stigma remains and damage control can therefore be only partial. What effect does the agency have on the parents? What feelings do these agencies arouse in parents? What demands do they make? Do these agencies help parents or do they burden them (with guilt, blame, unnecessary advice and requests)?

...

Socialization ... has been accomplished [but we have failed] to consider how children socialize their parents. Similarly, we have generally failed to inquire into the effect of children on parents. This gap in the general literature is reflected in the field of delinquency and is also magnified therein because the societal costs of delinquency are calculated from the costs that the delinquent incurs to the social system but only rarely to the familial system, and even more rarely, if at all, to parents (108–9).

So, instead of asking, "What kind of family produces delinquents?" Ambert says it is far more important to ask, "What kind of familial environments do delinquents produce?" (ibid.: 91). Katharine Davis Fishman echoes this concern: "It's important to see the direction of the effect: it's not the parents producing [the stressful environment]" (1992: 50). Because adolescents, as well as those who fall under the Young Offenders Act, often get away with the majority of their offences, parents are left to cope with their delinquent children on their own. This is what happened to the Verdans, when a judge appointed them to be their son Gerald's probation officers.

The family-systems approach, which understands delinquency in terms of the current family context and thus focuses on the entire family rather than on the person behaving deviantly, is coming under challenge. Stanton Samenow suggests that, in this therapeutic approach, where "the expectation is that changing the current patterns of behavior among family members will alter the behavior of the one member who is behaving deviantly," cause is being confused with effect (1989: 173). He adds: "Psychological maladjustment of the family system does not *cause* a child to be antisocial. In fact, it is the child's antisocial behavior that, in many cases, has disrupted a harmoniously operating family. In families where severe problems existed independently of the youngster's antisocial behavior, the antisocial behavior was not caused by those difficulties, but it did serve to intensify them" (ibid.: 174).

No one knows what makes one child in the family develop into an anti-social child. Harvey Armstrong states that "there are some children [who] exhibit antisocial behavior from a very early age and it gradually gets worse. Others are perfect until they hit adolescence when they suddenly veer dangerously out of control. Nothing the parents try to do works ... The [anti-social] child gradually gains all the power in the house and the parents are left helpless, depressed, anxious victims" (cited in Carey 1989: A1). He continues: "[These parents] are wonderful people, highly motivated, they loved their kids very much, had never had a failure. Now they were at each other's throats and they felt totally helpless ... We knew these parents were awfully depressed ... Their whole life was centred around the terrible tragedy this kid was causing. It was a barrier between them and their friends, employers and extended family ... The first process they had to go through was mourning the death of the child they had hoped for, often since before conception" (cited in ibid.: A22). Research especially needs to be done on the negative effects that out-of-control kids produce on the mother, who has always been seen as primary caregiver and thus thought to be the party responsible when things go awry.

There are other areas where more research is required, and they have been touched on in Armstrong's statement: the effects of guilt, especially that felt by the mothers, and grief. Because I struggled with guilt and Rod seemed quite clear about the fact that he had not, I was sensitive to this particular effect and when it emerged a number of times in the interviews. This is an area of much heartache and embarrassment and a central theme in the loss of a troubled child. The theme of grief has recently emerged in the literature. Most of the literature refers to the grief the adoptees experience, but parents' experience of grief is also real. In all the research done for this book, the only references I found to the grieving of adoptive parents was in the articles written about Parents for Youth. According to Armstrong, "the groups generally tend to do an enormous amount of mourning. They mourn the loss of the idealized child and must learn to accept that the child they had so many hopes and dreams for is a very troubled, abusive person that is in need of help" (cited in Petruccelli 1993: 21).

This kind of grief affects not just the adoptive parents of children who are out-of-control. Parents who have biological children with special emotional problems, such as attention-deficit disorder, conduct disorders, manic-depressive disorders, schizophrenia, and so on experience the same emotional upheaval and need a similar kind of help. Whether the children inherit the problem or whether it was as a result of a separation trauma because of illness, divorce, or death, the children are placed in a position similar to that of adopted children. And their parents, like adoptive parents, are faced with a situation where the child acts out. The result is that these parents, too, are confused, feel blamed, and grieve the loss of the idealized child.

More research also needs to be done on the effects of adopting older children. Older children have often been abused and neglected before they are apprehended and available for adoption. Parents who adopt older children with traumatic histories are blamed – and may blame themselves – unjustly for the children's problems and for the loss the adoption breakdown creates. In order to save the children *and* their families, expert diagnosis, extensive treatment, and extraordinary service based on informed judgment is needed, both before *and* after the adoption.

I would like to see more research conducted by men and women working as a team. Before 1989, most research was conducted by men, but a man-woman team can present a more complete picture of the phenomena I have discussed. Two examples of such teams are James Rosenthal et al. (1988) and Marianne Berry and Richard

Barth (1988; 1990). In the same way that Rod's presence in the interviews helped to draw out the fathers' perspective, when women are involved in this kind of research, a more balanced and holistic picture emerges about the details of the parents' experience in adoption breakdown. In the recent literature, I do not detect any of the mother-blaming that seemed so endemic to the earlier studies. These changes are positive.

In addition to the advances mentioned above, I would like to see further research in the following areas: the particular insight and interest teachers have in improving the lives of those around them (four of the six couples interviewed here had at least one teacher); the experiences of parents who have separated as a result of the adoption difficulties; the experiences of the adopted child's siblings with the adoption difficulties; and the nature of the adoptees' struggle and how they feel about their adoption experience. Research of this kind would be useful in furthering our understanding of all areas of the adoption experience. In order for its findings to be readily available to the adoptive parents and social agencies, they would have to be published, at least in part, in a popular format.

FACILITATING THE ADOPTION
OF NATIVE CHILDREN

It seems that both the adopted native child and the adoptive parents were victims of an ill-conceived government policy of assimilation. I still struggle with what I see as our naive participation in this plan.

The obscene marketing of native children has stopped. In the 1960s and 1970s, these children were marketed in local newspapers and on television, but it was done in a way that did not draw attention to the government policy of assimilation: for the parents, the thought was of "providing a loving home for one single disadvantaged child" (Wharf 1993; Johnson 1983). But the greatest wrong committed was perhaps not the advertising itself but the deception that adopting an older native child was no different from adopting a healthy newborn. The parents were not alerted to the potential difficulties: there was no frank discussion of expectations, no disclosure of the child's early experiences, no follow-up counselling, and no support structure to provide help for the parents as the child was growing up.

Either transracial adoptions should be discouraged outright – which few would support – or the parents involved should be fully provided with much more education, training, and support at all stages of the adoption procedure. There are thousands of foreign children being adopted in Canada every year. Surely, foreign adoptions, or transracial adoptions, are a fact of life today, and there are unquestionably many advantages and benefits for all parties concerned. But there must be far more recognition of the impact of cultural considerations on the formation of the child's identity and of the effects of any discrimination the child may encounter (Crumbley 1999; Reitz and Watson 1992; Wegar 1997). Any consideration of ethnic heritage was definitely understated during the 1970s when we adopted; currently, it has become a prominent issue, as ethnic minorities, women, and handicapped persons are becoming more vocal about having their rights and needs addressed.

Few of the adoptive parents I interviewed recognized the tremendous challenges that adopting a native child would present. Yet, although committed to take on and love a child, these parents were not able, for one reason or another, to provide the necessary cultural identity for the child or to make effective contact with local native people and cultural centres, although some tried. In some cases, misinformation was given. One of the participants in this study found out only recently that their adopted child was not Cree but Dakota; that his father had *not* given up the child, as indicated on the adoption forms; and that his mother alone had signed the papers giving the child up for adoption. These are important factors in establishing an adopted child's sense of identity. Provision for cultural education, and for participation in and exposure to a native community (if not the child's own community of origin), should be made for the adoptive parents and their native children by government agencies and by native groups.

There is no guarantee that the adopted native child will look up his biological parents or that, once located, meeting with these people will be wonderful. In many cases, reunions of adoptees and birth parents have been painful. However, such reunions do give the adoptee a clearer picture of his or her ancestry and roots, while also dispelling the myths, both good and bad, surrounding the adoption process and banishing the ghosts that sometimes hover over it. It is easier to resolve feelings of abandonment and rejection or of anger and grief when the true facts are available and when individuals originally associated with the child's early years can explain what happened. Whether or not the child continues the relationship is then entirely up to that child. In those situations where the child decides not to look up his or her birth parents, the fact that doing so is possible, that information is not being withheld, can help the child develop (or increase) a sense of self and of worth, as a person with a history, just like everyone else ("An Indian and a Québécoise Search for Roots").

A few parents who have adopted native children have been disappointed by the stance taken by some native associations. In 1983 the Ontario Native Women's Association, the Ontario Federation of Indian Friendship Centres, and the Ontario Metis and Non-Status Indian Association made a presentation to the provincial minister of community and social services outlining their concerns with the practice of allowing their children to be adopted by non-native families:

The imposition of "Euro-Canadian" middle class value systems on the people of very different cultural and social background, has led to the proactive removal of large numbers of Native children from their natural extended families and communities, the placement of them in non-native foster homes and/or their adoption by non-native people. This practice has not been attended with any high degree of success in terms of the happiness and well-being of the children. Many of them have suffered severe emotional and psychological stress, resulting in alienation and difficulties in social adjustment.

This removal of Native children from their natural community not only places the child under severe mental and emotional stress, with long-term, frequently permanent, damage to the individual, but also represents a real tangible loss to the Native community of Canada in general. It represents a constant draining away of the membership of the Native communal society and it represents a threat to the survival of the Aboriginal peoples in the world ...

Even under the best of conditions, Native children do not, generally speaking, become successfully "integrated" or "acculturated" or "adjusted" within the dominant societal framework, as a result of being placed in non-Native settings, either family or institution.

The kindest and best intended of "white" foster parents or adoptive parents find themselves at a loss to explain the high incidence of unhappiness, rebellion and so-called "anti-social" behavior exhibited by their Native-born children.

In simple words – it doesn't work ...

A major reason for this is that the Native child is a product of an ancient, deeply rooted North American culture, which is in almost every respect significantly at variance with the present Euro-Canadian cultural patterning.

There is a general assumption within the Canadian society at large, and reflected in the policies and programs of the provincial child welfare systems, that a child removed from its parental home because of abuse or neglect, and placed in a "good" nuclear family setting, either for foster care or adoption, will be, or soon become, happier, "better off," in every way.

It is confidently expected, that given kind care and a "nice" home, social stimulus, a "good education," etc. etc., that child will grow up to be a useful, happy well-adjusted citizen ...

Economic disadvantage, educational difficulties, poor housing, social maladjustment, alcohol and drug abuse, family breakdown, violence, conflict with the justice system, are only too prevalent in the life of Native people – individuals and communities.

There is now a sufficient body of evidence to show that this course of action actually aggravates, perpetuates, and institutionalizes the negative situations already existing.

The system continually creates new generations of dis-affected, dis-oriented, mal-adjusted individuals with a poor self-image, no strong sense of personal identity, lack of a sense of self-worth, dignity, or pride.

The system becomes a "set-up" for failure, a prescription for defeat. And a tragic loss to the Native community, and to the Canadian society at large (Ontario Native Women's Association ...1983: 17-21).

Accusations of genocide and racism have come to rest on the shoulders of adoptive parents and have filled them with feelings of guilt and of isolation. Although the children they adopted were those apparently unwanted by anyone else, the parents learned that the very native groups they thought would have supported them in their efforts were now against them. The opposition is aimed at the adoptions the parents had once been encouraged to believe were a benefit to everyone concerned. Not only have the parents' lives been thrown into chaos by the difficulties of the adoption, they have also had to face the charge that they were instruments in a government plan to destroy native culture.

Part of the plan was also assumed to include *taking away the right* of Indian bands to care for their own children. During the 1970s and 1980s across Canada, aboriginal people began a mammoth effort to reclaim their children and to take charge of their distressed native families. One successful measure – undertaken, for example, by the Spallumcheen band in British Columbia – has been for the native community to share the care and responsibility for their children and to disallow the adoption of their children by white families (Johnson 1983; Wharf 1993). Yet there are still many adopted children and adoptive parents who are struggling with the effects of the former practice. While every effort should be made to support these families in their efforts with their adopted native children, bands should also be supported, financially and publicly, in their efforts to provide care for all their children and to keep them within their own communities.

Although the evidence is strong that the mental health of native adoptees who were removed from their communities is not as good as that of their siblings who remained (Sarick 1994: A4), there is a great need to understand the problems that challenge so many young Canadian natives on reserves today. Governments are being pressured to do something about the devastating number of native suicides, a problem the government itself helped to create. The Royal Commission on Aboriginal Peoples states: "Within these documents there was a long march of compelling evidence that aboriginal people have been dying by their own hands much too often and for much too long ...[yet] aboriginal suicide has never become a high priority issue" (cited in Canadian Press 1995: A9). Natives kill themselves at about three times the rate of non-natives, but for native youth, that figure rises to six times, the report says. The reasons are a lethal potion of problems, including confusion about identity, poverty, alcohol and drug abuse, and family violence. It seems clear that, until native peoples are given more autonomy over their own lives and more resources with which to put into action their own policies concerning their young people, natives as a whole will continue to suffer (Fournier and Crey 1997).

CHANGES IN SOCIETY'S ATTITUDES

The changes that I have suggested would be necessary to facilitate future select adoptions of native children, and of other transracial adoptions, and that would offer support to past adoptions are really part of a larger picture. Only when society starts to take notice of the large numbers of children living on the streets, the epidemic of teenage pregnancies, the difficulties single parents encounter in raising their children, and the need for pre- and post-natal (or pre- and post-adoptive) leaves from the workplace and for regulated and affordable daycare will the foundation be there for the reforms I have proposed. Many parents are caught in a vicious cycle of under-unemployment, poverty, welfare, low-paying jobs, unaffordable daycare, and emotional separation from their children, and the real victims of these difficulties are the children. These circumstances then spawn further hardships, which the children are unable to transcend.

Society also no longer sets a predictable set of behavioural expectations for parents and for children:

Society lacks this kind of cohesive structure. Behavioural expectations are incredibly diverse, the values within the home are not supported by the community at large, and the feedback systems to parents are not very clear. The whole issue of society's refusal to set and enforce limits and boundaries has devalued parenting and disempowered parents. Legislation such as the Young Offenders Act does not have stiff enough penalties to deter juveniles. Consequently, parental attempts at discipline are lost on children who have learned to protect their rights by manipulating the system against their parents (Petruccelli 1993: 24).

Furthermore, society seems to have an elitist attitude and low tolerance for differences in people and for broken and troubled families. The parents profiled here did not find any validation for their struggle, and few in the social-service and judicial system recognized or respected the effort and investment the parents had made and were continuing to make with their troubled children. The blaming, isolation, misunderstanding, and loneliness adoptive parents and families experience must stop. These parents should be given the message that their difficulties are not their fault and that there is at least some support for them as they struggle and try to alleviate the pain, helplessness, and powerlessness. The parents do not need people telling them what to do, but rather they and their children need to be supported, in a general sense, by positive, society-wide attitudes and, in a more specific sense, with help as they and their children work through feelings of anger, sorrow, rejection, and identity confusion. Adoptive parents also realize that there are difficulties within the social-services system:

too few workers, too many caseloads, inadequate funding, time constraints, turnover of staff, and so on; however, there also needs to be changes in attitude. For this, education must take place.

Recently, street workers have changed the way they view the many deaths of young native people who live on the streets of Toronto. What were formerly called freak accidents are now viewed as a form of passive suicide. In 1992, the year Tim died, there were five similar deaths, and two years later, his girlfriend fell to her death from an apartment balcony. These young adults die from falls, car accidents, drug overdoses, reckless exposure to HIV infection, and other forms of suicidal behaviour and lifestyle. Tim had said many times that he was going to die young. He would say, "I'm not gonna live to be old, maybe twenty-five." It seems that he was on a deliberate downhill slide, and if he had not died when he did, he may have fulfilled his prophecy a few months later.

There are other areas in which society's attitude must change with regard to native people. These general changes would also set a basis, a context, in which other, more specific changes could be implemented. Only when native demands regarding aboriginal rights, land title, and financial compensation for past injustices become a political cause for the larger society will the federal government be pressed into acknowledging the deplorable conditions in which this country's aboriginal peoples have been languishing. As of January 1998, the federal government has offered an official apology to First Nations peoples for the way they have been brutally treated in the residential-school system, a system that was only a slightly veiled attempt at cultural genocide. This is a start. The report by Royal Commission on Aboriginal People makes 440 recommendations and proposes a twenty-year, $30-billion spending program aimed at addressing the high rates of poverty, family breakdown, suicide, and substance abuse that have plagued aboriginal populations for generations (DeMont 1998: 33). This report is now a few years old; it needs to be acted upon, and sooner rather than later.

Meanwhile, the oppression of parents with adopted native children, as well as those with special-needs children and those involved in other cross-cultural adoptions, continues. The only couple whom I contacted and who did not participate in this process was having too difficult a time. They were the parents of two adopted children who were experiencing severe problems and who had left home. The father, who had been under psychiatric care, had managed to reconnect with one of the children and was hoping to re-establish their relationship. However, at the time of my phone call, the son had not contacted his father. As a result, the father became distraught, took a leave-of-absence from his workplace, and left earlier than expected on his holiday. This situation, and the fact that participants for this study were relatively easy to find, clearly indicates that there are many other parents who are still floundering, as we had, and who need support.

Epilogue

This book has focused on the lived experiences of adoptive parents: their significant memories, their perceptions of adoption, their perception of their role in the breakdown of the adoption, the construction of their role after the disruption, and their healing. My objective has been to tell their stories. By making their stories known, I hope that the system that first promoted such adoptions, and then promptly ignored ensuing difficulties, will be inspired to make changes. If society is going to continue encouraging and/or promoting adoptions as an alternate means of caring for children, it is important that the experiences of adoptive parents and those of adoptees be clearly and sympathetically understood. In this respect, this book can be a resource for other adoptive parents, adoption workers, social-service agencies, and government officials who determine policies surrounding adoptions.

It is an impossible task to produce a complete picture or summary of the participants' struggle. We shared no more than ten hours with each couple, but our ideas have been altered through this process. Since then, time and new circumstances have altered and will continue to alter our horizons and our perceptions. It is my hope that readers have been able to capture the essence of the couples' experiences and that an understanding of the trauma of a disrupted adoption has been gained. The parents in this study had similar experiences because all of them adopted older native children; they encountered similar problems, underwent similar struggles, and felt similar emotions.

All the parents we interviewed still have difficult times with the breakdown of the adoption. However, they no longer visit courts and jails, search unsavoury areas, or participate in assessments and family therapy. Nor are they writing letters to politicians in an attempt to secure help for their children. Now, the challenge is to maintain or resolve the relationship with a son who is not often at home, perhaps in jail or not working and/or not in school.

Without exception, the participants admitted that they allowed Rod and me into their homes, lives, minds, and hearts *because* of our own experience. But there was another factor, too, that facilitated contact: our son had died, and so we were, in some way, off the playing field, no longer involved in our son's personal struggle. The participants wanted to help us, because we had experienced what they all feared for their son: his death. Through all the emotions the parents have experienced, and through all the changes they have undergone, the dissolution of the adoption is still a reality. Our particular story has ended, but the book is not closed on their stories. For most of the parents, while the nature of the challenge may have changed, the struggle – to help their sons live as healthy, happy, and self-sufficient adults, to accept their fragmented families, to rebuild their self-confidence, to accept the limitations of society, to heal relationships with spouses and other children – continues. I hope that this book will help to make their journey easier.

As the years went by, I knew that I must move on – shed the baggage of guilt, self-recrimination, disappointment, and self-directed anger. I knew that I must walk with a lighter step and enjoy the day and put the lost battle behind me. I had to remember the good times, and, yes, even the good, if naive, intentions. I had to try to laugh at the struggles and accept what I could not change. Now, I no longer agonize over the fact that the adoption did not work as planned and that maybe the adoption was a total mistake, or, as Rod once said, a net minus. I now accept it as part of my life. It has helped me appreciate and be thankful for what I *do* enjoy now, particularly my family.

My Personal Advice for Parents

Take care of yourselves. Take time for yourselves, individually and together. Take walks. Take breaks. Get away, even for short periods.

Keep fit. Eat well. Exercise regularly.

Retain your confidence. Continually remind yourselves of the things you do well: your job, cooking, sports, hobbies. Think of significant accomplishments.

Know yourself. Stay in touch with yourself. Experiment and find out what makes you feel good and/or feel good about yourself, and continue to do it.

Remember that you are not judged only by results with one child. You are a complex person with many talents.

Children are lent to us only for a short time, maybe twenty years. Our lives will continue after they have grown up and/or gone. This is only a short time in your lifetime. Keep this perspective even though it feels like forever.

Read whatever you can about your child's difficulty, about other people's experience with similar situations – those fighting an illness, job loss. Read self-help books.

Recognize that there are many theories about what causes certain types of behaviour and what method is best to treat them. These theories change over time. Do not be swept along by some new fad that does not seem to fit your situation. Accept the fact that there is probably no one cause and no one solution for the behaviour.

Do not listen to friends or family who give unwanted advice. Tell them frankly that you know they mean well, but you do not want them to tell you what to do. Tell them you would rather they listen and encourage you in what you decide to do. If they cannot do that, you do not want to talk about it with them.

Do not be intimidated by social workers, teachers, or judges. Do not accept the role of scapegoat.

Clearly identify and communicate what you want and need. Put it in writing and set it aside for a day, re-evaluate it, revise it, and then let your wishes be known.

Do the same with your children. Clearly identify the rules you can live with. Keep to the ones that you can monitor in your house. Be flexible and allow for some negotiating. Rank your expectations. Work only on the top two or three. Forget the others for a while. Do not deviate. Always follow through, no matter what the excuses.

Do not encourage and support your child's transgressions. There is no neutral. If you do not allow the child to accept the consequences for inappropriate behaviour, you are supporting the unacceptable and undesirable actions and fostering the idea that it is all right for him or her to act in this way.

Do not be manipulated. Recognize your own "hot buttons" and work out a strategy with your partner to avoid having them pushed. Be sure you both agree on how to handle a situation. Decide what you will do before it happens, call a time-out. Go to another room and discuss your options. Stay united.

Do not lose your self-control. This will destroy your confidence and self-image and increase your sense of helplessness. Leave the situation until you can handle it in a way that you will be comfortable with.

Do not be afraid to recognize your anger and to acknowledge it. Say, "I am very angry right now, so I am not prepared to discuss this any further."

Do not worry about the "what ifs" – the unknown. There are many children who drop out of school only to return in a couple of years, realizing the value of education if they want to have a good job and good income. Stay in the present. Deal with each situation as it comes to you.

If the situation is deteriorating, think of the worst thing that can happen and plan for it. That way, nothing can catch you by surprise.

Accept the fact that there are some things that you cannot control, that you cannot change. Life is not always fair.

Use parent-support groups and individual counselling. Do not let your pride or shame keep you from using the few resources that are available.

Shop around. Be selective. Use those resources that make you feel better about yourself.

Talk about your situation with the few friends you feel comfortable with. Do not hide it in shame and disgrace. There are others like you who have had or are having difficulty, who are feeling isolated and would welcome the opportunity to talk about it. Others will open up when you do. There are many people who appear in control but who are also struggling. It is helpful to share experiences. It is therapeutic to talk about it and helpful to listen. But do not waste your time on those who make you feel worse.

Talk to your other children about the issues. Keep them informed. Give them a chance to talk about their feelings of anger, frustration, and fear.

Remember that these situations are the norm in many families and other families face similar challenges. You are not alone.

Accept the fact that you and your family are experiencing a real trauma. Your emotions are real and deserve recognition. Do not disallow or erase your often overpowering emotions of anger, frustration, despair, helplessness, loneliness, and grief. Acknowledge them. Allow yourself to mourn, to grieve your loss. It is not self-pity. It is tremendous sadness for what should or might have been.

Recognize and accept the fact that you are good parents, because you love, provide for, guide, and support your children. Good parents do not stop their children from making mistakes, but they help them avoid mistakes or, if necessary, work through them. Most of our children grow into caring, independent adults. If they do not, this does not diminish your good parenting.

Remember that some children who had the worst parents have turned out to be marvellous people. It is not strictly cause and effect.

Do not take the responsibility for your child's decisions. In Parents for Youth we asked how parents who cannot get their child to brush his or her teeth can so willingly accept responsibility for failings in school or for running away. There is an important distinction between being a mother of an offender and being an offender. One is not guilty, the other is. Remember that you and your child are two separate people.

Do not take full responsibility for your child's failures. There are many experts involved: teachers, counsellors, doctors, social workers, and so on. If he or she is not improving, it means that these experts were also not able to help. (Tim had the best care that was available in Toronto. No one was able to stop his self-destruction.)

Parenting is not easy. Everyone struggles.

Trust yourself. You know your child best.

Remember and talk about the good times.

Bibliography

Adams, Judith. "When foster care doesn't work." Toronto *Star*, 20 January 1990: F1, F3.
– "Why some adoptions go wrong." Toronto *Star*, 22 January 1990: C1, C2.
– "Changes to adoption policy urged." Toronto *Star*, 23 January 1990: B1.
Ambert, Anne-Marie. *The Effects of Children on Parents*. New York: Haworth Press 1992.
Armstrong, H., C. Wilkes, L. McEvoy, M. Russell, and C. Melville. "Group Therapy for Parents of Youths with a Conduct Disorder." *Canadian Medical Association* 151: 7 (1994): 439–94.
Avery, Rosemary, ed. *Adoption Policy and Special Needs Children*. Westport, Conn.: Auburn House/Greenwood 1997.
Bachrach, Christine A. "Adoption Plans, Adopted Children, and Adoptive Mothers." *Journal of Marriage and the Family* 48: 2 (1986): 243–54.
Badia, P., S. Cuthbertson, and J. Harsh. "Choice of Long or Stronger Signalled Shock over Shorter or Weaker Unsignalled Shock." *Journal of the Experimental Analysis of Behavior* 19 (1973): 25–32.
Bagley, Christopher. "Transracial Adoption in Britain: A Follow-up Study, with Policy Considerations." *Special Issue: Adoption, Children Welfare* 72: 3 (May/June 1993): 285–99.
– "Native Adoptions." Interviewed on "As It Happens," CBC Radio, 7 September 1993.

Bandura, A. "In Search of Pure Unidirectional Determinants." *Behavior Therapy* 12 (1981): 30–40.

Barth, Richard P. "Adoption of Drug-exposed Children." *Special Issue: Research on Special Needs Adoption. Children and Youth Services Review* 13: 5–6 (1991): 323–42.

Barth, Richard P., and Marianne Berry. *Adoption and Disruption: Rates, Risks, and Responses.* New York: A. de Gruyter 1988.

– "Preventing Adoption Disruption." *Prevention in Human Services* 9 (1990): 205–22.

Bateson, Mary Catherine. *Composing a Life.* New York: Atlantic Monthly Press 1990.

Berry, Marianne B., and Richard P. Barth. "Behavior Problems of Children Adopted When Older." *Children and Youth Services Review* 11: 3 (1989): 221–38.

Blumer, H. *Symbolic Interactionism.* Englewood Cliffs, N.J.: Prentice Hall 1969.

Boldt, Menno. *Surviving as Indians: The Challenge of Self-government.* Toronto: University of Toronto Press 1993.

Bridges, William. *Transitions: Making Sense of Life's Changes.* Reading, Mass.: Addison-Wesley 1980.

British Columbia. Ministry of Social Services. *Adoption Newsletter,* July 1996. Victoria: Queen's Printer 1996.

Brodzinsky, David M., and Marshall D. Schechter, eds. *The Psychology of Adoption.* New York: Oxford University Press 1990.

Canada. Department of Indian and Northern Affairs. *A Guide for White Families Adopting Native Children.* Ottawa: Supply and Services Canada 1989.

Canadian Press. "Commission urges action on aboriginal suicide rates." Toronto *Star,* 2 February 1995: A9.

Carey, Elaine. "Parents refusing to accept the blame for bad kids." *Sunday Star* (Toronto), 28 May 1989: A1, A22.

Crumbley, Joseph. "Transracial Adoption: Love Is Not Enough." In *Adoptions Connections* (newsletter of Center for Adoption, Nashville, Tenn.), 1999, posted at web page of New York State Citizens' Coalition for Children (www.nyscc.org).

Daly, Kerry, and Michael P. Sobol. *Adoption in Canada: Final Report, National Adoption Study.* Funded by National Welfare Grants and Health and Welfare Canada. University of Guelph 1993.

DeMont, John. "Ottawa says it is sorry." *Maclean's,* 19 January 1998: 32–3.

DeMont, John, and John Geddes. "Aboriginal expectations." *Maclean's,* 29 December 1997, 5 January 1998: 70–1.

DiGiulio, Joan Ferry. "Self-acceptance: A Factor in the Adoption Process." *Child Welfare* 67: 5 (1988): 423–29.

DiLalla, Lisabeth F., and Irving I. Gottesman. "Heterogeneity of Causes for Delinquency and Criminality: Lifespan Perspectives." *Development and Psychopathology* 1: 4 (1989): 339–49.

Eichler, Margrit. "Family Change and Social Policies." In *Family Matters: Sociology and Contemporary Canadian Families*. Scarborough, Ont.: Nelson Canada 1988.

Fahlberg, V. *Attachment and Separation*. Lansing, Mich.: Department of Social Services 1979.

Fanshel, David. *Far from the Reservation*. Metuchen, N.J.: Scarecrow Press 1972.

Feldman, Robert. *Essentials of Understanding Psychology*. Toronto: McGraw-Hill Ryerson 1994.

Fishman, Andrea. *Amish Literacy: What and How It Means*. Portsmouth, N.H.: Heineman 1988.

Fishman, Katharine Davis. "Problem Adoptions."*Atlantic Monthly* 270: 3 (1992): 37–56.

Fournier, Suzanne, and Crey, Ernie. *Stolen from our Embrace*. Toronto, Douglas and McIntyre 1997.

Gelmych, A. "An Examination of Adjustment Difficulties in Adopted Adolescents." PHD thesis, University of Toronto 1991.

Gilligan, Carol. *In a Different Voice*. Cambridge, Mass.: Harvard University Press 1982.

Glesne, C., and Peshkin, A. *Becoming Qualitative Researchers: An Introduction*. White Plains, N.Y.: Longman 1992.

Groze, Victor, and James A. Rosenthal. "Attachment Theory and the Adoption of Children with Special Needs." *Social Work Research and Abstracts* 29: 2 (June 1993): 5–12.

Haag, Michael Arthur. "Identity and the Search for Origins: A Study of Adult Adoptees" PHD thesis, University of California (Santa Cruz) 1989.

Harlow, H.F., and M.K. Harlow. "Social Deprivation in Monkeys." *Scientific American* 207 (1962): 137–46.

Hehir, Michael G. "An Exploration of Family Adjustment in the Adoptions of Traumatized Children Who Have Behavioral and Emotional Problems." PHD thesis, Massachusetts School of Professional Psychology 1991.

Hewitt, John P. *Self and Society: A Symbolic Interactionist Social Psychology*, rev. ed. Needham Heights, Mass.: Allyn and Bacon 1997.

Hilborn, Robin. "Recommendations from Study of Romanian Orphanage Children." *Adoption Roundup: Journal of the Adoption Council of Ontario,* summer 1997.

Holtan, Barbara, and Tremitiere, Barbara. *Looking Back: How Have They Fared? An Outcome Study of Three Populations of Adoptees.* Study conducted for Tressler Lutheran Services (York, Penn.), 1996.

Hornby, Helaine C. "Why Adoptions Disrupt and What Agencies Can Do to Prevent It."*Children Today* 15: 4 (1986): 7–11.

"An Indian and a Québécoise Search for Roots." Ottawa *Citizen,* 3 May 2000.

Johnston, P. *Native Children and the Child Welfare System.* Toronto: Canadian Council on Social Development/James Lorimer 1983.

Kadushin, A. *Adopting Older Children.* New York: Columbia University Press 1970.

Karen, L., et al. *Family Matters.* Scarborough, Ont.: Nelson Canada 1988.

Karen, Robert. *Becoming Attached: Unfolding the Mystery of the Infant-Mother Bond and Its Impact on Later Life.* New York: Warner Books 1994.

Kellington, Charles, ed. "Child Abuse Can Have Life Long Effects. *Institute for the Prevention of Child Abuse.* Don Mills, Ont.: Rotary Club of Toronto, Don Valley 1993.

Kirk, David. *Shared Fate.* London: Free Press of Glencoe (Collier Macmillan) 1964.

– Adoptive Kinship: A Modern Institution in Need of Reform. Toronto: Butterworths 1981.

Kubler-Ross, Elisabeth. *Living with Death and Dying.* New York: Macmillan 1981.

Landy, Frank J. *Psychology: The Science of People,* 2nd ed. Englewood Cliffs, N.J.: Prentice-Hall 1987.

Lawder, E.A., K. Lower, T. Andresa, Elk Sherman, and J. Hill. *A Follow-up Study of Adoptions: Post-placement Functioning of Adoptive Families.* Vol. 1. New York: Child Welfare League of America 1969.

Lifshitz, Michaela, Ronnie Baum, Irith Balgur, and Chauna Cohen. "The Impact of the Social Milieu upon the Nature of the Adoptees' Emotional Difficulties." *Journal of Marriage and the Family* 37 (1975): 221–8.

Lifton, Betty Jean. *Journey of the Adopted Self: A Quest for Wholeness.* New York: Basic Books 1994.

McDaniel, Susan A. "The Changing Canadian Family: Women's Roles and the Impact of Feminism." In Sandra Bert, Loraine Code, and Lindsay Dorney, eds. *Changing Patterns: Women in Canada.* Toronto: McClelland and Stewart 1988.

Magid, Ken, and Carole A. McKelvey. *High Risk*. New York: Bantam Books 1987.

Mandell, Nancy, and Ann Duffy. *Reconstructing the Canadian Family: Feminist Perspectives*. Toronto: Butterworths Canada 1988.

May, Rollo. *The Courage to Create*. New York: Norton 1975.

Melanson, Joan. "Love Is Not Enough." CBC Radio AM, Toronto, 14 November 1993.

Merriam, Sharan B. *Case Study Research in Education*. San Francisco: Jossey-Bass 1988.

Miall, Charlene E. "Community Assessments of Adoption Issues: Open Adoption, Birth Reunions, and the Disclosures of Confidential Information." *Journal of Family Issues* 19: 5 (September 1998): 556–77.

Morgan, G., and L. Smircich. "The Case for Qualitative Research." *Academy of Management Review* 5: 4 (1980): 491–500.

Moustakas, Clark E. *Heuristic Research: Design, Methodology and Applications*. Newbury Park, Calif.: Sage Publications 1990.

Ontario Association of Children's Aid Societies. "CAS Facts – December 1966," no. 6 ("Issues in Ontario's Child Welfare System").

Ontario Native Women's Association, Ontario Federation of Indian Friendship Centres, and Ontario Métis and Non-Status Association. Letter Presented to the Minister of Community and Social Services, the Honourable Frank Drea. 1983.

Palmer, R.E. "Gadamer's Dialectical Hermeneutics." In R.E. Palmer, ed., *Hermeneutics*. Evanston, Ill.: Northwestern University Press 1969.

Pavao, Joyce Maguire. "A Study of the Themes That Appear in a Clinical Population of Adolescent Adoptees." PHD thesis, Harvard University 1989.

Perls, Frederick S. *Gestalt Therapy Verbatim*. Lafayette, Calif.: Real People Press 1969.

Peters, John F. "Adolescents as Socialization Agents to Parents." *Adolescence* 20 (1985): 921–33.

Petruccelli, Elizabeth. "Parents for Youth: Helping Parents of Children with Conduct Disorders." *Ontario Medical Review* 1 (1993): 19–24.

Reitz, Miriam, and Kenneth W. Watson. *Adoption and the Family System: Strategies for Treatment*. New York: Guilford Press 1992.

Rosenthal, James A., Dolores Schmidt, and Jane Connor. "Predictors of Special Needs Adoption Disruption: An Exploratory Study." *Children and Youth Services Review* 10:2 (1988): 101–17.

Rosenthal, James A., and Victor K. Groze. *Special Needs Adoption: A Study of Intact Families*. New York: Praeger 1992.

Samenow, Stanton E. *Before It's Too Late*. New York: Times Books 1989.

Sarick, Lila. "Good intentions breeding ground of tragic results." *Globe and Mail* (Toronto), 5 April 1994: A4.

Seglow, Jean, Mia Kelmar Pringle, and Peter Wedge. *Growing up Adopted*. England and Wales: National Educational Research 1972.

Seligman, M.E.P. *Helplessness*. San Francisco: Freeman 1975.

Senior, N., and E. Himadi. "Emotionally Disturbed Adopted Inpatient Adolescents. *Child Psychiatry and Human Development* 15 (1985): 189–97.

Smith, Susan Livingston, and Jeanne A. Howard. "A Comparative Study of Successful and Disrupted Adoptions. *Social Service Review* 65: 2 (June 1991): 248–65.

Sorosky, Arthur D., Annette Baran, and Reuben Pannor. *The Adoption Triangle*. New York: Anchor Press 1984.

Spitz, R.A. *The First Year of Life*. New York: International Universities Press 1965.

Terr, Lenore. *Too Scared to Cry: Psychic Trauma in Childhood*. New York: Basic Books 1990.

To Return: The John Walkus Story. Produced by Maureen Kelleher, Annie Frazier Henry, and Tom Konyves. Vision TV, May 2000.

Tremitiere, Barbara S. "Disruption: A Break in Commitment." Paper presented at the ninth North American Council of Adoptable Children conference, Chicago 1984.

Van Manen, M. *Researching Lived Experiences: Human Science for an Action Sensitive Pedagogy*. New York: State University of New York/Althouse Press 1990.

Wegar, Katarina. *Adoption, Identity, and Kinship: The Debate over Sealed Birth Records* (New Haven, Conn.: Yale University Press 1997).

Wente, Margaret. "Our poor ruined babies: the hidden epidemic." *Globe and Mail*, 7 October 2000: A17.

Westhues, Anne. Interviewed on "As It Happens," CBC Radio, 8 February 1994.

Wharf, Brian, ed. *Rethinking Child Welfare in Canada*. Toronto: McClelland and Stewart 1993.

Worchel, S., and W. Shebilski. *Psychology: Principles and Applications*. Englewood Cliffs, N.J.: Prentice Hall 1983.

Yalom, Irvin D. *The Theory and Practice of Group Psychotherapy*, 3rd ed. New York: Basic Books 1985.

Index

"acknowledgment of differences": thesis of, as set out by David Kirk, xxi–xxii, 146

Adams, Jeff, 3, 7, 8, 14

Adams, Joseph, 156

Adams, Lorie, 3, 7, 8, 156

Adams, Marie and Rod: adoption of Tim, 3, 7; background of Marie, 3–5; background of Rod, 5–6; birth of Lorie and Jeff, 7; death of Tim, 18; difficulties with Tim, 7–13; disruption memory of Rod, 14–15; effects of Tim's difficulties on family, 16–17; ideal-family memory of Marie, 14; lack of support from family and friends, 17–18; marriage of, 7; memorial service for Tim, 18–19; reasons for adopting, 3, 7; Tim's departure from home, 11

Adams, Melanie, 4 , 8, 132

Adams, Tim: adoption of, 3; background of, 3; behaviour of, 7–13; departure from home, 11

"adopted child syndrome": behavioural characteristics of, xx, xxiv; and native adoptees, xxvii–xxviii; statistics on behavioural difficulties, xxii; study by Katarina Wegar on, xx

adopting: reasons for, parents' views on, 101, 103

adoption: role of environment in ensuring success of, parents' views on, 96–8, 103, 105; role of parents' life experiences in shaping attitudes towards, 96–103

Adoption Council of Canada, 169

adoption disruption/breakdown: and acceptance, 119–20; and coping mechanisms, 159–68, 197–200; and denial, 108–10; differences in attitudes of women and men towards, 114–19, 123–4; as emotional journey, 105, 106–31, 154–9, 183–6; and frustration and anger, 110–13; and grief, 120–31; and guilt, 113–20; rate among natives, xxvii; rate among general U.S. population, 169; stages of, scholarly views on, 106

– factors in: age at adoption, 138–
9; heredity, 134–5; post-natal
abuse, 136–7; pre-natal abuse,
135–6; previous disruptions,
139–41; search for identity, 141–
5; sex of the adoptee, 137–8;
temperament and personality,
146–7

Adoption Helper, 182

adoption system, suggested
reforms to: access to birth
records, 141, 171–4; better
training of agency staff, 170–1;
changes in society's attitudes,
190–3; follow-up, 174–8; more
research, 182–6; more and
better support groups, 179–82;
recognizing native identity,
178–9

Adoptive Families, 182

Adoptive Families of America, 182

Ambert, Anne-Marie: effects of
adoption disruption/break-
down on parents, 183

Ames, Elinor. *See* adoption
system, suggested reforms to:
better training of agency staff

Anishnawbe and Native Child
and Family Services, 13

Armstrong, Harvey, xxiii, xxxi,
10, 17, 30, 89, 112, 115, 148, 166,
184–5

attachment theory, 97; as set out
by Melanie Klein and John
Bowlby, xxiii-xxiv, 138, 140–1,
145

Avery, Rosemary. *See* special-
needs adoptions

Bagley, Christopher. *See* transracial adoptions

Bandura, A. *See* adoption disrup-
tion/breakdown, factors in:
temperament and personality

Barth, Richard. *See* adoption
disruption/breakdown, factors
in: pre-natal abuse

Barth, Richard, and Marianne
Berry. *See* family-systems
approach; adoption system,
suggested reforms to: follow-
up; more research

Bateson, Mary Catherine: on
women and guilt, 114–16

Blumer. H. *See* symbolic interactionism

Boldt, Menno. *See* government
policy: towards natives

Bridges, William: on grief, 129–30,
162

Brodzinsky, David, and Marshall
Schechter. *See* adoption system:
suggested reforms to: follow-up

Brooks, Allan, 35, 40

Brooks, Donna, 35

Brooks, Jamey, 35, 41

Brooks, Jon: adoption of, 35, 39;
background of, 39–40; behaviour of, 40–3, 45, 46; departure
from home, 45; relationship
with parents today, 46–7

Brooks, Kelly, 35, 40, 46

Brooks, Mary and Arnold: adoption
of Jon, 35, 39; background of
Arnold, 37–9; background of
Mary, 35–7; difficulties with
Jon, 40–3; disruption memory
of Mary, 44–5; effects of Jon's
difficulties on family, 46; ideal-
family memory of Arnold, 43–4;
Jon's departure from home, 45;
reasons for adopting, 35, 39; relationship with Jon today, 46–7

Brooks, Von, 35

Children's Aid Society, 3, 12, 17,
22, 29, 50–1, 69, 71, 113, 139,
174–6, 181

Chudley, Albert. *See* fetal-alcohol
syndrome (and effect)

Cline, Foster. *See* attachment
theory

Cole Elizabeth S. *See* adoption
system, suggested reforms to

Dalewood, 26–7, 121, 150
disruption memories: explained,
    xxxvi–xxxvii

early pre- and post-natal care:
    importance of, xxiii
Erikson, Erik. *See* adoption
    disruption/breakdown, factors
    in: search for identity

Family Court Clinic (Toronto),
    10, 30, 69, 150, 154
family-systems approach: to
    adoption disruption/break-
    down, xvii–xix, 145, 184
Fanshel, David, and Christopher
    Bagley. *See* transracial adoption
Feldman, Robert. *See* adoption
    disruption/breakdown, factors
    in: heredity
fetal-alcohol syndrome (and
    effect), xxiii, 135–6
Fishman, Katherine Davis: effects
    of adoption disruption/break-
    down on parents, 183. *See also*
    family-systems approach
Fournier, Suzanne, and Ernie
    Crey. *See* adoption disruption/
    breakdown, factors in: pre-natal
    abuse. *See also* government
    policy; transracial adoption

Gilligan, Carol: on gender differ-
    ences, 114, 115, 117–19
Glesne, C. and A. Peshkin. *See*
    adoption disruption/break-
    down: and coping mechanisms
government policy: towards
    natives, xxv, 144–5; in encour-
    aging native adoptions, xxvi–
    xxviii, 128, 186–90
Graves, Cindy, 59
Graves, Ella and John: adoption
    of Ken and Grace, 48, 50–1;
    background of Ella, 48–9, 56;
    background of John, 49;
    difficulties with Ken, 51–6;

disruption memory of John,
    56–8; effects of Ken's difficulties
    on family, 55, 59–60; ideal-
    family memory of Ella, 56;
    Ken's departure from home,
    56; lack of support from family,
    friends, and social agencies,
    60; marriage of, 49; reasons
    for adopting, 50, 59; relation-
    ship with Ken and Grace today,
    58
Graves, Grace: adoption of, 48,
    50–1; background of, 50;
    behaviour of, 51, 56; relation-
    ship with adoptive parents
    today, 58
Graves, Ken: adoption of, 48,
    50–1; background of, 50; behav-
    iour of, 51–6; departure from
    home, 56; relationship with
    adoptive parents today, 58
Graves, Will, 54

Harris, Monty, 10
Hehir, Michael. *See* adoption
    disruption/breakdown, factors
    in: post-natal abuse
Hewitt, John P. *See* symbolic inter-
    actionism

ideal-family memories: explained,
    xxxvi
Indian Eskimo Assocation, 61
interviews: importance to families
    profiled in this book, 150–4

Kadushin, A. *See* adoption disrup-
    tion/breakdown, factors in:
    temperament and personality
Klein, Melanie, and John Bowlby.
    See attachment theory
Kubler-Ross, Elisabeth: and grief,
    105, 129; and anger, 110, 114

Laurence, Margaret, 142
Lifton, Betty Jean, 142–3
Lydia (Tim's social worker), 167

McKuen, Rod, 142

Magid, Ken, and Carole McKelvey. *See* adoption disruption/breakdown, factors in: previous disruptions. *See also* attachment theory

Manen, M. Van: and phenomenological research, xxxiii

May, Rollo. *See* adoption disruption/breakdown, factors in: search for identity

Moustakas, Clark: and heuristic theory, xxxiv

National Association of Homes for Children (U.S.), 169

National Native Association of Treatment Directors, 136

Native Brotherhood, 33, 61

Native Child and Family Services (Toronto), xxvii

native identity: as factor in adoption disruption/breakdown, 143–4

Ontario Association of Children's Aid Societies, 176

Ontario Federation of Indian Friendship Centres, 188

Ontario Metis and Non-Status Indian Association, 188

Ontario Native Women's Association, 188

Palmer, R.E. *See* adoption disruption/breakdown: and coping mechanisms

Parents for Youth, xxii, xxxvi, 115, 148, 150, 185

parent-support groups: importance of, 148–50

Pelligrini, Victoria and Lou: adoption of Vincent, 75, 79; background of Lou, 76–8; background of Victoria, 75–6; difficulties with Vincent, 79–84; disruption memory of Lou, 86–7; disruption memory of Victoria, 85; effects of Vincent's difficulties on family, 87–8; ideal-family memory of Lou, 84; lack of support from family, friends, and social agencies, 87–8; marriage of, 78; reasons for adopting, 75, 79; relationship with Vincent today, 88–90

Pelligrini, Vincent: adoption of, 75, 79; artistic talent of, 82, 88; background of, 79; behaviour of, 79–84; relationship with adoptive parents today, 88–90

Post-adoption Helper, 182

Project Opikihiwawin, 181

Reitz, Miriam, and Kenneth W. Watson. *See* family-systems approach

Richard, Ken, xxvii–xxviii

Roethler, Alison and Georg: adoption of Donald, Rebecca, and Jimmy, 22; background of Alison: 20–1; background of Georg: 21; difficulties with adopted children, 23; disruption memory of Alison, 31–2; effects of adopted children's behaviour on family, 24, 27–8; ideal-family memory of Georg, 31; marriage of: 21; reasons for adopting, 21–2; relationship with adopted children today, 33

Roethler, Donald: background of, 22; behaviour of, 23–4, 30–1

Roethler, Jimmy: background of 22; behaviour of, 23–6

Roethler, Rebecca: background of, 22; behaviour of, 23–4, 29

Royal Commission on Aboriginal Peoples; 190, 192

Samenow, Stanton. *See* family-systems approach

scholarly literature: on adoption, shortcomings of, xvii

"Sixties Scoop," xxvi–xxvii
Spallumcheen band (B.C.), 190
special-needs adoptions, xx, xxii
Street Outreach Service Programs,
167
support: lack of in adoption disruption/breakdown, from family, friends, and social agencies,
125–8, 148
symbolic interactionism: theory
of, in influencing author's
approach and conclusions, xxx,
146–7, 161; as elaborated by
John P. Hewitt, xxxi–xxxii, 146;
as set out by H. Blumer,
xxix–xxx, 146, 162–3

Terr, Lenore: on guilt and shame,
120
Thistletown, 11
Tough Love (support group), 150
transracial adoption, xxiv–xxvi,
xxviii–xxix, 159, 178–9
Tremitiere, Barbara: as example
of successful adoption agency,
176. See also adoption system,
suggested reforms to: follow-up

Verdan, Diane, 61, 70
Verdan, Elaine and Edward: adoption of Gerald, 61, 65; background of Edward, 62–3;
background of Elaine, 61–2;
difficulties with Gerald, 61,
65–70; disruption memory of
Edward, 71–2; effects of Gerald's difficulties on family, 70,
73–4; ideal-family memory of
Elaine, 71; lack of support from
family, friends, and social agencies, 66–7, 73–4; marriage of, 63;
reasons for adopting, 61–2,
63–4; relationship with Gerald
today, 72–3
Verdan, Gerald: adoption of, 61,
65; background of, 61, 64–5;
behaviour of, 61, 65–70; relationship with adoptive parents
today, 72–3
Verdan, Jim, 61
Verdan, Mathew, 61, 69–70

West Detention Centre (Toronto),
84, 86, 89
Westhues, Anne. See transracial
adoption
women: as primary caregiver,
views of H.F. and M.K. Harlow
on, 117

Yalom, Irvin: on support-group
therapy, 150–2
Youthdale Crisis Centre, 12, 30–1